IN THE SHADOW OF GLORY

In the
SHADOW
of
GLORY

THE THIRTEENTH MINNESOTA IN THE
SPANISH-AMERICAN AND PHILIPPINE-
AMERICAN WARS, 1898 TO 1899

Kyle Roy Ward

NORTH STAR PRESS OF ST. CLOUD, INC.

Library of Congress Cataloging-in-Publication Data
Ward, Kyle Roy, 1969-
    In the shadow of glory : the thirteenth Minnesota in the Spanish-American and Philippine-American wars, 1898-1899 / Kyle Roy Ward.
    220 p. 25 cm.
    Includes bibliographical references and index.
    ISBN 0-87839-138-X
    1. United States. Army. Minnesota Infantry Regiment, 13th (1898-1899)
2. Spanish-American War, 1898—Regimental histories—Minnesota. I. Title.
E726.M7 W37 2000
973.8'94--dc21   00-055000

ISBN: 0-87839-138-X paper
ISBN: 0-87839-153-3 cloth

Cover Photo: Flags of the Thirteenth Minnesota Volunteer Infantry 1898
Courtesy of the Minnesota Historical Society

All photos on page 17 and in Appendices from *Campaigning in the Philippines*
by Karl Irving Faust, 1899

Printed in the United States of America
by Versa Press, Inc., East Peoria, Illinois

Published by
North Star Press of St. Cloud, Inc.
P.O. Box 451
St. Cloud, Minnesota 56302

Contents

Chapter 1

"Crisis at Hand"

With the ninteenth century coming to a close, many Americans, especially those who were born after the Civil War, needed some catalyst to change how they looked at themselves. This was as true for the youth of Minnesota as it was for any other group in the United States. However, for the Minnesotans involved in the events which soon transpired, their contributions helped change not only their own but also a great many other Americans' impressions of their country. These actions also became the catalyst for many Americans to question not only the wars fought in the Philippines at the turn of the century but also the United States' newly developed imperialistic foreign policy.

With the nation suffering from a terrible economic depression and this generation dealing with feelings of inadequacies due to the fact that they did not have even one event, like the Civil War, to put their names in the history books, they were desperately seeking something to uplift them. Fortunately for them, a crisis was brewing in the world in the last half of the 1890s, one which many hoped would not only solve the economic and emotional depression in the country, but one that would also cure the national division still left over from the Civil War.

Not only would this generation have to help heal the wounds from a war fought some thirty years earlier, they would also be forced into fighting any future battles with the same mythical patriotism and valor that the Civil War generation had. It was this enthusiasm that those who enlisted to fight at first took with them. In a near carnival atmosphere this generation went off to fight their war. Unfortunately for them, by the time they returned to American soil, this excitement had all but vanished. These men quickly found that the war they had been sold was not the one they would end up fighting.

This changing of views happened in part because of what was taking place in their nation's capital. Even as the nineteenth century was coming to an end, many American politicians did not seriously plan for America's future, often leaving many of their newly developing foreign policies rather vague. With no serious, concise plan coming out of President McKinley's administration, most of the plans for the United States and the government were being formulated by low-level government officials, military leaders, or an over-zealous group of Americans who wanted to see America expand its territorial holdings.

With little or no direction from the top officials, America's foreign policies were often then formed as events progressed, usually with the help of one of the above mentioned groups. This lack of direction not only caused problems for President McKinley, but it also created issues for this generation of Americans who were never quite sure what direction their country was taking them. At a time when a definite foreign policy needed to be formulated, this generation of Americans never knew for sure where their government stood. This questioning by many American citizens of what it was their government was trying to accomplish, only further complicated things for the men who went off to serve their nation in a time of war.

The problems facing this generation of Americans were tremendous. With a government unsure of itself, pressure coming from an older generation, and the desire to finally heal the wounds of past transgressions, they needed an enormous event through which they could solve all the problems plaguing them. When they did get their opportunity to act, most did so with the belief that they were going to be given the chance to "spread the blessings of their exceptional civilization to the world." A crusade with this concept as its backbone would not only be seen as noble but might also lift them and their nation out of their current malaise.[1]

Their prayers of getting that one major event would come true, but the answers which came from it were far from what they expected. Instead of getting what they wished, this generation of Americans found themselves changing forever the way the nation looked at itself. For, by 1900, Americans not only found themselves at the beginning of a new century, but they were also able to witness the arrival of a new and more powerful nation on the world stage.

The opportunity for all this came in the form of a crumbling Spanish Empire. Since their discovery of the "New World," the Spaniards had held a vast empire in both the Americas and in the Pacific. Unfortunately for the Spanish government of the 1890s, this empire was beginning to fall apart. Rebels in Spanish colonies such as Cuba and the Philippines, who were trying to expel the Spaniards, placed Spain in a precarious position. Having more military might than its colonies, Spain could try, over time, to suppress these revolts and return these nations into the fold, but the more they tried to put down these revolts the more attention they received from around the world, especially from the United States.

Of all the Spanish possessions, the island of Cuba garnered special attention from the Americans, primarily because it lay only ninety miles off the coast of Florida. Having started a number of revolts against their colonial masters throughout the 1800s, with the start of a new revolt in 1895, the Cubans found themselves aided immensely by three different groups of sympathizers in the United States— American businessmen, a minority of Republicans, and certain East Coast newspapers.

In 1893, America had suffered from the worst economic depression in its history. In order to get America out of this depression, many business leaders began to argue that the country needed to keep its labor force working. To do this, they believed, they had to continue to make products from the surplus of goods coming in from around the nation. In order to keep these first two goals alive, many businessmen, along with a group of politicians, argued that America needed to increase exports.

Along with America's business world pushing for intervention, the Cubans were also aided by the fact that America, in 1896, elected William McKinley as President, re-establishing Republican rule in the White House. Since McKinley and certain key members of his party, such as Theodore Roosevelt, held both expansionistic beliefs and pro-Cuban tendencies, he and the Republicans were able to put the Cuban cause in the forefront of American thought at the end of the nineteenth century.

However, of the three groups aiding the Cuban revolutionaries, the main culprit in leading America to war with Spain was the world of print journalism. What started out as a simple business competition between two rivals, in the end would lead to all-out war.

During the 1890s, the market for newspaper supremacy in New York City was a closely fought battle between two men, William Randolph Hearst and Joseph Pulitzer. In order to grab more readers, thereby gaining more circulation and money, neither was above over-sensationalizing an event. Believing that "stark contrasts of black and white would sell more papers than bland shadings of gray," these editors portrayed the Spanish as "unspeakable villains, who committed murder, torture, and rape against innocent Cuban women and children."[2]

This tabloid war, and the type of sensationalistic reporting called "yellow journalism," was aided by the events unfolding in Cuba. Both Hearst and Pulitzer believed, correctly, that there was nothing like a war to capture readers' attentions, and if the actual events were not exciting enough, they would then print their own exaggerated versions of what may or may not have happened.

Although pro-business, President McKinley still did not want to send America to war. But with intense pressure mounting on him from newspapers, Cuban sympathizers, a small but vocal group of politicians, and a growing sentiment for action across the nation, it became harder and harder for him to stay above the fray and try to solve things diplomatically. Trying to maintain the peace while certain segments of the United States were lobbying for war was difficult enough, but diplomatic crises, which were beyond President McKinley's control were quickly used by those looking for a fight, forcing him to set America on a path for war.

During the spring of 1898, the three groups lobbying for action were further aided by three events that help set the course, not only for what would take place in Cuba, but in various other spots in the Caribbean and half way around the world. These events, making their biggest impact in Washington, quickly developed a ripple effect that spread, first to the larger East Coast newspapers, then, subsequently, throughout the rest of the United States.

In a day and age when local newspapers were the only way one could obtain news, the editors of these papers became the source for all that the general public knew. As it was in New York, so it was throughout the state of Minnesota. Minnesotans, many believing they had more civic pride than people in other states, followed what was happening both in their state and in the national government. When it came to the three events that led America into war, Minnesota newspapers not only reported about them, but they also had an effect on those who later signed up to fight the war.

The first of the three incidents leading to war was the de Lome affair. In a simple personal letter to a Spanish minister, Dupuy de Lome, Spain's ambassador to the United States for three years and a well-respected diplomat, claimed that he felt President McKinley was "weak and catered to the rabble of his party." He further added that the president was also "a low politician, who desires to leave the door open to me, and to stand with the jingoes of his party."[3] Dupuy de Lome had been in his position long enough that his gaffe, once discovered, was unpardonable.

Had the letter not fallen into the wrong hands, it would not have caused the problem it did for the Spaniards. The letter had been sent through the regular mail system and was stolen by a Cuban sympathizer. It was quickly forwarded to a pro-Cuban group in New York City. Going through a series of channels (no one wanted to take responsibility for getting it published), it finally ended up on the desk of William Randolph Hearst, where it made front page news with the headlines: "WORST INSULT IN AMERICA'S HISTORY."[4]

While the Hearst and Pulitzer newspapers immediately beat the drums for war, Minnesota took a much more watchful approach to the de Lome situation. The *Moorhead Daily News* was far less excited about the event than its New York counterparts and reported it much like the rest of the state's newspapers. Not only was the story of this "diplomatic crisis" over the de Lome letter located on the second page, it also followed a page-one story with the headline, "Ole Pederson went to Fosston Monday morning." The Moorhead paper, like a number of others, focused its concern more on whether the translation of the letter had been accurate. While the East Coast tabloids were ready for war right then and there, Minnesota's newspapers originally took a much more cautious approach to the events unfolding.[4]

Not wanting war over this issue alone, some Minnesota newspapers, depending on their political affiliations, even agreed with de Lome's characterization of President McKinley. The *St. Cloud Daily Times* said in an editorial on February 11, 1898, that this letter told the ". . . exact truth . . ." in regard to the president's character. Even in his own administration, McKinley was being berated for his character. McKinley's Assistant Secretary of the Navy, Theodore Roosevelt, had himself gone on record saying, ". . . that his chief had the backbone of a chocolate éclair."[6]

De Lome, being an astute diplomat, had resigned his position before any official actions could be taken. With de Lome out of the picture and the Spanish government's apology accepted by a war-leery McKinley, the incident began to slip from the forefront of people's minds. It had not become the spectacular catalyst of war that many "yellow journalist" hoped it would be. For their part, Minnesota's newspapers remained levelheaded about the whole affair and were able to report the de Lome story with little sensationalism. Unfortunately for those who did not want war, stories about de Lome were replaced by a more horrible story, and the pro-war yellow journalists in America latched onto it and did not let go until the country was finally at war.

With diplomatic tensions heightening, President McKinley, under the guise of dispatching ships on regular naval visits to other countries, began to send American war vessels to Cuba in January. The first of these ships was the *U.S.S. Maine.* The Spaniards in Cuba, for their part, were not too threatened by the ship's arrival. In fact, when the *Maine* arrived in Havana harbor on January 25, 1898, "[T]he Spanish commander sent a case of fine sherry to the Maine's Captain and officers."[7]

Three weeks later, the peace and tranquility that the sailors of the *Maine* might have enjoyed upon first arriving in the island, quickly vanished. At 9:45 P.M., on the night of February 15, 1898, an explosion ripped through the bow of the *Maine,* killing 260 of her men and injuring many more. Hearst's reporters were some of the first on the scene. They immediately telegraphed the news to New York where a messenger brought the report of the *Maine* incident directly to Hearst. He, in turn, called his editor to find out what the next day's headlines would say. His editor responded ". . . the *Maine* as well as the other big news of the day." Hearst replied, ". . . there [is] no other big news . . ." and instructed the editor to fill

4

the front page with the news of the *Maine.* Hearst, knowing that this was the story for which he had been looking, cryptically added: "[T]his means war."[8]

The news of the *Maine's* sinking was the story of the day, and it was quickly circulated around the nation by the Associated Press, to which most, if not all, of Minnesota's newspapers belonged. This service, invaluable as it was to Minnesota editors, also had a terrible flaw to its system. The Associated Press often carried stories picked up from Hearst's *New York Journal,* which was famous for its yellow-journalist tradition. Consequently, Minnesota's papers reflected this taint of yellow journalism in their stories on the *Maine* incident.

Although a great many of the early reports out of Havana stated that the explosion was an accident and noted the aid given by the Spaniards in rescuing the survivors, this was readily overshadowed in the days to come. Other sources claimed that the mine had been planted by the Spaniards, who purposely set out to destroy the *Maine.* No matter what the truth may have been, the yellow journalists quickly molded the incident into the sensationalistic story they wanted, and they were going to run with it.

Back in Minnesota, the citizenry followed the story of the *Maine* in their local newspapers just as closely as anywhere else in the nation. For Minnesotans though, the sinking of the *Maine* was seen as horrific, but most editors continued to take a cautious approach to the event. This sentiment was reflected in an editorial in the *Mankato Daily Free Press,* which stated that the *Maine* incident: "has caused a thrill of horror to pass over the nation." The editor then went on, pleading with his readers not to be swayed toward sensationalism, although he agreed it was easy to ". . . turn suspiciously toward the Spanish." In the end, he hoped his readers would heed the advice of the *Maine's*

Captain Sigsbee when he warned people to withhold judgment ". . . until a thorough investigation . . ." was conducted.[9]

During this time, Minnesotans found themselves aroused to anger, but they were also uncertain what significance the *Maine* affair had. Those who wanted action found an outlet for quickened emotions in the work of Cuban relief. Around the state, one could find constant reports on Cuba in the newspapers along with lectures at church services and socials. Although not ready for war, Minnesotans found themselves getting emotionally prepared for one if it were to happen.[10]

While pro-Cuban sentiments were beginning to develop across the nation, back in Washington McKinley and his administration had their hands full diplomatically. Although personally wanting to claim the *Maine* incident as being purely accidental, McKinley knew full well that the American press would not let it stand at that. The day after the incident, McKinley gathered his cabinet together, and they decided upon their official policy. They agreed there would be a board of inquiry to examine the situation, which would then report its findings to the president. The official White House line until then was that the destruction of the *Maine* had been due to an accident. President McKinley also promised the "public [that they] would know the real truth as soon as he did himself, and until then he asked [for] a suspension of judgment."[11]

With many politicians and various newspapers around the nation clamoring for war, some of the Minnesota newspapers began to agree and started to print articles in favor of war with Spain. The *Moorhead Daily News* changed its cautious view when it stated that "[T]he sentiment of the country is overwhelmingly in favor of prompt, decisive and adequate action on the part of our government."[12]

While in Duluth, the *News Tribune* felt that "[T]he destruction of the battleship *Maine* has stirred this country from coast to coast, not so much because of the disaster itself, . . . as because of the strained condition of affairs." Because of these "strained conditions," America found itself being led by jingoistic politicians and journalists, heading toward a war with Spain over Cuba, a war that neither the McKinley administration wanted nor the Spanish government could afford.[13]

Putting all of that aside, throughout America, in the last few weeks of the month of February and the first week of March a new debate developed that focused on whether or not the Spaniards had sunk the *Maine,* and, if so, what the United States should do. Although the sinking of the *Maine* put many Americans on the threshold of support for a war, Minnesotans, due to their own stoicism and the lack of sensationalism in their newspapers, continued to remain cautious and levelheaded. Ironically, it would take something far more mundane than any diplomatic faux pas or even a naval explosion to make the citizenry of Minnesota stand up and prepare to take arms.

On March 7, 1898, the United States Congress passed McKinley's "Fifty-Million-Dollar Bill," which would be the third and final step in preparing America for war. President McKinley hoped this bill would solve a number of his problems. First, he hoped, it would calm the yellow journalists by making it look as if he had a "backbone" and would stand up to the Spaniards. He was all too aware that war was quite possible and wanted the nation to be prepared. Also, the bill "was designed primarily to deter Spain from continuing intransigence." The hope was that they would see that America was completely prepared for war and then back down.[14]

Unlike either the de Lome letter or the *Maine* incident, the passing of this legislation did much to help unite, first newspapers, then the people from across Minnesota. With the passage of this bill, a feeling of patriotism began to surge, not only in Minnesota but across the United States. Suddenly, there emerged a sense of unity among Americans not felt since the days preceding the Civil War. This unity was first reflected in the House of Representatives, with its vote on McKinley's "Fifty-Million-Dollar" bill. As the *St. Cloud Daily Times* headlines exclaimed on March 9, 1898: "AYES 311, NOES 0." The *Times,* along with numerous other newspapers, thrilled to the fact that, with this vote, "[P]arty lines were swept away. . . ." All Americans were once again united over a single cause.[15]

In an article the following day, the *St. Cloud Daily Times* continued with its unity theme. "The enthusiasm with which [the Fifty-Million-Dollar Bill] was hailed everywhere—n, s, e, w—is notice to all people that, however Americans may differ as to party politics, they will be united as one man when the nation is threatened. If war should really come . . . the rush of men to arms, would surpass anything the world has ever witnessed." For many Americans, the memory of the Civil War still lingered in their conscience. Since 1865, many had been looking for something to finally reunite the nation under one theme and one flag. For those people, this bill was it. It showed that it was time to unite against a common enemy and forget past transgressions. With a large portion of the United States still holding onto old hatreds, for many the Civil War would be concluded with a victory over Spain.[16]

This third event on the road to war was the one that inspired Minnesotans (or at least their newspapers) to climb aboard the patriotic bandwagon and call for the defeat of the Spaniards. One of Minnesota's own Congressmen, Representative McCleary, in a speech before the United States House of Representatives, even claimed, ". . . if war must come, all lines of division among us will be forgotten. There will be no North, no South, no East, no

West, but one united country." He then concluded by telling the rest of the House, "[A]nd if war shall come, the North Star State . . . will again be found in the forefront in the hour of danger and the sons will emulate the glorious achievement of their sires at Gettysburg and Chickamauga."[17]

This speech was met with a thunderous round of applause by all sections of the House. Although wrapped tightly in patriotic zeal, not only did this speech stir sentiments in both the House of Representatives and in thousands of Minnesota men, it spoke more truth than Representative McCleary knew, for those who would go off to fight the Spaniards would not only help conclude the Civil War in the minds of many Americans, they would also have to live up to the tradition of the Civil War soldier, both real and mythical. These proved to be shoes nearly impossible to fill.

McCleary's words also spoke the truth about how Americans felt about themselves. At the turn of the century, "it is questionable whether a Minnesotan thought of himself primarily as an American, or whether he identified himself as a farmer, a Midwesterner, a Norwegian, a Lutheran, or perhaps a Republican." The sectionalism that had divided the nation back in the 1860s was still alive and well. With few in the United States considering themselves and those around them to be Americans, many in this post-Civil War generation believed it was up to them to find that one national cause which would, once and for all, unite all Americans.[18]

While the money had been appropriated by the Congress, the final act of declaring war would have to wait until the Board of Inquiry, established to find out the cause of the U.S.S. Maine's explosion, gave its report to McKinley, who was himself still trying to stave off war at all costs. By the end of March 1898, this inquiry had been completed and was on its way to

Washington, D.C., for presidential viewing. Whatever the results of the Board of Inquiry's report, it seemed that most Minnesota's newspapers, as well as most of America's, had already come to a conclusion—not so much as to whether or not the Spanish had sunk the Maine, but rather how the United States would fair in a war with Spain. As the St. Cloud Daily Times reported on March 26, 1898: "[T]he time for idle speculation is past—the period for active and energetic preparations for offensive operations is at hand. . . ."

The Daily Times concluded by saying: "[T]here can be but one result, victory for this nation, and yet this does not detract from the momentousness of the occasion, when it is remembered that many lives will be lost and millions of treasure expended." Having staved off the influences of East Coast jingoism for weeks, Minnesota's editors had succumbed to the allure of tantalizing articles used to inspire the masses.[19]

The report reached Washington amidst an almost carnival atmosphere of reporters all trying to get the scoop. On March 25, 1898, President McKinley met with his cabinet to discuss the report of the Naval Court of Inquiry. Having known for a week what the report would say, this document held no surprises for the president. Still hoping for a last minute miracle, McKinley was aware that the whole nation knew he had the report and that he had to send it to Congress. He knew the findings almost certainly meant war, since even though the report did not name names, it did blame the sinking of the Maine on an external explosion. To most Americans that clearly pointed to the Spaniards.

McKinley and his cabinet decided to hold onto the report over the weekend, thereby allowing him a couple more days in which to conduct some last minute negotiations with the Spanish government. If that failed, he knew that the patriotic feelings flowing throughout the

Congress and the nation at large would surely sweep him and the nation off to war.[20]

With no last minute miracle to stop the war, the report was made public, and the machinery of war began to spin rapidly. On April 11, 1898, President McKinley sent a message to Congress asking for the authority to intervene in Cuba. This message was received in the Senate and referred to the committee on foreign relations, chaired by Minnesota's own Senator Cushman K. Davis. Two days later, Davis, in the committee report, said that Spain was guilty either by an ". . . official act of the Spanish authorities or was made possible by a negligence on their part so willing and gross as to be equivalent in culpability to positive criminal action." In Senator Davis', and the committee's, view it was now time to start the war and free the Cubans. This resolution was adopted by the full Senate on April 16, 1898, and was accepted with few changes.[21]

While Davis remained a strong imperialist throughout the war and after, he by no means represented the entire state of Minnesota, for, while Senator Davis was pushing for war, another Minnesotan, Archbishop John Ireland of St. Paul, was waging a war for peace. Having been contacted by the pope (who wanted to avoid the bloodshed of Catholics from Spain, Cuba, the Philippines, as well as the United States) to try and find a peaceable ending for the current diplomatic deadlock, Archbishop Ireland went to work.

Ireland had been chosen by the pope because of his American citizenship, his "undoubted loyalty to his country, and [his] friendly personal relations with the president and members of the cabinet." Once in Washington, Archbishop Ireland was courteously received by President McKinley and his staff. Even with all the pleasantries among all involved, the Ireland talks with McKinley proved futile. Anti-war groups believed that, since the pope, many Spanish officials, and even President McKinley all desired peace, Ireland, playing intermediary, would be able to convince all parties of the war's irrationality. Unfortunately for the archbishop and his cause, war fever had grabbed hold of the nation and neither religious nor political leaders were going to curtail it.[22]

Having failed as a diplomat, Archbishop Ireland returned to Minnesota to continue his duties with the Catholic Church. With war nearing and his peace initiatives failed, Ireland, being a patriotic American, began to support the war to the point where his church sermons began to reflect the righteousness of war and those who fought in it.

Even with the last-ditch efforts to avoid a conflict, McKinley knew that the majority of Americans, having been misled by both jingoistic politicians and newspapers, wanted war. He also knew that if he continued to seek peace at this late date, the Republican Party would be split and his administration would lose some of its popularity and self-confidence. Also, being a first-term president, McKinley had another election coming up in just two years, and he knew if he wanted to be re-elected, his choice was simple, send America to war or lose the White House.[23]

Therefore, on April 25, 1898, McKinley asked the Congress to declare war, to which it whole-heartedly complied by passing a resolution that said that war had existed since April 21.[24] It was little wonder, though, that the country demanded war. Most Americans, having followed the Cuban Insurrection and the developing diplomatic crisis in their local newspapers, had had months of patriotic indoctrination by continuously hearing how evil and treacherous the Spaniards were and how easily they could be defeated by the superior military of the United States. This belief, coupled with the concept that the nation would be fighting a just war and could bring the blessings of liberty to the Cubans, made many Minnesota youths excited for war. So, once the call went out for soldiers, the young men of this state and nation were all too ready to respond.

Before Minnesotans could join the military and head toward Cuba, another event of major significance began to unfold half way around the world. On May 1, 1898, Admiral George Dewey, with orders from Washington, sailed from Hong Kong and reached Manila Harbor in the Philippines. (The Philippines had been a part of the Spanish empire since the days of Ferdinand Magellan's world voyage when he claimed the islands for Spain.) Dewey's orders were to attack the Spaniards in these islands primarily to prevent them from setting sail and bringing either their Pacific navy, or their troops stationed there to aid in the fighting in Cuba. In what was considered one of the greatest naval victories in American history, Dewey's ships completely destroyed the Spanish fleet in a matter of hours, whereas the Americans only lost one man to heat exhaustion during the entire battle.

News of this victory spread quickly to the United States where Dewey was made an instant hero. Having no idea about what to do next, Dewey awaited orders from his superiors in Washington. They, too, had little inkling of what to do with this situation. Outside of defeating the Spanish navy in the Philippines to prevent it from sailing to Cuba to help their troops there, American leaders were at a loss to know how to direct Dewey.

Slowly, though, a plan began to develop, one in which Dewey tried to gain control of the city of Manila, the capitol of the Philippines and a Spanish fortified outpost. While wanting to accomplish this, Dewey feared that his small contingent of troops could not take and then hold the city. On May 7, he telegraphed Washington informing them that in order for him to take Manila, he needed more troops. American political and military leaders knew that if they listened to this request, they would completely open up another front in the war. This in turn would force America's military strategists to completely rethink their strategy for victory. After a brief debate, leaders in Washington decided to go along with Dewey's request, and began to develop plans to send troops to the islands.

Although new to the American military leaders, this war in the Pacific was anything but new to its participants. The Filipinos, like the Cubans, had been fighting an insurrection against their Spanish colonizers for some time. They were waiting for their chance to strike a decisive blow and force the Spaniards out of the islands. Also like the Cubans, they would see their best opportunity come with the arrival of the Americans. With Dewey's overwhelming victory in Manila Harbor, the Filipinos saw their chance and again began to attack the Spaniards. With lightning-quick military movements, the Filipinos were able to cut off large numbers of Spanish troops and were also able to force a large contingent of Spaniards into Manila, where the war would stalemate for months.

Americans, wanting and needing the assistance of the Filipino insurgents, contacted exiled Filipino leader Emilio Aguinaldo, who was then living in Singapore. With American promises of aid, friendship, and Philippine independence, Aguinaldo agreed to sail back to his homeland and begin again his war against the Spaniards.

American leaders in Washington sent orders to Dewey and others who had contact with the Filipino leader to avoid all alliances with the revolutionaries. But they were too late, for American diplomat E. Spencer Pratt (one of just a handful of American diplomats working in Asia at that time) had already vaguely promised Aguinaldo independence and offered assurances that America would not colonize the Philippines. All of these statements were reinforced by the fact that the United States Navy had already brought Aguinaldo, on an American ship, back to the Philippines, thereby giving his authority some credence.[25]

Lacking any serious plans for dealing with the Spanish in the Philippines, and paying even less attention to the Filipinos, President McKinley mistakenly gave much of America's diplomatic duties over to the military officers who were currently, or would soon be, in the islands. This absence of direction from Washington would not only cause serious problems during the Spanish-American War but was also a considerable hindrance when more serious events arose that next spring.[26]

Weeks later, President McKinley confided to a friend: "[I]f old Dewey had just sailed away when he smashed that Spanish fleet, what a lot of trouble he would have saved us." Dewey did not, however, and America found itself not only fighting a war on two fronts but also its first overseas war. For most Americans, this one-sided victory in the Philippines reaffirmed their superiority over the Spaniards. It also meant that America would need even more troops to fight its war, thereby giving more Americans the opportunity to show off their patriotism and courage. Finally, by having another front in the Pacific, Americans could have an additional opportunity to export its version of liberty and democracy to another nation suffering under Spanish oppression.[27]

At this moment in time, it seemed as if almost everyone was getting their wish. Jingoistic newspapers and politicians were getting their war, and the Cubans and Filipinos hoped they were going to get their freedom. The United States set itself on a course for international involvement and all that would come with it. But, before they could dive into the realm of international relations and become one of the world's superpowers, the young men of America would have to don military uniforms and go off and fight for the right of America to make these claims. With patriotic fervor sweeping the nation, Minnesota's own were also caught up in this tidal wave of emotions and attitudes that would carry them to the other side of the world, where they would have to fight three wars, one against the Spanish, another against the Filipinos, and a third against the memory of a war fought some thirty years earlier.

NOTES

*The title of this chapter comes from the *St. Cloud Daily Times,* March 24, 1898. The article forewarned about coming hostilities between Spain and the United States.

[1]Stanley Karnow. *In Our Image: America's Empire in the Philippines* (New York: Random House, Inc., 1990), p. 80.

[2]H.W. Brands. *The Reckless Decade: America in the 1890s* (New York: St. Martin's Press, 1995), p. 307.

[3]*St. Paul Pioneer Press,* April 14, 1898, p. 2. Other Minnesota newspapers used in this research were the *Duluth News Tribune, Mankato Daily Free Press, The Minneapolis Tribune, Moorhead Daily News, Red Wing Daily Republican, St. Cloud Times,* and the *Stillwater Gazettee.* These newspapers were used either because they represented the cities which had specific companies that belonged to the Thirteenth Minnesota or because they represented large geographical areas of the state in which I hoped to get a good cross-section of how most Minnesotans felt about certain events as they arose.

[4]Philip Seib, *Headline Diplomacy: How News Coverage Affects Foreign Policy*

(Westport, Connecticut: Praeger Publications, 1997), p. 5.

[5]*Moorhead Daily News,* February 10, 1898, p. 2.

[6]*St. Cloud Daily Times,* February 11, 1898, p. 1. Michael Emery and Edwin Emery, *The Press and America: An Interpretive History of the Mass Media* (Englewood Cliffs, New Jersey: Prentice Hall, 1988), p. 237.

[7]Seib, *Headline Diplomacy,* p. 6.

[8]Chiasson, *Press In Times,* p. 104.

[9]*Mankato Daily Free Press,* February 18, 1898, p. 2.

[10]Franklin F. Holbrook, *Minnesota in the Spanish-American War and the Philippine Insurrection. Vol. 1* (St. Paul: The Riverside Press, 1923), p. 9.

[11]Charles Henry Brown, *The Correspondents' War: Journalists in the Spanish-American War,* (New York: Scribner, 1967), p. 122.

[12]*Moorhead Daily News,* February 23, 1898, p. 2.

[13]*Duluth News Tribune,* February 17, 1898, p. 4.

[14]David Trask, *The Spanish-American War* (New York: Macmillan Publishing, Co., 1981), p. 34.

[15]*St. Cloud Daily Times,* March 9, 1898, p. 1.

[16]*St. Cloud Daily Times,* March 10, 1898, p. 2.

[17]*St. Paul Pioneer Press,* March 10, 1898, p. 1.

[18]Peter Mickelson. "Nationalism in Minnesota during the Spanish-American War, 1899-1902," *Minnesota History* (Spring 1968), p. 2.

[19]*St. Cloud Daily Times,* March 26, 1898, p. 2.

[20]G.J.A. O'Toole, *The Spanish-American War, an American Epic—1898* (New York: Norton, 1984), p. 150.

[21]Holbrook, *Minnesota in the Spanish-American War and the Philippine Insurrection,* p. 5.

[22]Ibid, p. 3.

[23]Seib, *Headline Diplomacy,* p. 9.

[24]Since some fighting had already taken place, by pushing the actual starting day of the war back, legislators felt they were covering themselves diplomatically.

[25]Brian McAllister Linn, *The United States Army and Counterinsurgency in the Philippine War, 1899-1901* (Chapel Hill: University of North Carolina, 1989), p. 6.

[26]Karnow, *In Our Image,* p. 110.

[27]Ibid., p. 106.

Chapter 2

"Valiant Sons of Valiant Fathers"

With Minnesotans, and the nation, on the edge of their seats and ready for war, the question became not who to fight, but rather who would do this fighting. With pro-war sentiments as strong as they were that spring of 1898, it was not hard, once war had been declared, to find the necessary bodies to go and fight. In Minnesota, as across the nation, throngs of young men rushed to the nearest recruiting offices to sign up for military service.

Although their reasons varied for why they wanted to serve, some common threads existed for why most signed up to serve their nation. Probably the biggest factor was that most of them had, at one time or another, sat and listened to stories about the Civil War from either their fathers, uncles, or grandfathers. Born years after the Civil War ended in 1865, this generation, which would go off to fight the Spanish, had been raised on stories of what war was like. Throughout history, one of the most peculiar issues about war is how veterans remember it. The Minnesota veterans of the Civil War, along with a large portion of the state, sold warfare to this younger generation as more of a combination of summer camp and a classic adventure story rather than recalling the horrors which always come with war.

Along with the glorious stories they were told, this younger generation also saw how their communities and state held these veterans, and the memories of those who had died, in such high esteem. Those who fought in the Civil War were the bravest of the brave, and they had sacrificed all for the glory of the Union. For many who enlisted in 1898, it was this, attainment of personal glory and respect, which was the catalyst for them to go off and fight the Spanish. For those who desired adventure and glory, this war would be their ultimate dream. It would allow them to attain honor for themselves, and their country, by showing bravery in some far-off battlefield, and, they hoped, place them in the upper echelon of society, much as it had done for an earlier generation.[1]

The Civil War veterans, with war drawing near, proudly showed their patriotism and stood behind their stories of the past. Few, if any were to come forward and try to warn these boys about the possible dangers that lay ahead. For some, the persistence of peace was not a source of national pride, but rather one of concern. A number of the veterans from the Civil War even went so far as to say that the lack of war was detrimental to the creation of a "praiseworthy national character." Many of these veterans felt this younger generation was growing up without having to prove its manhood, thereby implying that these boys had a life that was far too easy.[2]

Those who turned over their civilian clothes for those of a soldier also saw this conflict as an opportunity to travel and see the world. From the letters sent home during the first days of camp, it is obvious that a great many of those who joined had never been more than a few miles from their homes in their entire lives. By joining the army or navy, many believed they would be given the one and only chance in their lives to see different parts of the United States and the world.[3]

The final reason for this generation of Minnesotans to go off to war was because of what their newspapers and politicians had been telling them. Getting all of their information about the outside world solely from their local newspapers, those who signed up had for months read stories about the evil Spanish empire, and even more important, stories of how weak and decrepit the Spanish soldiers were. In their minds then, America was on an altruistic mission to save the Cubans and Filipinos from the horrid Spaniards, not only freeing them from their oppressors, but also bringing them American liberty. By joining the military, they would not only be doing their patriotic duty but, maybe even more important, they would be doing the right and just thing. It was this that their politicians and newspaper editors had been telling them for months, and it was this notion that these soldiers brought with them into the field months later.[4]

With the questions of whom they would fight and who would do that fighting answered, the next question the government had to ask itself was how were they going to do this fighting. The regular army, all but dissolved in the years following the Civil War, had in the latter half of the nineteenth century been made up primarily of smaller units doing their service in a series of forts in the West. With war imminent, the debate then arose between President McKinley and some on his staff over the size of the army needed in this war. In the end, knowing that this shrunken regular army would not be adequate, McKinley and his Secretary of War, Russell Alger, turned to the National Guard units to fill in the necessary numbers.

Although neither Secretary Alger nor Major General Nelson A. Miles, the army's senior officer, held the state National Guard units in high esteem, they did see them as being somewhat useful. Both agreed that the National Guard would not make up any fighting units, but rather could be used primarily as a police force to protect the coastal defenses during wartime.[5]

In their estimation of the National Guard as being basically useless, they were probably not too far off. Until 1898 the Guards had been "primarily [a] social and political club," used more for social gatherings and political patronage than anything else. Most National Guard units also "had little equipment, an easy going type of discipline . . . and scarcely any cavalry or artillery." Worst of all was the fact that few, if any, knew anything about war, much less how to fight one.[6]

By April 9, 1898, General Miles devised a plan to fight the war that consisted of using all the Regular Army and asking for 40,000 to 50,000 volunteers. Knowing that the National Guard just did not have the numbers they needed, Miles devised this plan calling for volunteers to come from the states immediately following any declaration of war, much as they had done during the Civil War. Most of these volunteers, it was hoped, would come from the state National Guard thereby giving the state governments the power to organize the regiments and select their officers.[7]

On April 13, Congress enacted this plan and six days later, on April 19, the same day Congress authorized armed intervention in Cuba, a bill was brought to both the House and Senate that asked for the creation of an all-volunteer army. The government would not only get the required number of troops they felt they needed, but they would also tap into a vein of patriotism not known in the United States since before the Civil War.

Even before Congress passed legislation for the establishment of this all-volunteer army, and even before war had been declared, patriotism in Minnesota ran rampant. With war fever having gotten the best of them, many wanted to do their part and proudly display their patriotism. From March, until war was officially declared in April, Minnesota Governor David Clough's office was deluged with requests from all across the state with citizens asking that they be given their chance to do their duty.

In order to do their duty though, a great many wanted and asked for some kind of political patronage from the governor. Knowing that Clough was to be in charge of the decisions of who would lead the state's regiments, many wrote to him requesting that they, or their son, be mustered in at one rank or another. Typical was D. M. Neill's letter to the governor of April 9, 1898, in which he informed Clough that his son, Edmund P. Neill, had forwarded his "application for a Lieutenancy in the volunteer service. . . ." He went on to explain that his son would make an excellent leader and that Edmund would do himself and the governor credit. Although not brought in as a lieutenant, the younger Neill was made a corporal in the Volunteers.[8]

Another man seeking a position within the volunteer organizations was the Reverend Charles A. Cressy. A veteran of the Civil War, in which he served with the Fourth Regiment New Hampshire Volunteers, this Episcopalian preacher's exciting life was far from over, and he wished to be part of this new adventure. After "respectfully apply[ing] for a position as Chaplain in the State troops," the reverend closed his letter to the governor's office by explaining that he desired, "most earnestly to Serve [his] country."[9]

Patriotism was not monopolized in Minnesota by only those in the metropolitan areas of Minneapolis and St. Paul, but it was also found in the northern part of the state. From Park Rapids came a letter to the governor requesting that the writer, P. D. Winship, a Civil War veteran, be given command of the troops from Hubbard County, since they were ready for war. He also informed the governor that, due to his past experiences, he was the obvious choice as their leader. Caught up in, and reflecting the jingoistic tendencies found in even the most patriotic newspaper in New York, Winship concluded his letter to the governor by saying that if "[W]ar with Spain [is] inevitable [then] every American Heart Burns with Patriotism (sic) and wants only the call to arms to spring to the front and avenge the wrongs and insults that Spain has heaped upon the nation." Through these letters, it is obvious that the work of newspaper editors clamoring for war had been very successful.[10]

Where some Minnesotans could not hide their patriotism, others could not hide their uniqueness. Again coming from the north, this time from Duluth, an overly ambitious group of citizens requested that the governor admit them to the volunteer units because they had a unique talent that could help win this war. This ability that made them unique was that they were entirely made up of a company

15

of bicyclers. The letter stated: "I have the honor to tender the services of from fifty to one hundred wheelmen for the support of the government. . . ." To the surprise of probably few on his staff, Clough did not accept this company into the new volunteer units.[11]

But, for every one thousand super-patriots found across the state, there was always one who saw things in a different light. In a letter dated March 1, 1898, Hook Maglook wrote the governor saying: "I notice from the daily papers, that your mail of late is from men who want to command the first company in the first regiment enlisted. In order to break the monotony of the same I tender my service as the last private in the last company, of the last regiment." If Hook's wish was that his sarcasm would keep him away from any fighting, it worked; he never served in the volunteers.[12]

Although Hook Maglook's letter was the one oddity in the thousands of letters sent to the governor that spring, most of the rest resembled those shown earlier. Groups such as the Young Men's Democratic Club, Sons of Veterans, USA, and men who had served in the Civil War and wanted the honor again, deluged the governor's office with requests for membership in the new volunteer units. Along with these specific groups of people, Clough also received letters from cities all across the state, including Duluth, Willmar, Worthington, Crookston, Tower, Hector, Osakis, and East Grand Forks, all requesting that their towns be represented in the pending fight.[13]

With patriotism at an all-time high across the United States, and would-be soldiers from all walks of life preparing for war, it was just a matter of time before the government led these men off to war. The anticipation of war peaked in those last days of April, and was reflected in a *Minneapolis Tribune* article that stated that "[W]ar strikes no terror to the heart of

the Minneapolis man. It rather awakens him to the fact that he is a citizen of the greatest republic on earth and that as such he has an opportunity now of proving his loyalty to his country." It was this type of super-patriot rhetoric that not only helped recruit Minnesota's boys for this "great adventure," but also kept the regular citizenry at a fever pitch for war.[14]

On April 23, 1898, the news had finally come that answered the prayers of volunteers across the nation when President McKinley, under the just-passed legislation, requested that states recruit volunteers for the war against Spain. In a surprising move, McKinley, instead of requesting the 60,000 volunteers that the War Department had originally planned, asked for 125,000 volunteers, double of what was originally intended.

President McKinley's supporters cite three reasons why he asked for such a large volunteer force. First, and probably most important, many of his advisors had warned him not to make the same mistake Lincoln had made during the Civil War. In the first few weeks of the Civil War, Lincoln had called up too few volunteers right away and then tried to get more later, a delay that proved costly for the Union. Second, McKinley wanted to impress Spain with America's vast military manpower, still hoping that he could frighten the Spaniards into a diplomatic solution. Third, the President knew that he had to jump on the bandwagon and take advantage of the wave of patriotism sweeping across the nation. Somebody had to take credit for this war, and, with the presidential campaign coming up, it might as well be him.[15]

The call from the president was met with great enthusiasm throughout Minnesota. At the Minneapolis Armory, where a number of the boys from the Minneapolis National Guard companies had gathered, the word that they had been called was met with a "cheer that shook the rafters of the

University of Minnesota students who joined the Thirteenth Minnesota

rickety old building. . . ." The Minneapolis companies also received word that one of their own, a Colonel Charles McC. Reeve would be appointed colonel of the regiment, which received another thunderous round of cheers.[16]

Despite all of the enthusiasm for war, Minnesota troops were not ready to fight a war. Under the new legislation, the volunteer units were to resemble their counterparts in the Regular Army. The Minnesotans, as well as other state's units, were nowhere near this. Whereas the Regular Army had companies of approximately eighty to one hundred men, most newly formed volunteer units resembled Company C of the future Thirteenth Minnesota Volunteers. As late as April 23, 1898, this company "had on the rolls 50 men; of these 38 immediately volunteered . . ." the rest had excusable reasons not to go off and fight. This left Company C, much like the other state companies, with less than half the required numbers to be mustered in. To fill these gaps, men came from literally right off the street to sign up for military service and began preparing to fight a war.[17]

Brigadier-General C. McC. Reeve

17

Even though they were accepting a wide variety of recruits, there were requirements that had to be met before these men could become volunteers. The military was looking for men who were "between the ages of 18 and 35, of good character and habits, able bodies, free from disease and must be able to speak the English language." They also wanted, if possible, to avoid married men, minors (who needed their parents consent), only surviving parents, and non-citizens.[18]

On April 25, 1898, the die was cast, and America declared war on Spain. That same day Secretary of War Alger telegraphed the state governors, explaining to them exactly what portion of the 125,000 volunteers they were to raise, and specifically what number of regiments, companies, or batteries each was to organize. He finished his telegram by requesting that as many of these volunteers should be recruited from each state's respective National Guard units, as Miles and Alger had discussed earlier.[19]

The wire from the secretary of war to St. Paul clearly informed Governor Clough that "[T]he number of troops from your State under the call of the President . . . will be three regiments of infantry." Clough replied that same day that Minnesota could supply the three regiments, but they would need supplies. Minnesota, as he informed Alger, had "about half the required number of rifles, gun slings, bayonets, belts, haversacks, blanket bags, blankets, overcoats, blouses, trousers, campaign hats, caps, leggings and meat-ration cans. . . . The troops however, he stated, were ready for muster at once."[20]

The original three regiments were not up to standards according to the Hull Army Reorganization Bill, which was passed on April 26. This bill, dealing with the new volunteer army, specified that each regiment should consist of twelve companies each. As for Minnesota's, both the First and Second Regiment, formed two days before, had ten companies each, whereas the Third only consisted of eight. This put Minnesota eight companies short. Meeting the required number of soldiers for the nation's cause was not to be a problem, for once word got out that they needed more men, recruiting offices were again thronged with willing volunteers.

While finding men was never a problem, what was going to cause some difficulty for many Minnesotans was that even though they were to be mustered in and paid by the United States Government, they still wanted to be known as a state organization. As one *Minneapolis Tribune* article stated, "[T]his was the plan followed during the Civil War. Each state filled its quota and received credit for the regiments it furnished and followed their careers and preserved their records with pride." The Civil War veterans continued to cast a large and influential shadow over anything these new units ever tried to do. This comparison to the Civil War soldiers continued in an article written in the *Minneapolis Tribune*, entitled "Valiant Sons of Valiant Fathers." This report described how this generation would serve its nation as well as their fathers had thirty years earlier. Having enlisted for two years, or for the duration of the war, "the boys leave their homes and employment in glorious uncertainty as to when they will return."[21]

With the organization of the regiments decided, and how many each state should provide to the cause, the next decision lay in the hands of each state's government. The question before them was where to set up training camps for the volunteers. State government and military leaders decided that the best place to set up camp for these three regiments was the State Fairgrounds. Believing there would be enough room there, they renamed it Camp Ramsey, after the state's first territorial governor, who was still alive. The next thing state officials had to do was to get the troops congregated in their new home.

Cashing in on the patriotic sentiments, the plan was to have all three regiments meet at the state capitol and from there march to Camp Ramsey. This gave the people of the Twin Cities the opportunity to cheer on their men, and also gave Clough more recognition, for he, much like McKinley, also had a political campaign coming up.

With the orders to meet at the state capitol on the morning of April 29, 1898, some could not help but to continue to point out the similarities between the Civil War and the current war. One astute observer noted that the First Minnesota Regiment was mustered in on April 29, 1861, and, exactly thirty-seven years later, on the very same day, the three regiments for the war with Spain were mobilized at the state capitol.[22]

Upon the arrival of the other three companies from outside the Twin Cities, the regiments lined up in parade formation at the capitol and headed out toward Camp Ramsey. With Colonel Joseph Bobleter and the Second Regiment in the lead, they were off. To get to Camp Ramsey, this newly formed army had to wind its way through the crowds of well-wishers that lined the city streets. As they started out, they passed in review of the governor with bands playing and crowds cheering them on.

Even with the festive atmosphere, it was not a joyous occasion for all involved. Due to an unseasonably warm April day in Minnesota, some of the soldiers who were not use to the excitement or conditioned for marching "dropped out during the march and covered the remainder of the distance in street cars." Upon reaching the camp, soldiers found themselves exhausted "and immediately sought the shade."[23]

After the hours of parades, speeches and numerous ovations for their bravery, they reached their destination, and it was now time to get to work. The first order of business was where to put everyone.

Lacking the number of tents needed to accommodate all the troops, the camp commanders decided on rather unique barracks. With enough tents for one regiment, they had the men of the Second Regiment "pitch their tents . . . on the grounds occupied by the gun club, immediately east of the racetrack, and on an eminence which will overlook the entire grounds (today know as Machinery Hill)." They were more creative in their placement of the First and Third Regiments. They decided that the remaining two regiments could easily fit into the state fairground's stock barns. "Each of the barns for horses contains 54 stalls, and bunks for two men could readily be placed in each." Of course the two regiments would move into their luxurious new surroundings only "after the floors had been swept [and] the buildings clean[ed]. . . ." Those cleaning out the barns grumbled about this duty until the traditional Minnesota spring weather returned, and those in the tents had to deal with the wind, the cold, and the rain.[24]

Private Lewis Burlingham of Company K from Stillwater, in one of his first letters home to his parents (he was only seventeen and too young to enlist without consent from his father) told them about life in the barns and the lack of creature comforts there. "We are in barns and sleep in the stalls, have straw to sleep on. There are four or more men in each stall and when one wants to turn over he has to holler and the rest of us turn at the same time."[25]

Once the soldiers were moved into their new homes, the next order of business was to start making them into an army. The first thing that the camp leaders decided the men needed was a set of rules. Posted on the second day all around the camp was the soldiers' first taste of army regulations. General Order I set forth what exactly a day at Camp Ramsey would look like:

"The following daily routine will be observed.

Reveille, 6:00 A.M.; breakfast. 6:45 A.M.; fatigue, 7:30 A.M.; sickcall, 7:45 A.M.; guard mounting, 8:00 A.M.; squad and company drills, 9:00 A.M.; first sergeants call, 11:30 A.M.; dinner, 12:00 n[oon]; officers school, 2:00 P.M. squad and company drills, 3:00 P.M.; supper, 5:45 P.M.; guard mounting, 6:45 P.M.; retreat, 7:30 P.M.; tattoo, 9:00 P.M.; taps, 9:30 P.M."[26]

Even though many of the volunteers had little or no training, for the most part they were in good hands when it came to their commanders. Colonel Charles McC. Reeve, commander of the First Regiment was given high marks by the *Minneapolis Tribune* when they told their readers that "[H]e has an eye out for the welfare of the private as well as the officers, and as long as they do their duty they will fare well at his hands." This New York born and Yale educated soldier had been a part of the First Regiment since 1883, and rapidly made his way up the ranks to colonel by 1892.[27]

Even with commanders who wanted strict military control, these volunteers could not escape the feeling that they were more at a summer camp than a military boot camp. For their relaxation, the YMCA set up a reading room where the soldiers could go and read or use the "[c]urrent magazines, the home-town newspapers, writing materials and Testaments. . . ." Weekends were even more relaxing for the soldiers. On the first weekend, much like those that followed, approximately 15,000 people showed up to see the troops. Family, friends, girlfriends, and well-wishers from all over came either to see a soldier or see the spectacle swirling around the camp. For the soldiers, these weekends were not spent preparing for war but rather picnicking, going on excursions to local sites (this was the first time in the big city for a good number of these soldiers) or playing games. The atmosphere at Camp Ramsey resembled a Fourth of July picnic more than a military institution.[28]

After a weekend of festivities, the boys woke up on Monday morning, May 3, 1898, knowing that that day would decide the fate of a great many of them. Over the next two days, the physical examinations would begin for the soldiers. All knew that this was the cut off, and, by failing this, the first of many tests put before them, their dreams of achieving Civil War-style heroism would be destroyed before they even left the state.

A great many of the soldiers, knowing that their physical condition was nowhere near what was needed to pass, tried to make up for months, maybe even years of inactivity, by whipping themselves into shape hours before the exams began. Some of the soldiers, trying to get ready were, "at one of the barns . . . jumping up and down on one foot showing how their limbs would be tested, and at another heavy knapsacks were strapped on their backs, just to see if they could carry weight gracefully."[29]

The man the soldiers most feared that day was a Major Harry, who oversaw the physical examinations for the 3,755 officers and men. To meet the War Department's standards, Minnesota had to have eighty-one enlisted men in each company, or a total of 3,096 officers and men for all three regiments. With so many men having signed up, an added fear was put on those trying to make the cut, for all knew that under current War Department requests, at least 659 Minnesota volunteers would be sent home, healthy or not.

As Major Harry wound up his physical examinations, the commanders began to get a better look at what they had. They discovered that thirteen companies "were found to be more or less short of enough able-bodied men to make up their quotas, seventeen companies reached full strength, but apparently with none to spare; and only six companies [were] said with certainty to

Men of the Thirteenth Minnesota waiting for their next meal at Camp Ramsey, St. Paul (state fairgrounds). (Courtesy of the Goodhue County Historical Society)

have dismissed men—some sixty in all—who were acceptable but for whom there was no place in those companies." Ironically, those who were dismissed, but were still healthy, did not join other companies in sufficient numbers to fill in the holes in those units.[30]

As the commanders scrambled to fill in the gaps in their units, a political struggle was developing that would have an effect upon these regiments. The same Civil War veterans, who had squawked that the lack of any wars had made this generation soft, now began to complain that they did not want their units names tied up with these soldiers' unknown future. Going to their state legislators and the governor to file their grievances, Civil War veterans complained that these newly recruited

troops had taken their regiments' numbers (the First, Second, and Third Minnesota Volunteers) and did not deserve them. The old veterans feared that this "lazy" group of kids might so badly besmirch the good name of such regiments as the First Minnesota that history would forever remember it as being a failure, and not the gallant unit it once was.

Still holding much political and sentimental clout throughout the state, the veterans got their way. On May 4, 1898, the governor reorganized the three regiments starting with number Twelve, after the eleven regiments that had served during the Civil War, thereby not stepping on any toes. From that day forward, the First, under Colonel Reeve, became the Thirteenth, while the Second, under

21

Colonel Bobletter, became the Twelvth, and finally the Third, under Colonel Van Duzee, was renumbered the Fourteenth.[31]

For the next few days, the newly organized regiments continued their drills, waited for much needed supplies from the War Department, visited with friends and families and patiently awaited word that they would soon be sent to Cuba to fight the Spaniards. Along with the monotony that developed over the next few days, illness was another developing problem. Due to it being very windy and the nights getting quite chilly, many began to suffer from colds. To coincide with this garden-variety sickness, the camp was also hit with the more serious problems of measles, pneumonia, and meningitis. But overall, and especially compared to other camps around the nation, the overall health of the Minnesotans remained good.[32]

Found in almost every military camp throughout history, the rumor mill was one of the first organizations established. Stories rapidly began to spread about which regiment was to leave first, who would go to Cuba, who would be sent to the coastal defenses, and so on. By the end of the first week and with news of Dewey's victory in Manila, new rumors began to spread that one regiment was slated for duty in the Pacific. Jumping at the chance to get involved, Colonel Reeve became a one-man lobbying machine by contacting his political and military connections and by "keeping the wires hot between Camp Ramsey, New York, and Washington." All in hope that the Thirteenth might see some action before the war was over.[33]

Before any regiment was going anywhere though, all of them had to be mustered into the service of Uncle Sam. Starting on May 6, the official mustering in was to take place. With the staff being sworn in earlier, each brought forth their companies to the camp headquarters, where their

"commander was questioned as to the character of the men presented. . . ." After the commanders responded in the affirmative, Captain Swigert, the regular army officer who mustered them in, "made a personal inspection of the line, [after which] the roll was then called. . . ." After each individual was called forward, all of them, as a unit, took off their hats and raised their right hands and in chorus swore allegiance to the United States, obedience to the president and of the officers appointed over them. Once officially made volunteers of the United States Army, they were then ordered back to their barracks or tents.[34]

After all were mustered in, the Thirteenth Minnesota consisted of fifty commissioned officers and 978 enlisted men, in the required twelve companies. These companies consisted of five companies from Minneapolis (A, B, F, I, L), four from St. Paul (C, D, E, H), and one each from Red Wing, Stillwater, and St. Cloud (G, K, and M, respectively).

With the momentary excitement of being made official soldiers over, the men quickly went back to the routine of camp life and awaited their assignments. By May 7 the rumors about the Philippines had become so frequent that many soldiers began to talk only of going to Manila to fight. The *Minneapolis Tribune* reported that "the boys are even digging up statistics and information as to the Philippine Islands so as to find out what they will see if they go there, [since] they seem to think they will."[35]

Before they could go anywhere though, the boys still had to learn how to be soldiers. In order to do this Colonel Reeve knew that his troops needed the necessary equipment with which to train. Part of Reeve's requests was met when, in the first part of May, he received an issue of 75,000 cartridges. In cooperation with the other two regiments, they established a shooting range at Camp Ramsey where the men could improve their marksman-

Members of the Thirteenth Minnesota (probably Company C). (Courtesy of the Minnesota Military Museum, Camp Ripley)

ship. In addition, the commanders continued to work on other training including close order drills and all around discipline.[36]

Even with the new drills, the weekend excursions, and the rumors that they were soon to embark upon their great adventure, camp life was becoming terribly monotonous for many of the men. As one soldier from Company G told the Red Wing newspaper, he either wanted ". . . to fight or go home. . . ." This statement expressed not only his feelings but probably most at Camp Ramsey. Not only was this sentiment to be expressed while idling away the time in Minnesota, but it was to be a constant theme of the soldiers throughout the war.[37]

By May 12 all the problems they had suffered—the lack of supplies, the monotony, and the illnesses—were quickly forgotten when word came from the Adjutant General of the Army to Governor Clough that Minnesota troops were needed. In a telegram dated May 12, Clough read "[I]n fitting out the expedition for the Philippines, Secretary of War desires that one infantry regiment from your state be placed enroute for San Francisco soon as it is able to travel." The telegram went on to state that they were not expected to be fully armed or equipped, since most of the equipment would be at San Francisco.[38]

While the telegraph told Clough what to send, it did not specify which unit was to go. Although the Twelfth was actually more prepared to leave in a moment's notice, it was to be the Thirteenth Minnesota Volunteers that went, due to Colonel Reeve's lobbying of both state and national legislators, which gave them the governor's final approval. Along with Reeve's persistence, it was believed by most that the Thirteenth was the best equipped and drilled. With the official word being quickly handed down the chain of command, by the time it reached the soldiers, the news was met with a raucous celebration in the barn-barracks.[39]

With the assignment of the Thirteenth to the Philippines, they, more than their counterparts the Twelfth and Fourteenth regiments, captured the attention of the press and the public. Almost immediately, citizens came out to see the honored Thirteenth and to contribute money to a fund set up for them. Citizens from both Minneapolis and St. Paul continued their rivalry by trying to give more money than the other to Colonel Reeve and a board of officers from the Thirteenth Regiment. The smaller cities of St. Cloud, Red Wing, and Stillwater also sent money to help their companies. Of all the money cities sent and the individual contributions given, one stood out above the rest. The Honorable James J. Hill, the Minnesota lumber, railroad, and newspaper giant donated $7,500 from his own personal fortune to the Thirteenth's fund.[40]

Before heading to the Philippines to fight, the government had decided to have all the volunteers heading to Manila stop in San Francisco for further training. For the members of the Thirteenth, the trip to San Francisco was to be taken by trains. Besides the men, the trains were to carry "15 horses, 47,000 pounds of public property, 3,500 pounds of rations, 2,000 pounds of forage, etc. . . . " The officers were to take the "palace sleeping cars," while the enlisted men had to travel in the "emigrant coaches."[41]

Before they boarded the trains to San Francisco, the boys of the Thirteenth Regiment were going to receive a lesson in military preparedness. The complaint down through the ages by the common soldier is that most of military life is made up of being told to hurry up and then having to sit and wait. With orders being received on May 12 to be ready to go as soon as possible, the Thirteenth packed fervently, and then waited four days before they boarded the train.

After four days of killing time, the Twelfth, Thirteenth, and Fourteenth Regiments all boarded trains on May 16 for their destinations. The Twelfth left first, but with no ceremony, followed by the Fourteenth, departing from the fairgrounds depot. The Fourteenth did receive some cheers, but most of those came from people who had gotten there early to see the Thirteenth off. Both the Twelfth and Fourteenth left in virtual anonymity, and that is how their military careers would stay throughout the war. Both were sent to Camp Thomas in Georgia, where they

remained until the war was over, suffering terribly from the diseases, boredom, and heat that plagued these camps.

While the Twelfth and Fourteenth faded into the distance with little recognition, the Thirteenth's send-off was quite different, for they not only had a crowd of well-wishers, but also were given two large demonstrations. "One when the regiment entrained that evening at the camp, and another when the troop trains passed through the union depot in St. Paul where other crowds had been waiting for hours for a glimpse of the Thirteenth." With the last train carrying the Thirteenth out of sight, Camp Ramsey, the one time thriving military camp and hub of excitement in the Twin Cities, was by 9:00 that night completely deserted.[42]

The trains that carried the Thirteenth away from family and friends were made up of four sections. For those young men, most of whom had not been farther than a few miles away from their homes, these trains were to take them across much of the western United States to California. Traveling across new lands, their excitement was still at fever pitch, since for many this was what they had signed up to do. For them this was all part of the adventure, taking them away from their mundane lives back in Minnesota.

Due to a railroad mix-up, the four sections of trains were split up. On May 28, while the first two sections were reaching San Francisco, the last two were still in Utah. Even though met by crowds at every stop, the trip to San Francisco was a rather uneventful one for the Minnesotans, with the exception of an incident that occurred while outside a small town in Utah. There, as John Butman, reporter from the *Minneapolis Tribune* wrote, "[T]he Minnesota boys had a hot time at Wadsworth, chasing Indians. They got after one buck who was so frightened that he jumped on top of the train to get away from them. He was finally run down by the

Men of Company G leaving from the Red Wing depot. (Courtesy of the Goodhue County Historical Society)

yelling mob, but the officers made the men release him." He then cryptically added at the end of the article, "[T]hey also captured a Chinaman."[43]

The first step of their military careers was over, and for most the adventure had already begun with their trip across the United States. What lay ahead was another camp and then, they hoped, service in the Philippines, where they might finally attain the glory needed to get out from underneath the shadow of the Civil War veterans. Before that could take place, however the men of the Thirteenth Minnesota Volunteers would have to come face to face with their racial biases and notions of superiority, clearly shown in the incident in Utah. Ironically they would have to face these issues in a land where they, for the first time ever would be the minority.

Although the trains headed toward California had forced these boys from Minnesota to leave behind their friends and families, it did not separate them from their own racial stereotypes and prejudices that were seen as being common and justifiable beliefs in the late 1890s. What also could not be seen for these men was a definite clash of cultures on the horizon that these Minnesotans, no matter how hard they tried, could not avoid. This clash would, in the end, help shape their opinions of themselves, their nation, and the world.

NOTES

[1]Richard Severo and Lewis Milford, *The Wages of War: When America's Soldiers came home—from Valley Forge to Vietnam* (New York: Simon and Schuster, 1989), p. 189.

[2]James Brands, *The Reckless Decade: America in the 1890s* (New York: St. Martin's Press), p. 317. Severo and Milford, *The Wages of War*, pp. 189-190.

[3]Lewis Saum, "The Western Volunteer and 'The New Empire.'" *Pacific Northwest Quarterly* (January 1966), p. 19.

[4]Ibid, p. 22.

[5]Joseph Smith, *The Spanish-American War: Conflict in the Caribbean and the Pacific, 1895-1902* (New York: Longman, 1994), p. 99.

[6]Leon Wolff, *Little Brown Brother: How the United States Purchased and Pacified the Philippine Islands at the Century's Turn* (Garden City, New York: Doubleday, 1961), p. 90.

[7]Graham A. Cosmos, *An Army for Empire: The United States Army in the Spanish-American War.* (Columbia: University of Missouri Press, 1971), p. 99.

[8]Minnesota. Governor. *Records, 1895-1898.* Letter from D. M. Neill to Governor Clough, April 9, 1898. Minnesota Historical Society, St. Paul, Minnesota.

[9]Ibid., Letter from Reverend Charles A. Cressy to Governor Clough, April 18, 1898.

[10]Ibid., Telegraph from P. D. Winship to Governor Clough, April 19, 1898.

[11]Ibid., Letter from Wilson and Wray Law Offices, April 21, 1898.

[12]Ibid., Letter from Hook Maglook to Governor Clough, March 1, 1898.

[13]Ibid., Survey of all letters written to Governor Clough in the spring of 1898.

[14]*Minneapolis Tribune,* April 23, 1898, p. 5.

[15]Graham Cosmos, *An Army for Empire*, p. 109. David Trask, *The War with Spain in 1898* (New York: MacMillan, 1981), p. 152.

[16]*Minneapolis Tribune,* April 23, 1898.

[17]Hiram David Frankel, *Company 'C,' First Infantry Minnesota National Guard: Its History and Development* (Brown, Treacy and Speary, Co.), p. 35.

[18]Trumball White, *Pictorial History of Our War with Spain for Cuba's Freedom* (Freedom Publishing Co., 1898), p. 372.

[19]Cosmos, *An Army for Empire, p. 109.*

[20]Holbrook, *Minnesota in the Spanish-American War and the Philippine Insurrection,* p. 16.

[21]Virginia Brainard Kunz, *Muskets to Missiles: A Military History of Minnesota* (St. Paul: Minnesota Statehood Centennial Commission, 1958), p. 120. *Minneapolis Tribune,* April 27, 1898, p. 2.

[22]Kunz, *Muskets to Missiles, p.* 120. *Minneapolis Tribune,* April 29, 1898, p. 1.

[23]Holbrook, *Minnesota in the Spanish-American War and the Philippine Insurrection,* p. 19. *Minneapolis Tribune,*

October 8, 1899, p. 2.

[14]*Minneapolis Tribune,* April 30, 1898, p. 5.

[15]Lewis Preston Burlingham to Parents, May 2 1898. Burlingham, Lewis P., 1879 to 1951, Letters, Minnesota Historical Society, St. Paul, Minnesota.

[26]*Minneapolis Tribune,* October 8, 1899, p. 2.

[27]*Minneapolis Tribune,* May 1, 1898, p. 4.

[28]Holbrook, *Minnesota in the Spanish-American War and the Philippine-Insurrection,* p. 123.

[29]*Minneapolis Tribune,* May 3, 1898, p. 7.

[30]Holbrook, *Minnesota in the Spanish-American War and the Philippine Insurrection,* p. 21.

[31]Ibid, p. 20.

[32]Ibid, p. 20.

[33]*Minneapolis Tribune,* May 6, 1898, p. 10.

[34]Holbrook, *Minnesota in the Spanish-American War and the Philippine Insurrection,* pp. 21-22.

[35]*Minneapolis Tribune,* May 7, 1898, p. 2.

[36]Kenneth M. Davies, *To the Last Man: The Chronicle of the 135th Infantry Regiment of Minnesota* (St. Paul: The Ramsey County Historical Society, 1982), p. 56.

[37]*Red Wing Republican,* May 13, 1898, p. 1.

[38]Holbrook, *Minnesota in the Spanish-American War and the Philippine Insurrection,* p. 23.

[39]Ibid., pp. 23, 47.

[40]Tew, *Official History of the Operation of The 13th Minnesota Infantry,* p. 2.

[41]*Minneapolis Tribune,* May 14, 1898, p. 3.

[42]Holbrook, *Minnesota in the Spanish-American War and the Philippine Insurrection, p.* 25.

[43]*Minneapolis Tribune,* May 28, 1898, p. 2. (There was never any mention of the "Chinaman" again, so no word on what ever became of him or the Native American gentleman.)

Chapter 3

"... Well Equipped and Excellently Drilled"

After having traveled across the western half of the United States, all of the men of the Thirteenth Minnesota Volunteer Infantry had reached San Francisco and were beginning the second leg of their journey to the Philippines. In San Francisco, the War Department planned to assemble its troops into the VIII Army Corps. It was also here that the government hoped it could turn this hodgepodge of volunteers into an army, then send them halfway around the world to destroy the Spaniards.

On May 25, 1898, President McKinley made another decision that had an effect on these volunteers and the states from

Members of the Thirteenth Minnesota unloading their train. (Courtesy of the Minnesota Military Museum, Camp Ripley)

which they came. On that day, McKinley and the War Department decided to increase the army's numbers by calling up another 75,000 volunteers. The reasons for this decision were threefold. First, McKinley and the army would have reserves, something Lincoln did not have in the early days of the Civil War. Next, with all the patriotism flowing throughout the nation, more citizens would be given the opportunity to enlist and serve their country. Finally, being a wise politician, McKinley knew that more regiments meant governors could commission more officers and pay off more political debts. With the next presidential campaign always in his thoughts, the more political debts he could collect, the better chances he felt his campaign had.

The only group upset with this plan was the Regular Army. They pointed out, the Act of April 22 "... forbade the acceptance of new regiments from states whose existing units were under strength. ...." In their view, these new recruits should reinforce the first regiments called, which were grossly undermanned in their current condition. In the end, McKinley concurred with the Regular Army and told the governors to fill up existing units first, then they could begin the process of mustering in new ones.[1]

Once McKinley and the army decided they should recruit more soldiers, they then informed each state as to its new quota. Since few companies in the original three regiments were up to the required 106 enlisted men, most of the 2,000 men, newly recruited from the North Star State, were to be sent to those units already established. Those who remained would be mustered into the newly recruited Fifteenth Minnesota Volunteer Infantry.[2]

Although many politicians wanted these new recruits to be used as political gain for many state governors, including Clough, this decision was seen as being both irritating and embarrassing. In a May 28 telegram to the Secretary of War, Clough argued: "Minnesota acted in exact accordance with your letter of April twenty-fifth in regard to [the] number of men to be mustered into each company in first call. I don't want it understood that shortage was any mistake of mine." Clough was afraid that this new request would make him and other governors look incompetent. But, not wanting to ruffle any feathers in Washington, he also added: "[H]owever, will be pleased to furnish shortage of nine hundred and ninety men. . . ." When it came down to it, Clough, a crafty politician himself, knew this war was a political windfall and wanted to take advantage of it as much as the next politico.[3]

While some of the men from the Thirteenth Minnesota were sent back to recruit soldiers to fill up their ranks, the rest of the men were just getting into San Francisco and were setting up camp. In the early morning hours of May 20, the Thirteenth arrived in Oakland where they had to march ". . . up hill it seemed all the way . . ." carrying an excess in bags and equipment, due to the fact that "[T]hey had not yet learned the act of getting along without things . . ."[4]

After marching through the city, they then headed to Camp Merritt, named after the Philippine Expeditionary Forces' commander, General Wesley Merritt. The general, much like the camp that bore his name, did not appear too friendly toward these volunteers. In a comment made on May 16, Merritt "complained publicly of his distaste for volunteer troops and asked that regular units then in Florida be directed to his expedition."[5]

Until Dewey's smashing victory in Manila Harbor on May 1, the government's, as well as the public's, full attention was focused on the events transpiring in Cuba. Having focused all of their attention on the island south of Florida, few, if any, of America's military strategists had ever made plans for the army going anywhere else but Cuba. With the decision to fight in the Philippines, the War Department, already grossly unprepared to fight and having already sent almost all of its Regular Army to the southeastern United States to prepare to invade Cuba, had to rely on these volunteers from the Western states to fight the war in the Pacific.

Merritt, originally welcomed his assignment, but, by the time his expedition had assembled at San Francisco, he had seriously begun to regret it. A Civil War veteran and a career military man, he did not want to face the logistical problems of moving an army that size, especially one which was almost completely made up of amateurs. Not only would he have to try and train a nonprofessional army, but he also had to supply 15,000 men from government stores that were depleted when most of the equipment had already been sent to the Regulars in Florida. Finally, Merritt had to deal with the fact that this group was embarking on America's first war to be fought overseas. Due to isolationist policy, the army and navy had never built, nor did they own, any troop transport ships. It would be up to Merritt and his staff to find the necessary transportation to take this citizen army across the Pacific.[6]

If the camp's namesake was not thrilled to have the volunteers, the camp itself was even less welcoming. According to one Thirteenth Minnesota historian, "[T]here was not a single natural advantage about Camp Merritt to recommend it as a place for troops. Each regiment was quartered on a sand lot without trees or grass. The streets surrounding the grounds were overrun with salons and disrespectable haunts of all kinds."[7]

The camp, "located four miles west of the main part of San Francisco, a mile from the ocean, and just north of the Golden Gate Park . . ." was also unpopular because it was situated atop an old racetrack, also filled with fine sand. Whenever the wind blew in from the ocean, which was frequently, the men and their equipment were covered in sand. These impromptu sand storms, combined with the "unseasonably cold weather and frequent fog" prevented the soldiers from drilling in this area. In order to alleviate the men of drilling in such horrible conditions, the commanders decided to send them to the Golden Gate Park or on Presidio Hill to finish their training.[8]

For the men, the difficulty of having a commander who was not thrilled with them, coupled with the foul weather, all paled in comparison to the problem of the lack of supplies. Although there were a few modern guns, most of the recruits were given the army's old 1873 Springfields, while a handful had the newest weapon, the superior bolt-action Krag-Jorgenson.[9]

Although this lack of supplies was irritating to the Minnesotans, it was more of a problem for other states' units. Those volunteers not only came without uniforms, but a great many soldiers made it to camp without such essentials as shoes, hoping the government would supply them once they got there. The Thirteenth was fortunate that their state's National Guard stores did have a fairly large supply of

equipment and that through their fund they were able to purchase many other needed things.

The final problem the volunteers faced during their time at Camp Merritt was that of illness. This was a problem that plagued not only Camps Ramsey and Merritt but every military camp during this war, whether it was in the Unites States, Cuba, Puerto Rico, or the Philippines. As Martin

Men of the Thirteenth Minnesota posing for a picture. Notice the Minnesota flag in the background. (Courtesy of the Minnesota Military Museum, Camp Ripley)

The troops lining up at Camp Merritt. (Courtesy of the Minnesota Military Museum, Camp Ripley)

Tew, the official historian of the Thirteenth, was to point out, in Camp Merritt, "at one time 198 members of the regiment were incapacitated for duty by reason of sickness." These illnesses passing through the camp would bring the first death to the

Thirteenth. On May 30 typhoid fever claimed the life of Corporal William W. Ray of Company I, the Thirteenth Minnesota's first casualty of war.[10]

Even with all the negative things going on around them, the Thirteenth, along with all the other volunteers encamped at San Francisco, was able to find one bright spot. This morale booster came in the form of the good people of the city. Showing undying civic pride, many San Francisco citizens opened up their hearts and doors to the volunteers. Rarely did a day go by when a San Franciscan did not either bring food and or conversation to the camp, or even invite a young soldier to share a home-cooked meal.

A variety of stories came from the time in San Francisco, detailing how the soldiers were treated during their stay, especially by the women. A *Minneapolis Tribune* article that ran May 29 stated that ". . . at present Minnesota has the most popular camp, and the women are rapidly finding out their good qualities."

While many of these women were of upstanding character, there were also those who had converged on these camps to ply their trade to these boys who were ripe "off the farm!" As quickly as the military camp was built, houses of prostitution encircled.[11]

Private John Bowe, a Minneapolis man, originally from England and serving with Company B, also commented on how well the people of San Francisco had treated them. In a diary, which he kept throughout the war (and which he published afterward), he described the soldiers' feelings about the out-pouring of emotions. Bowe claimed that the San Franciscans "all tried to make us feel welcome and at home, and I think they succeeded, for many of the boys would rather be here than at home." He was right, for after the war a great many of the men of the Thirteenth returned to San Francisco either to find work or to reunite with some of the young women they met while on their brief stint in the city.[12]

Company C posing for a picture in camp at San Francisco.

Company G on parade for the people of San Francisco. (Courtesy of the Goodhue County Historical Society)

Like the other volunteers encamped at Camp Merritt, the Minnesotans did receive a great deal of attention from the people of San Francisco. But the Thirteenth stood out compared to the other Western volunteers for three reasons. First, all reports commented on the fact that the average Minnesotan was considerably taller than volunteers from other states, boasting to have men who stood as tall as six feet, six inches. Second, due to their state's surplus and their regimental fund buying much of their supplies, the Minnesotans had a more professional look than other units. Third, even with their brief training period in Minnesota, they did have excellent leaders who trained them well. Therefore, they stood out in comparison to units who were less well equipped and had not had time to train.

While they stood out in California for the above reasons, many things in Camp Merritt reminded them of life back in Camp Ramsey. Camp Merritt, like Camp Ramsey, was more of a social setting than any kind of serious military training facili-

ty. In order to kill the dead time between the few hours of drill and policing duties, the men had to find other things to occupy their time. Fortunately there were plenty. One of these diversions was sporting events, primarily the numerous baseball games that the Minnesotans readily joined. Private Bowe, in his diary, even commented that on June 10, "[O]ur regiment played the S.F. boys a game of ball yesterday and got done up to a finish, 25 to 5." Whereas they never backed down to a challenge, neither did they always come out on top.[13]

Another big diversion was the town and people of San Francisco. Few if any of the local citizenry ever complained of having the soldiers in and around the city. For the volunteers, San Francisco had an exotic feel and needed to be explored. Local businessmen were able to sell almost anything to these soldiers who had little else to do with their money, other than send it home or purchase things in the city. The happiest of all these businessmen had to be the local saloon owners, for at these establishments ". . . the men sang, drank, and celebrated in the immemorial ways of soldiers on the eve of battle."[14]

The final group pleased with this situation was the prostitutes who converged on the city by the hundreds. Present-day numbers show that, along with these ladies, came an alarming increase of venereal disease found among the soldiers. In order to keep the good name of its men and so as not to embarrass them or their families back home, not a word of any member of the Thirteenth being afflicted was ever printed. By looking at how hard other regiments were hit, however, one has to assume that the Minnesotans were not all at church during their free time, thereby probably becoming afflicted with the same ailments as all the other units.

Even though the Thirteenth had departed the state weeks before, those in Minnesota did not forget them. One group, the Custer Circle Grand Army of the Republic (G.A.R.) of Minneapolis sent Mrs. L. A. Runge to present the Thirteenth with a regimental flag. This flag, made in Minnesota, "was a superb specimen of needlework, white silk, elaborately embroidered on both sides with the Coat of Arms of the state."[15]

After the flag was handed over and unfurled, the men gave a boisterous cheer. Then, after thanking Mrs. Runge and the good people of the state, Colonel Reeve pledged the crowd gathered there that "every drop of blood in the veins of the boys of the 13th before they would allow the flag to be dishonored." Again the men cheered. Still thrilled with the idea of going off to fight a war, ironically this enthusiasm was one of the first casualties of war when America's policies changed that next spring.[16]

On June 6, 1898, Major John Friedrichs, Captain Corristan, and

Lieutenant Merrill, accompanied by twelve enlisted men, left San Francisco and returned to St. Paul and Minneapolis for the purpose of recruiting an additional 300 recruits. This was in accordance with the War Department's recent requests to get all companies up to 106 men. When these fifteen men returned to Minnesota, recruitment was not a problem. By this time all had heard that the Thirteenth was heading to the Philippines to fight, and enlistment with them meant almost certain action. Whereas Friedrichs' group had no problem getting the needed 300 men, the Twelfth and Fourteenth Regiments had a little more difficulty since they had received no word as to whether or not they were to leave their camps and go to Cuba.

After gathering their recruits, these officers had them mustered in on June 14,

The flag of the Thirteenth Minnesota on display at Camp Merritt (both flags can still be seen in the rotunda of the state capital). (From *Campaigning in the Philippines . . .*)

1898, and sent to San Francisco on the sixteenth. After four days on the trains, these new soldiers were greeted at Camp Merritt by Colonel Reeve, his staff, and the regimental band. These "rookies," as those with only six weeks of experience called them, were "equipped as no volunteers entering San Francisco had yet been equipped, and so soldierly in bearing and appearance that they attracted attention on every side." In just a matter of weeks the Thirteenth had distinguished itself as being a unique unit in a unique army. This was something of which they were very proud and were not going to allow the "rookies" to do anything to hurt.[17]

By June 20, with the new recruits settled in camp, along with the twenty-one men who enlisted to be part of the Thirteenth in San Francisco, the total number of both men and officers in the regiment was 1,349. Meeting all standards required of them by the War Department, the only thing they had to do now was to sit and wait.

The troops began to get tired of the monotony of drills and the boredom of daily camp life. As the *Minneapolis Tribune* wrote in its June 16 edition, "[T]he Minnesota boys are growing sad. The main trouble is due to too long a camp in one place without anything in particular to relieve the monotony. There is also the general disappointment caused by the selection of this or that regiment to go to the Philippines, said regiments being manifestly inferior to that sent out by Minnesota." Feeling that they were superior to their comrades in arms from other states, sitting in camp watching "inferior" regiments heading out, only intensified their boredom and dislike for Camp Merritt.[18]

This boredom would be reprieved quickly though with a single visit from General Merritt to the Thirteenth on June 15. On his official visit, Merritt said "many complimentary things in regard to the regiment . . ." but most important of all he told them that he had ". . . asked for its special detail . . . to accompany his expedition . . ." to the Philippines. Since April, the Minnesotans had had plenty to cheer about, but it was this news, that they were finally going to go fight, that received the most boisterous cheer from the men. Now they were going to get their chance at gaining glory and honor, fighting in a war in a far off land. The stigma of not being as worthy as their fathers and grandfathers, would, they hoped, finally be washed from them on the distant island shores of the Pacific.[19]

Although they received word on June 15 that they were slated to leave, it would take almost a week before they were to set sail. In the meantime, the regiment continued to drill and was even asked to give an exhibition drill for the benefit of the California Red Cross, which was attended by hundreds of northern Californians. They put on such a fine show that one San Francisco paper would say of them; "[V]ery fine looking men those Minnesota boys, well equipped and excellently drilled. They are an example of what volunteers may be and are surpassed by few regulars." It was these kinds of soldiers that General Merritt, the man who gave little credence to the ability of volunteers, wanted for his campaign in the Philippines.[20]

Whereas the Thirteenth continued to get ready by drilling, packing and writing letters home, the camp's commanders prepared by seeking out transportation to take these troops across the Pacific. The relatively small number of American vessels that sailed the Pacific made this task difficult. They were able to come up with steamers that were primarily passenger ships built for voyages to tropical climates. One of these, the *City of Para*, which belonged to the Pacific Mail Steamship Company, was chosen to take the Thirteenth to the Philippines.

By June 25, both the ships and the men were ready to depart. As the *Minneapolis Tribune* reported that day, "[T]he

13th Minnesota regiment is on waiting orders. Everything possible is loaded on the boats, and nothing remains but orders to strike tents." By that night, the orders had come down that it was time to break camp. With the exception of the new recruits who still needed more training, the rest of the regiment headed toward the docks.[21]

Those leaving on the *City of Para* and the other two steamers, made up the third expedition of United States troops heading for the Philippines, the first two having been sent earlier that summer. This expedition, included the Minnesota Volunteers, troops from Idaho and Wyoming, twelve companies of regulars and the Astor Battery (a mountain artillery unit privately equipped by John Jacob Astor and manned principally by college students).[22]

In what was becoming a common occurrence, crowds lined the streets cheering the departure of the volunteers. Marching through the streets of San Francisco, the Minnesotans received flowers, fruit, and kisses from the young ladies in attendance. Much like their march from the state capitol to Camp Ramsey, the day turned out to be a hot one, but with the assistance of the citizens who brought them water, this time none dropped out.

At the time of embarking onto the *City of Para*, the troops' excitement was at a fever pitch. After entering the ship and seeing their new home for the next few weeks, this excitement lost some of its luster. As the diarist, John Bowe wrote: ". . . it [the ship] was hastily fitted up for a troopship. She has three decks; the upper, having state-rooms, was occupied by the officers; the middle by the band, hospital corps, and some choice selected non-coms; while on the lower deck, in long rows of bunks, three tiers high, with only width for one man to pass through, was the rank and file. . . ."[23]

Quickly nicknamed the "Black Hole," the lower deck received instant consternation from all who saw it. The *Minneapolis*

Tribune reported how one man's complaints about the soldiers' accommodations placed him in trouble with the brass. "As Dr. [Walter] Beck, Co[mpany] I, marched into the hold of the steamer *Para* yesterday afternoon he remarked that it was an outrage to put men in such a place, and added: 'They treat cattle better than that.' Col. Reeve was behind him and said 'steady.' Beck thought it was a private talking and talked back very emphatically." Then to try and continue what he deemed a high standard of discipline for his men, "Col. Reeve . . . ordered him put in irons."[24]

While the men were slowly getting accustomed to their new home, the ship's captain and crew pulled anchor and headed out of the harbor. This did not stop the well-wishers from trying to get in one last cheer for the departing troops, though. "Yachts, small steamers, and boats of all kinds, chartered by groups of admirers, passed and repassed near enough to the transport to bombard the passengers with fruit and farewell messages." Then as they hit the last stretch before leaving the United States, the expedition was met with whistles, cannons, bands playing and crowds cheering, with a large convoy of boats following them. Finally, with the United States behind them and only their futures ahead of them the Thirteenth set sail for the Philippines.[25]

With the California coastline quickly disappearing, the boys of the Thirteenth soon discovered that the days of social picnics and leisurely military drilling were coming to an end. As Bowe recalled in his diary, "[A]s soon as we got outside the Golden Gate the trouble began. The boat commenced to rock, the boys to feed the fishes [they were vomiting], and all our presents, pie, cake, shoes, etc., that were lying under our bunks, were washed into the scupper."[26]

Ironically, those from a state whose sons often boasted of having direct lineage

Men of the Thirteenth on the *City of Para* as it departs San Francisco. (Courtesy the Minnesota Military Museum, Camp Ripley)

to the great sea-faring Vikings of Scandinavia could not find their sea legs. George W. Kurtz, Company I, wrote home explaining the sight.

> I saw dozens of poor soldier boys pale as death, looking as though they had lost their last friend, holding their hands over their stomach, waiting for their turn to come to deposit their last rations overboard. There must have been two or three hundred sick the first night and the odor below must have been terrible to those who were not sick. Not laughing at his fellow comrades Kurtz was quick to point out at the end of his letter that, "[A]lthough so sick myself I wanted the boat to sink . . ."[27]

Those who fell victim to seasickness bore the brunt of the jokes of those who initially withstood the first few hours. Besides feeling deathly ill, the sick were berated with mock commands such as, "[L]ine up according to height!" "Fire by squads!" "Ah, Sergeant, your stripes did not save you!" But these jabs quickly abated for, within twelve hours, a vast majority of the men, both enlisted and officers "had joined the grand chorus of woe."[28]

Within a couple of days, although still not old sea dogs, most of the Thirteenth were back on their feet and able to swallow and completely digest a whole meal. As Reverend Cressy wrote and told his wife on July 3, "[T]he boys are all in good spirits— and hungry. One of them said he could 'Eat a fried rat.'" With that situation fixed, the boys then found other things for their complaints. Private Bowe, who was originally unhappy with the *City of Para,* later wrote that in the Black Hole, "[T]here was scarcely any ventilation; the place smelled like a rabbit warren, and it was oppressively hot."[29]

After a couple of days, most of the men were able to get accustomed to sealife and found themselves trying to keep busy. In order to pass the time on board, a number of activities were set up for the men to do. The commanders insisted on daily drills and calisthenics in order to keep the men in shape. There was also the band, singing groups, reading rooms, educational lectures, and Bible study classes run by the regimental chaplain, Charles Cressy.

Cressy not only oversaw the Bible classes but also gave most of the sermons on Sundays. Doing all of these tasks did not keep Cressy from his other mission while on board ship. His goal was to try and keep the boys from swearing and playing sinful card games. Both, according to letters, were prevalent during those long summer days. As the reverend was to tell his wife in a letter: "[C]ard playing—and some gambling (on a small scale) goes on among the men. The Col[onel] does not see fit to interfere with the latter. My impression is that this is contrary to Army regulations and that it should be stopped." He informed his wife that he would later have to talk to the colonel about this. Reeve's reaction was not recorded.[30]

As for profanity, Cressy believed it was "one of the most common evils among the men." While on board, he charged that "the profanity with which the decks and baths echoed from morning till night was simply shocking to sensitive ears." Profanity, he went on to say "is a vice that needs reforming." He tried to set up an Anti-Profanity Association in each company, but no record survived to tell if anyone signed up.[31]

The profanity issue and the boredom of the men were to be temporarily forgotten only a few days out to sea when an event occurred that would make news not only among the Thirteenth, but also in Minnesota and the nation. In a book written after the war, a story entitled "Perseverance of a Woman," told how Colonel Reeve's wife (no first name given) "could not bear his going on the long and hazardous journey. Having done everything in her power to gain permission from the government to accompany her husband, she found that the rule was inviolable. Women were not allowed on the transports and there could be no exception."[32]

After two days stowed away, Mrs. Reeve appeared on deck and, with a show of mock terror, asked if they were going to throw her overboard. How she got on board was an issue of much debate among the soldiers, as well as in the newspapers at home. Mrs. Reeve claimed she had hidden in the cargo hold until her food ran out, but most of the men argued that she was hidden away in Colonel Reeve's stateroom until they were too far out at sea for her to be sent back.

At first, most of the enlisted men were shocked, then they became disgusted with this turn of events since the presence of a lady on board meant they had to put their shirts back on and were forced to curtail their swearing. After arriving in Hawaii, some of the other commanders told Mrs. Reeve she would have to stay in the islands and find her own way home. As Lewis Burlingham wrote home and explained the situation to his mother, "[A]t the last moment while the anchor was being raised Mrs. Col[onel] Reeve started ashore in a boat with a native during the morning. I haven't heard whether she will stay on the island or go back to the states." Being extremely tenacious Mrs. Reeve would actually do neither, for a few days after the troops left Hawaii she took a ship to Hong Kong and then on to Manila.[33]

It is highly unlikely that a lady like Mrs. Reeve could have slipped by the sentries and lived in the cargo hold for a few days without being noticed, especially since she never mentioned the company she would have had below decks, for in the cargo hold of the *City of Para* were three other stowaways. Not only would these additional stowaways prove that Mrs. Reeve could not have held up in the cargo hold of the ship, but what transpired when two of them were found once again shows

the kinds of racial attitudes these western volunteers were bringing with them to the Philippines.

Their stories unfolded in the July 19, 1898, issue of the *Minneapolis Tribune*. The article first tells how the twenty-five "negro" cooks "have been in a panicky condition owing to the discovery of a stowaway, a little 'coon' about 12 years of age, who was discovered the third day out." How this boy got on board and what happened to him was not discussed in this article, but how the second stowaway came to be part of the Thirteenth was described in elaborate detail.[34]

The article went on to describe how one Minnesota citizen was fairing in his journey. The story reported that "'Snowball' Mason, the mascot of the regiment and Major Friedrichs' orderly, [were] still with the 13th." The story of Snowball Mason, is both extremely interesting and tragic at the same time, while conveying a great deal about the attitudes the men of the Thirteenth had at this time.

The regiment first had contact with Snowball back in Minnesota, during their stint at Camp Ramsey. When it came time for the Thirteenth to leave, just before they boarded the train Snowball jumped aboard and hid in a barrel and was not discovered until they were some thirty miles out of town. At that point he was unceremoniously kicked off the train. It was not until Major Friedrichs returned to recruit more soldiers that Snowball's story started again. As the newspaper reported it, "'Snowball' made such a pathetic appeal to that officer to be taken along that the kind-hearted major agreed to take him as his orderly. . . ."

With the Thirteenth about ready to board the *City of Para*, the officers agreed that they did not want Snowball to be allowed on board. Having come this far, Mr. Mason was not going to be deterred. With the same tenacity as Mrs. Reeve, he climbed aboard the night before the ship's departure using the ropes on the side of the ship, and hid below deck. He did not come out until he was sure they could not turn around and send him home and he became too hungry to stay hidden. He was "allowed" to stay only after both Companies F and I decided to "take care of him," and make him their mascot.[35]

Concluding this article was the very brief statement that a man from San Francisco had stowed away also, but when he was found he was ceremoniously mustered into service with the Thirteenth. In a sad and ironic twist of fate Snowball, an actual Minnesotan, was not allowed to serve with the Thirteenth due to the color of his skin, whereas the white man from California, who was never questioned as to how he got on board, was quickly made a soldier, and not a "mascot." These racial attitudes that many of these Minnesota volunteers had would manifest themselves in the foreign nation of the Philippines. There they continued to grow and often made the Americans behave in less than altruistic ways.

After a few days at sea, the expedition stopped at the Hawaiian Islands so that the ships could re-coal and the men could stretch their legs. Having moved into the more tropical climate of the Pacific, the soldiers on board received new uniforms to better deal with the heat. The new attire, to many of the soldiers, looked like ". . . brown duck uniforms . . ." and were believed to be, ". . . about as ugly looking garments as the most fevered imagination ever pictured. . . ." Fortunately for the soldiers though, they were, ". . . loose and baggy and consequently comparatively cool," in comparison to the blue wool ones they had been wearing.[36]

From Hawaii, the convoy headed to the Ladrone Islands before changing direction for the Philippines. Day after day of doing the same thing once again became the Thirteenth's major gripe. The only difference in this last half of their voyage was a sight beheld by all the Minnesotans for the first time in their lives. As one soldier put it, "[J]ust as it was getting dark we passed within a quarter of a mile of what turned out to be an island, and for the first time of my life I beheld an active volcano, spitting forth fire and smoke, and I doubt if ever in the history of one's life anyone will witness a more beautiful sight."[37]

With all the excitement of seeing the volcano, and knowing that they were in striking distance of the Philippines, many of the soldiers seemed to forget that it was a war they were heading to and not another drill exhibition for a civic group. With a death on board the ship during the last days of July, many were snapped back into the reality of what they were doing, at least for a few moments. With Chaplain Cressy conducting the service, Musician Fred Buckland of Company E, who had died of pneumonia, was buried at sea. As quickly as the dead soldier was swallowed by the waves, the gloom that hung over the boys quickly dissipated, and they immediately went back to their mundane lifestyle.

Two days after Buckland's burial, the men of the Thirteenth were awakened on the early morning of July 29 to see the island of Luzon. Two more days of travel brought them to the spot where history had been made just three months earlier. Hardly a soldier who was there could resist writing to the people back home that they could see the remains of the Spanish fleet, twisted, tangled and jutting out of the Manila harbor. In their minds, they were there, standing on the threshold of history, where the "greatest" naval commander in all of history had destroyed the dastardly Spanish. Most of them, as they wrote home, had a sense that it was here, in the Philippine Islands, that they too would be able to make their own history, just as Dewey had.

Notes

[1]Graham Cosmos, *An Army for Empire; The United States Army in the Spanish-American War* (Columbia: University of Missouri Press, 1971), p. 135.

[2]Franklin F. Holbrook, *Minnesota in the Spanish-American War and the Philippine Insurrection, Vol. I* (St. Paul: The Riverside Press, 1923), p. 25. *Minneapolis Tribune*, May 26, 1898, p. 4.

[3]Ibid, p. 26.

[4]Martin E. Tew, *Official History of the Operation of the 13th Minnesota Infantry, U.S.V. in the Campaign in the Philippine Islands* (S.I.: S.N., 1899), p. 3. Hiram David Frankel, ed., *Company "C." First Infantry Minnesota National Guard: Its History and Development* (Brown, Treacy and Speary Co.), p. 36.

[5]David F. Trask, *The War with Spain in 1898* (New York: MacMillan Publishing, Co., 1981), p. 383.

[6]Stanley Karnow, *In Our Image: America's Empire in the Philippines* (New York: Random House, Inc., 1990), p. 117.

[7]William C. Fitch and General C. McC. Reeve, *13th Minnesota Vols.: Historical Record in the War with Spain* (Minneapolis: Price Bros. Printing Co., 1900), p. 16. Obviously written by a commander who disliked the distractions, for no enlisted man ever complained about the life outside of Camp Merritt.

[8]Margaret Inglehart Reilly, "Andrew Wadsworth, A Nebraska Soldier in the Philippines, 1898-1899" *Nebraska History* (Winter 1987): p. 187.

[9]Karl Faust, *Campaigning in the Philippines* (New York: Arno Press, 1970 [c1898]), p. 59.

[10]Tew, *Official History of the Operations of the 13th Minnesota Infantry,* p. 4.

[11]*Minneapolis Tribune*, May 29, 1898, p. 4.

[12]John Bowe, *With the 13th Minnesota: In the Philippines* (Minneapolis: A.B. Franham Printing and Stationary Co., 1905), p. 11.

[13]Bowe, *With the 13th Minnesota,* p. 12.

[14]Leon Wolff, *Little Brown Brother; How the United States Purchased and Pacified the Philippine Islands at the Century's Turn* (New York: Doubleday, 1961), p. 93.

[15]Fitch, *13th Minnesota Vols.,* p. 18. *Minneapolis Tribune,* June 13, 1898, p. 2. This flag is still on display in the rotunda of the Minnesota State Capitol.

[16]*Minneapolis Tribune,* June 13, 1898, p. 2.

[17]Fitch, *13th Minnesota Vols.,* p. 18.

[18]*Minneapolis Tribune,* June 16, 1898, p. 2.

[19]Fitch, *13th Minnesota Vols.,* p. 18.

[20]Holbrook, *Minnesota in the Spanish-American War and the Philippine Insurrection,* p. 48.

[21]*Minneapolis Tribune,* June 25, 1898, p. 2.

[22]William Thaddeus Sexton, *Soldiers in the Sun; an Adventure in Imperialism* (Harrisburg, Pennsylvania: The Military Service Publishing Co., c1939), p. 25.

[23]Bowe, *With the 13th Minnesota,* p. 14.

[24]*Minneapolis Tribune,* June 27, 1898, p. 2.

[25]Holbrook, *Minnesota in the Spanish-American War and the Philippine Insurrection,* p. 49.

[26]Ibid., p. 49.

[27]Mouraine Baker, ed., *Dear Folks at Home: Wright County's View of the Spanish-American War,* George W. Kurtz, Co. I, July 21, 1898, p. 8.

[28]Tew, *Official History of the Operations of the 13th Minnesota Infantry,* p. 5.

[29]Charles Cressy to wife, July 3, 1898. Cressy, Charles A., 1861-1916. Papers. Minnesota Historical Society, St. Paul, Minnesota.

[30]Ibid.

[31]Russell Roth, *Muddy Glory: America's "Indian Wars" in the Philippines 1899-1935* (West Hanover, Massachusetts: Christopher Publishing House, c1981), p. 41.

[32]Marshall Everett, *Exciting Experiences*

in our Wars with Spain and the Filipinos (Chicago: Quadrangle Books, 1964), p. 187.

[33]Lewis Burlingham to Mother, July 8, 1898. Burlingham, Lewis Preston, 1879-1951. Papers. Minnesota Historical Society, St. Paul, Minnesota.

[34]*Minneapolis Tribune,* July 19, 1898, p. 2.

[35]Ibid., p. 19.

[36]Ibid., p. 2.

[37]Frankel, *Company "C," First Infantry Minnesota National Guard,* p. 61.

Chapter 4

"... With Coolness, Intelligence, and Courage"

On July 25, 1898, after weeks of traveling the Pacific, the *City of Para* was able to anchor off Cavite about seven miles south of Manila. Unfortunately, the Minnesotans reached the Philippines the same time as the monsoon season, making it impossible to undertake disembarkation until August 7, 1898, when they landed at Paranaque. Until then, however, they had to sit on board and continue to view the war from a distance, which was especially irksome for the Minnesotans as they could hear skirmishes taking place between the Americans and the Spaniards. As Private John Bowe wrote: "[W]e heard the Americans and Spaniards fighting the whole night long and some of the boys were afraid the war would be over before we landed."[1]

Luckily for the glory-seeking members of the Thirteenth, these minor skirmishes amounted to very little. In the meantime, the weather broke, and the third expedition was able to go ashore. In order to get all the men and their equipment on land, the Americans had to rent small Filipino boatmen who used *cascos* (small Filipino boats that worked excellently in the harbor) to land the men and their equipment. Even though they were now "experienced" seamen, going from ship to *casco* to land proved to be another adventure. As Private Bowe recalled on that August 7th day, "... troops had problems timing their getting into the *cascos*, had to get in on the crest of the wave. Col[onel] Reeve stood there, cussing and swearing at the men, and using language that would make an old Mississippi steamboat Capt[ain] turn green with envy." Reeve's anger did not alleviate any of the problems, and probably added to them. Although no group ever got the timing part down to reach the boat at the same time the crest pushed it up, they did manage to finally get ashore.[2]

Once the entire regiment was ashore at Paranaque, they marched northward a mile and a half and pitched their tents on the south end of a peanut field named Camp Dewey. The peanut field, far from being the most luxurious camping grounds they had yet seen, was the best spot available due to the fact that it was the only "... solid, open ground in a region full of rice swamps and bamboo thickets."[3]

After setting up camp, the Thirteenth was given two days to rest and try to get acclimatized to the Philippine tropics, which, to their consternation, they quickly discovered was a combination of rain, intense heat, and high humidity. All of this was coupled with the fact that the constant rain, which plagued them the entire time they were in the islands, made the ground stay in a constant state of mud, which quickly ruined shoes, clothes, and morale.

Lewis Burlingham, finding time to write his mother, told her about life in Camp Dewey. "We pitched our tents in a peanut field and got beds from the natives, which they made out of bamboo, and slept on them because the ants there were a great deal worse than the mosquitoes and goodness knowes [sic] they were bad enough." As the two days slowly passed, the oppressive heat and rain kept pounding down upon the men, making it impossible for them to remain dry.[4]

The final problem the weather caused was illness. The heat made them perspire constantly, forcing a loss of body salts and inducing chronic fatigue. In addition, the troops also had to deal with the ever increasing problems of dysentery, malaria, cholera, and dengere fever.[5]

Besides the weather, there were a number of other disadvantages to Camp Dewey. Drinking water was a problem because of the contamination occurring in un-boiled water in the tropics. Cooking was also a problem since there was an extreme scarcity of dry wood anywhere. Finally, all the rain that kept the men and their clothes wet made the leather in their equipment mildew and become stiff when it dried.[6]

While the soldiers had plenty to complain about—the weather, food, camp life—and they did, General Merritt still insisted that no matter what the current conditions, they still had to act like gentlemen and soldiers. On August 9, he issued a general order to all the troops stating: "[I]t is not believed that any acts of pillage, rapine or violence will be committed by soldiers or others in the employ of the United States, but should there be persons with this command who prove themselves unworthy of this confidence, their acts will be considered not only as crimes against the sufferers, but as direct insult to the United States flag, and they will be punished on the spot with the maximum penalties known to military law." These orders would stand throughout the duration of the volunteer's tour of duty in the Philippines.[7]

By August 10, a day after the orders were given and just three days after their landing, the Minnesotans were put on guard duty in the trenches south of Manila. Although the men of the Thirteenth were looking for a fight, what they found was that they would have to battle the rain and mud long before they fought the Spaniards. Guard duty consisted of twenty-four hours of patrolling and standing in mud. After their duty was done, they would be relieved by another regiment and given twenty-four hours off. Lewis Burlingham later explained to his family at home that on one of his patrols: "[I]t was a bad night as it rained nearly all the time and when you wasn't [sic] on the lookout and wanted to sleep you couldnt [sic] on account of there being so much mud and water and rain to contend with."[8]

John Bowe further described the situation by writing in his diary: "[O]ur location was opposite to and within three hundred yards of Spanish Block House No. 14, where we put in twenty-four hours, crawling in and out of trenches. If we get into a trench, the water would drown us out, and if we got out of it, the Spaniards would take a 'pot shot' at us." It was a dilemma they had to endure for at least a few more days.[9]

With the third expedition under General Merritt setting up camp just south of Manila, Emilio Aguinaldo and his soldiers began to have growing suspicions about the American's intentions in the islands. The American leaders in the islands too, began to have doubts about their Filipino allies. Having come half way around the world to "free" the Filipinos from Spanish oppression, most were under the impression that they would have to either take Manila without the help of the Filipinos or end up fighting them before it was all done.

Unfortunately for all sides involved, the United States did not have any professional diplomats in the islands to deal with the Filipino revolutionaries. These relations were then left up to professional military men "who were ill-suited to play diplomatic roles due to their training and temperaments." Use to having things done once an order was given, the realm of international relations, with its constant give and take, was extremely both-

ersome and a continual annoyance for them.[10]

Chief amongst these soldier/diplomats was General Merritt, who came to the Philippines to assume overall command. Merritt, known as an "imperious leader devoid of any diplomatic inclinations," forbade any communication with Aguinaldo's headquarters. By doing this, Merritt found himself in a dilemma, for he could not attack Manila without getting permission from the Filipinos to use their trenches, which by this time completely encircled the city. On the other hand, he could not diplomatically deal with them since this went against his own order of not talking to Aguinaldo. With McKinley's orders to maintain the peace with the Filipinos at all costs, Merritt had to resort to trickery in order to get what he wanted.[11]

The Filipino guerrilla army outside Manila just before the attack on that city. (Courtesy of the Minnesota Military Museum, Camp Ripley)

45

Merritt sent General Greene to talk to Aguinaldo's staff in order to suggest a deal with the revolutionaries. The deal was that the United States would give the Filipinos much needed pieces of artillery for a sector of trenches immediately south of Manila. Knowing they needed the artillery, General Noriel, a member of Aguinaldo's staff, sent an aide to Aguinaldo's headquarters to receive his approval. Aguinaldo said he would go along with the deal just as long as Merritt signed the request.

Knowing that Merritt would refuse to sign anything dealing with the Filipinos, Greene told the Filipino leader that he would forward the document as soon as the Filipinos withdrew from the trenches. Aguinaldo, still believing that the United States and his people were truly allies, and were completely trustworthy, conceded to the demand. Sadly, neither the document nor the artillery were ever forwarded, but the American troops did move into the trenches.[12]

Tension between the Filipinos and the Americans was not lost on the Minnesotans. George W. Kurtz, Company I, wrote home on August 1 telling his family about the presumed plans to attack Manila. In it he claimed that the "[I]nsurgents don't want our help and everybody thinks we will have to fight them as soon as Manila is captured."[13]

Two days later, Captain Oscar Seebach, Company G, wrote home telling his family in Red Wing that he believed, ". . . there is not a shadow of a doubt but that we will have to fight them [the Filipinos] a great deal more than the Spaniards after Manila falls. . . ."[14]

Finally, Sergeant Alexander Kahlert, Company D, spelled out the situation in his diary when he wrote, "[W]hat preceded us have landed and are engaged in throwing up earthworks between Coirto and the insurgents, This [sic] makes it a [three-] cornered fight. The rebels are not friendly towards [and] the chances are we will have the most trouble with them.[15]

The most interesting thing about these commentaries, and others like them, is that they were written either while the Minnesotans were still on the ship or had just landed and were setting up camp. Having not been in the islands for more than a few hours, how was it that they were so sure that they would be fighting the Filipinos? Was this just personal sentiments expressed by a few adventurous soldiers looking for more excitement, or was it an already understood policy that they would have to take on the Filipinos before their duty was done? Either way these statements did reflect America's constantly changing policies towards the Filipinos and the Philippine Islands.

No matter what their personal feeling were, these men had another war to fight before having to deal with the Filipinos. With the third expedition established in Camp Dewey, Merritt had 8,500 men in position to attack the fortified city of Manila. These men, along with the navy sitting and waiting in Manila Harbor, knew that the Spaniards had no sign of relief coming to help them. With this knowledge, the Americans deemed it time to prepare for their invasion.

On August 6, 1898, both Dewey and Merritt sent a joint letter to Captain General Jaudenes [Spanish commander in the Philippines], notifying him that he should remove all non-combatants from the city within forty-eight hours. In a return message to his American counterparts, Jaudenes thanked the Americans for giving the civilians the chance to leave. This being a formal and public letter between the two warring nations, it was not the only communication these two camps had with each other in the days before the fighting broke out.

The Spaniards, held up in Manila and under attack from the Filipinos since May, were in a precarious situation. Under siege for three months, Manila was suffering from disease, starvation, and a lack of water, to say nothing of poor morale. The Spanish officials knew the situation was hopeless, but, due to a "quaint code of honor, a court-martial awaited them unless they put up a fight. So a sham battle with the U.S. forces had to be contrived to save them from disgrace." This code of honor was not to be taken lightly. Back in July, for simply suggesting a surrender, Governor Augustin was replaced by General Fermin Jaudenes as governor of the islands.[16]

Negotiations then began and were secretly conducted between Dewey, Merritt, and Jaudenes through an intermediary, Edouard Andre, a member of the Belgian counsel. The negotiated deal was laid out as follows: in order to save Spanish honor, the American fleet would have to shell the city (preferably doing very little damage), while the land forces were to keep the Filipinos out of the battle, since the Spaniards utterly refused to surrender to them. If the Americans could do these two things, the Spaniards then would only lightly defend the outer line of trenches and blockhouses and would not use their heavy guns to attack the navy.[17]

If the operation succeeded after a fixed number of shots from the navy, the *Olympia*, Dewey's command ship, was to steam forward and fly the international code for surrender, "DWHB." Then the Spaniards were to hoist a white flag, and the battle would be over. All of this was to take place without a single loss of life . . . unfortunately, even the best-made plans of mice and men go awry.

It is interesting to note that the whole "sham" battle and all the secret negotiations that were conducted were not for the benefit of the Spaniards, the Filipinos, or even the Americans. None of these groups involved truly wanted a fight and cared less about how the war was concluded but, rather, this whole battle was a show for a contingency of foreign naval vessels harbored off the coast of Manila.

At the time of the hostilities, the German, English, and other international navies had converged upon the Philippines, all looking for that proverbial piece of the pie. Jaudenes, fearing word might get back to Spain from one of these other nations that he had "cowardly" surrendered, insisted some kind of display of force be shown. Knowing that the Americans would most likely defeat the Spaniards, these other nations, wanting their chance at setting claims on the Philippines, hovered around waiting for their chance to strike.

While all of these secret negotiations were taking place, the Minnesotans and the rest of the VIII Army Corp prepared for a real battle. The original date set for the attack was to be August 10, but since Merritt did not believe his troops to be fully prepared, they re-scheduled the attack for August 13.

In accordance with the secret negotiations with General Jaudenes, Dewey, and Merritt, who had already removed the Filipinos from their well-dug trenches, were now telling them that they could not fight and help finish off the war they had started years before. To make it official, on the night of August 12, Merritt sent Aguinaldo a letter that instructed the Filipino leader to keep his troops out of the battle.

Most of the volunteers knew about the deal to keep the Filipinos out and felt it to be a good idea. Lieutenant Colonel Ames, in a letter published in the *Minneapolis Tribune*, told Minnesotans: "[G]eneral Merritt and Admiral Dewey do not intend to act in conjunction with the insurgents because it is [a] well known fact that they intend to sack and pillage the city, ravish the women, and murder the Spaniards if they once succeed in getting inside." He went on to say that if Spain were to surrender it would "result in our defending the people and the city from the bloodthirsty insurgents." During those first few days in the Philippines it seems many of the volunteers had to be reminded that they were there to "free" the Filipinos, and not to fight them.[18]

By August 12, the soldiers knew that the next day would be their chance to gain the glory about which they had been dreaming since they enlisted back in Minnesota. Angus McDonald, Company K, summarized these sentiments in a letter home, saying that, "[T]he night of the 12th we received the long looked for and joyful news that on the morrow we would make a general advance while Admiral Dewey bombarded the city. No one slept much that night."[19]

Carl Stone, Company F, also took time to write home that night and told his parents that "[T]he 13th Minn. [and] the 18th regulars have the post of honor [and] also of danger, although the general opinion seems to be that we are going to have an easy time without much fighting." Although the rumor mill was in full force, and ironically, fairly accurate, the Minnesotans were to find next day anything but an "easy time."[20]

The next morning, those who had joined the volunteers to see the adventurous side of war were to get their wish, for the battle of Manila was about to commence. Describing what took place those early morning hours was Private Bowe and his diary. "Reveille at 4:30, had a thin breakfast, then stowed away twelve hardtacks, a canteen full of coffee, and one hundred rounds of ammunition, and started to capture Manila." For him and countless other soldiers, this was their time to pay their "little tribute to the memory of the *Maine* . . ."[21]

Bowe and his comrades were awakened that morning by a bugle call and were also met with a not-too-surprising rain, which, by the time these soldiers were up and ready to go, had turned the roads into porridge. They were ordered, as Bowe recalled, to take "one day's cooked rations, canteens filled with water, and a

minimum of 100 rounds of ammunition for the Springfield rifle and 150 for the Krag-Jorgenson."[22]

By 6:00 A.M. the soldiers had dressed, eaten, grabbed their equipment and headed toward their position in the trenches. Colonel Reeve's later reported: "I moved with my regiment, comprising three battalions of four companies each, from Camp Dewey . . . and marched through the town of Pasai, along the direct road to Manila." At 7:45 A.M. the Thirteenth arrived at the general line of earthworks where they were to replace the North Dakota Regiment, who had been on guard duty throughout the night.[23]

To reach Manila from Camp Dewey, the Americans had but two choices: the Calle Real, a road toward the city that was rarely more than a few hundred yards from Manila Bay, or a road a half mile inland from the Calle Real parallel to it, running north through the villages of Pasai and Cingalon, before reaching the fortified city of Manila.[24]

The American plan to take Manila consisted of splitting the VIII Army Corp into two brigades. The main attack, led by Brigadier General Francis V. Greene, was to head up the Calle Real, whereas the second brigade, which was in support and led by General Arthur MacArthur,[25] was to go through Pasai and Cingalon and meet up with Greene in Manila.

Prepared for a real war for centuries, the Spaniards had an elaborate defense system set up around Manila. Half way between the walled city and the camp, sitting at right angles, was the Spanish outer defense—a line of earthworks extending from Fort San Antonio de Abad on the coast to Blockhouse No. 14 commanding the Pasai road. The Minnesotans, being within a few hundred yards of the Spaniards, were split up into battalions, each receiving different orders from Colonel Reeve. The Second Battalion (Companies C, H, D, and E) and the Third

Battalion (Companies I, F, B, and A) were ordered to stay behind while the First Battalion (Companies K, L, M, and G) were ordered to the extreme left of Blockhouse No. 14. Just as the troops got into position, the tropical sun of the Philippines broke through the clouds, and what had been a soggy, muddy terrain, quickly turned into a steamy, humid one.[26]

While the troops, who knew absolutely nothing about the sham battle, got into position to attack, the navy in the harbor began its part of the plan. At 9:30 A.M. the battle was joined when Admiral Dewey's command ship, the *Olympia,* began shelling the city of Manila. At the same time, the infantrymen hauled themselves out of the muddy entrenchments and proceeded through Manila's southern suburbs toward the city.[27]

While Greene's second brigade headed up the Calle Real through Malate, past Fort San Antonio de Abad and on to Manila, their support to the east was also on the move. MacArthur's first Brigade, with the Thirteenth Minnesota, who were ordered to take the lead, also consisted of the Astor Battery, and the Twenty-third Infantry, who were also sent to the front. Held in reserve, MacArthur had one battalion of the Fourteenth Infantry, two battalions of the First North Dakota, two battalions of the First Idaho, and one battalion of the First Wyoming, all ready and willing to move up if needed.

Although the entire field of operations hardly covered more than a square mile, the terrain was horrible. The Americans had to contend with barbed-wire fences, bamboo jungles, paddy fields, swamps, streams, and sharpened pickets before reaching the outer defenses. While not necessarily as big a problem for Greene's troops (who were having an easier time of it on the left), for MacArthur and the men of the Thirteenth, the terrain posed serious obstacles in what was turning out to be a rather interesting day.[28]

The Walled Fortress of Manila. Built by the Spanish as a fortified position in the islands. (From *A Wonderful Reproduction of Living Scenes in Natural Color Photos of America's New Possessions*)

Rare photo of members of the Thirteenth Minnesota in the trenches just outside Manila, August 13, 1898. (Courtesy of the Minnesota Military Museum, Camp Ripley)

Always under the notion that this was a real battle, MacArthur's brigade had more than just the terrain with which to contend. Because of the deal with Jaudenes, Dewey's fleet could not effectively shell the far right flank, nor did they have any intention to do so. With no shells hitting the Spanish defense, the Spaniards stayed in their well-entrenched fortifications, waiting for the Americans to attack. After having struggled through terrible weather conditions and rough terrain, the First Brigade then had to face the Seventy-third Spanish Regiment, "whose favorite boast was that it had never retreated."[29]

Captain Charles Metz, Company D, noted the problem with the Naval bom-

bardment, while writing home to a friend after the battle, saying that the Thirteenth had taken their "position on the right of the American line, that position being furthest from the Bay and out of reach of the Guns [sic] of the fleet. . . ." As for the landscape, Metz also noted that "the 13th was in it [and] we fought our way for fully a mile through mud and water many times up to our waist."[30]

While things were going pretty much according to the secret negotiations, an intangible came into play that morning, something for which neither the Americans nor the Spaniards had planned. On MacArthur's right flank, still occupying parts of the trenches they built, were

A more common picture of the men of Company G awaiting orders to advance. Taken in the trenches outside Manila, August 13, 1898. (Courtesy of the Minnesota Military Museum, Camp Ripley)

Filipino soldiers. Having fought the Spaniards for years, many either did not get the word from Aguinaldo to stand down, or could not contain their excitement. Either way, early in the morning on August 13, many began to exchange fire with the Spaniards. In order to deal with this, MacArthur began to send detachments to various points to stop the Filipinos from firing. This caused one of the most bizarre and unprecedented situations ever found on a battlefield. There, in the midst of a battle to free the Filipinos from Spanish tyranny, stood American soldiers pointing their guns at and threatening to kill any Filipino who tried to join in the battle.

Although a unique situation in and of itself, it was not the only one the Minnesotans encountered that day. Not knowing about the negotiations, and unable to see any white flags being displayed on the extreme left, MacArthur's Brigade, as well as the Spaniards they faced, proceeded throughout the day not knowing that what was developing was completely unnecessary.

While this bizarre situation was developing on the right, Greene's troops advanced on Fort San Antonio Abad and occupied it around 10:25 A.M. With the situation on the left quickly settled, the Thirteenth Minnesota, under orders from MacArthur, moved the First and Second

Battalions (Second had been called up a few minutes earlier) past the earthworks and toward the Spaniards. Because of the earlier fighting with the Filipinos, who were now under control by the Americans, the Spaniards were now directing their fire upon the Americans. To counter this, Colonel Reeve sent out Companies E and L to form a strong skirmish line. While under light fire from a handful of Spaniards, Companies E and L moved forward slowly until they discovered that the Spaniards were abandoning their trenches.

When it appeared that the Spaniards were retreating, the two companies were quickly ordered forward. Continuing to move toward Manila these Minnesotans soon found out that the Spaniards were not retreating but had actually set up an ambush from within the dense bamboo stands in the area and from another series of trenches. Slowing their advance, Companies E and L were again able to push the Spaniards back with desultory fire toward the center of the Spaniards defense, Blockhouse No. 14. These blockhouses, which encircled Manila, were "thirty feet square, two stories high, built on raised ground . . ." and built out of heavy planks and a mixture of earth and stone, with a bottom lined with steel.[31]

Colonel Reeve then ordered the company from St. Cloud toward the Blockhouse. This movement, by Company M, was supported by the Astor Battery whose 3.2-inch guns began to place some well-positioned volleys into the blockhouse. Although there were intense moments, most of the fighting for Blockhouse No. 14 was over once the fusillade from the Astor Battery ended. Company M (with Company A in support) quickly stormed the fortification, and by 11:20 A.M. the United States flag was placed upon it. For the rest of the day's fighting, these two companies were to hold their positions at the blockhouse while the other six pressed on toward Manila.[32]

As Private Bowe, who was in the thick of it, wrote; "[O]n reaching the corner near the little stone wall, we ran into such a hail of bullets that we got orders to lie down flat upon the road." It was here that Captain McQuade (McWade) was ordered to go take his Company A and support Company M in a hot fight with the Spaniards. As Bowe tells it, "[I]nstead of obeying orders, Capt[ain] McQuade, [McWade] hugging the stone wall, replied that he was sick and could not go ahead." At the first sign of fear by a Minnesotan during the battle, the companies' honor was saved when Lieutenant Donaldson, jumped to the front and cried, "[C]ome on boys follow me!"[33]

Pleased with their first victory over the Spaniards, the Thirteenth did not have long to revel in their glory, for they were quickly ordered to move out again toward Manila. Before they could celebrate the capture of the Philippine capital, however, they first had to go through the village of Cingalon.

At 11:20 A.M., with Blockhouse 14 under American control, MacArthur ordered the general advance to resume. With the Thirteenth still in the lead and the Astor Battery supporting them, the Second Brigade continued toward the front. Along their path toward Manila, the drive was again suddenly slowed by another Spanish blockhouse. This time, instead of the Spaniards drawing fire on them, it was the blockhouse itself that caused the problems. Having caught fire during the battle, and with a large store of ammunition inside, the blockhouse began to explode, sounding much like a Fourth of July fireworks display. Fearing for the safety of his men, MacArthur ordered his troops carefully to go around the blockhouse.[34]

As the Thirteenth tried to work its way around the exploding blockhouse, MacArthur ordered the Astor Battery to join them at the front. Due to a barrier placed by the Spaniards, the Astor Battery

Photo of Blockhouse 14, one of the obstacles the men of the Thirteenth Minnesota had to overcome during the battle of Manila. (Courtesy of the Minnesota Historical Society)

was unable to move their artillery and awaited help. With the assistance from Lieutenant March and his Regular Army troops, the Astor Battery was finally able to move its equipment over the gun emplacement that made up the barrier and obstructed the road.

Once past the burning blockhouse, and with the Astor Battery able to continue, the Second Brigade was able to advance into the village of Cingalon. There the retreating Spaniards again set up another ambush and began firing on the advancing Americans, "which increased as the forward movement was pressed, and very soon the command was committed to a fierce combat." Again the Minnesotans and their comrades found themselves fac-

ing another heavy fight from fortified Spaniards, this time from a church and the entrenchment that surrounded it.[35]

Facing the church with his six companies of the First and Second Battalion, and being far ahead of the rest, Reeve "was commanded to throw out a line of skirmishers to the right and the front, and to establish a point in the road immediately in [the] front, along which [the Thirteenth] had been advancing." He quickly detached Company K to take up position on the right, and then he sent Companies C and H to the left. Leaving Lieutenant Lackore of Company L, along with eight men and a sergeant to man the point, which was established on the road in front of the church.

Once the two St. Paul companies reached the left flank, they quickly discovered that the Astor Battery was under a hot fire from the Seventy-third Spanish Regiment. In order to protect their artillery pieces, Company H, under Captain Bjornstad began a rapid fire and saved the Astor Battery from being torn to pieces.[36]

Meanwhile, Lieutenant Lackore, with his small band of men, with little or no protection, was finally ordered out of the thick of it by Captain Spear of Company E. Having been under heavy fire since entering the village, this group was ordered to act as reinforcements for Company E, while the men from Red Wing's Company G, were sent forward to help strengthen the line. With Companies C and H pouring fire in from the left, and Company K putting pressure on the church from the right, the battle was a virtual stalemate until the Astor Battery, slowed by the Spanish obstructions, could establish themselves in the village. With orders to move back 100 yards, the four companies retreated to a safer position while the Astor Battery shelled the church. With the completion of the bombardment, Company H, retaking its position on the left, again began firing at the barricaded Spaniards until approximately 1:30 that afternoon, when the "cease-fire" command was given.[37]

With two companies guarding Blockhouse 14, and four more assaulting the church in Cingalon, soldiers from the remaining two companies were able to assist in the taking of Blockhouse No. 20. While the rest of the regiment was fighting around the church, some men from the Thirteenth Minnesota and the Astor Battery, along with Captains March and Sawtelle were ordered to take the blockhouse, which was not far from the church. They advanced toward their objective while "under [the] cover of their comrades' fire, edging their way through bamboo groves, rice paddies, and clutches of small palm-thatched huts to within eighty yards of the blockhouse."[38]

Coming out that close to the Spaniards and under such heavy fire, these Minnesotans believed they would have the element of surprise with them. In that regard, they were sorely mistaken, for as soon as they emerged from the jungle, they ran into a hailstorm of bullets and were driven into the center of the village of Cingalon. There, under extreme duress, they improvised hastily erected defense works to protect themselves from the hail of bullets.

With these fifteen men in the center of town holding onto the temporary firing line for dear life, MacArthur, who just learned what was happening, ordered the Astor Battery placed behind the village church where they were to start shelling Blockhouse 20 immediately. He then ordered troops forward to help protect this small band trapped in the open. The supporting infantrymen rapidly ran to their defense and began digging in behind stone walls. With the Astor Battery finally in position, they began shelling the blockhouse from which most of the firing was coming. Once the guns behind them roared in support, March and Sawtelle kept their men intact, allowing the shells to strike the blockhouse and nearby trenches with deadly accuracy.[39]

Deciding they had only two choices, stay in this open position and let the Spaniards shoot at them or charge the blockhouse, they decided that they would do what their forefathers had done during the Civil War; they attacked the Spanish defenses. With bayonets and revolvers, this small but courageous band of outnumbered soldiers got up from their positions and charged the Spaniards.

One Stillwater soldier, John T. Wheeler, one of the fifteen men, later described the battle by saying,

> [T]en minutes after the bombardment began our whole line moved forward with a grand charge captured the first Spanish entrenchments and raised the American

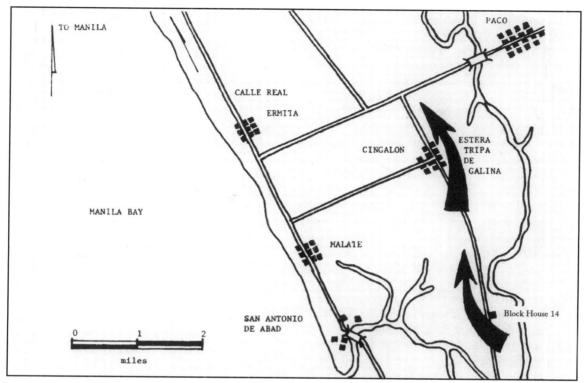

Route of the advance of the Thirteenth Minnesota at Cingalon, August 13, 1898. (Courtesy of the Ramsey County Historical Society)

flag amid deafening shots. When we reached them they had been driven from their guns but they with revolvers drawn and we with bayonets fixed, charged the Spanish line and recaptured the guns. In about five minutes the regulars came up and the firing ceased.[40]

Although the day, and the glory that went with it, belonged to the Minnesotans, all could not rejoice, since, due to some confusion in orders, the Third Battalion and the detached companies from the First Battalion which had captured Blockhouse No. 14, remained in their positions and took no part in the capture of Cingalon. By 1:30 P.M. the Second Brigade under General Arthur MacArthur had secured Cingalon and awaited their next orders.

While this was transpiring on the right flank, it was a completely different story on the left. By 11:20 A.M., Admiral Dewey had spotted the white flag flying over Manila and immediately sent his aides, Lieutenant Brumby and Lieutenant Colonel Charles A. Whittier of Merritt's staff to arrange the terms of surrender with General Jaudenes. By 2:30 P.M. the Americans reported the surrender, and by 5:43 P.M. the American flag was gently waving over the city of Manila. Unfortunately for those who did their fighting over on the right, they could not see the white flag being raised, nor did any of them know that this battle was pre-arranged and need not have been fought.[41]

The casualty list for the day's battle read that six Americans had died and forty-three were wounded. Of the dead, two were from the Thirteenth Minnesota Volunteers. Archibald Patterson, bugler, Company I, was shot and killed while the

Third Battalion was moving between Blockhouse No. 14 and the Cingalon Church. Lewis Burlingham reported this death to his mother, recalling: "Patterson [had been] shot through the neck by a sharpshooter in a tree who was afterward brot [sic] down from his perch by an American bullet. . . ."[42] The second to die was Sergeant Charles Burnson, Company G. He was able to live for three days after the battle, but the wounds he received were too severe. The tragedy of this death is that Burnson, who had probably left for war to become a hero, lost his life from wounds suffered on August 13, his twenty-eighth birthday.[43]

Despite the deaths and casualties, nothing was going to mar this day for the men of the Thirteenth Minnesota, for they had had their chance for glory. While all the men felt good about what they had accomplished, some no doubt to the envy of their comrades, they received additional recognition from Colonel Reeve when he issued a memorandum of exceptional actions on the part of individual members of the Thirteenth Minnesota Volunteers. These included:

—Capt. A. W. Bjornstad, Co. H—Took personal command of the firing line in the road at the church, without cover, and again formed another line in the same place in the most exposed portion of the road partly screened by two small logs in their front, at which point he and three members of his company were wounded.
—Capt. Oscar Seebach, Co. G—Crossed the road under heavy fire at the head of his company, deployed to the front, occupying the advance line about one hundred and twenty-five yards from the Spanish earthworks: severely wounded.
—Lieut. H. D. Lackore, Co. L—In command of the point, advanced up the road to within one hundred yards of the Spanish earthworks, where he remained firing at the enemy until warned that the guns were about to be discharged.
—Lieut. E. G. Falk, Regimental Adjutant—Constantly exposed to heavy fire, both at the front and along the line of

communications to the rear. He was at the front during almost the entire action.
—Battalion Sergt. Major J. H. Loye, Second Battalion—Was the first to respond to the order of the General Commanding, to carry a log into the street to protect Capt. Bjornstad and his men.

Along with these officers, nine privates were also mentioned for bravery for their action of occupying the firing line in the street, while being protected by only two logs. These were:

Privates W. D. Bowen, Co. H; Berndt, Co. C; Peake, Co. D; Thorsel (wounded), Co. H; Widman, A. J. Weidle, W. J. Worthington, L. H. Wallace (wounded), and Corporal E. O. Cowden, all of Co. H.[44]

Colonel Reeve finished his report to Major-General MacArthur by indicating that due to the "peculiar nature of the ground . . . it was impossible for me to observe the individual conduct of the men under my command." But, he wanted to assure MacArthur, even though his men were, "[E]xposed to a withering fire from an unseen enemy, all did their duty with coolness, intelligence and courage. . . ." Just for good measure, he added that the Thirteenth's heroism was, ". . . inspired by the example of the general commanding, whose utter disregard of personal danger prevented what otherwise might have been a serious disaster."[45]

With the fighting halted, the Minnesotans were ordered to march through Paco into Malate, both suburbs of Manila, where they halted at 6:00 P.M. and were quartered in barracks. There they were told to take up outpost duty for very specific reasons. The Filipinos, being extremely upset over not being allowed into Manila or take part in the fighting, immediately after the battle tried to beat both Greene and MacArthur's brigades into strategic positions around the city. They did this in hope that, by taking possession of the suburbs, they could at least try to maintain their strategic positions. MacArthur's Brigade, having just been in battle, was not successful in cutting off the Filipinos from these positions. With only a few minutes rest, the Minnesotans were put on guard duty to stop the Filipinos from advancing any further.

By 7:00 P.M. on August 13, 1898, less than two hours after the Spaniards had surrendered, the Minnesota Volunteers found themselves facing 4,000 angry Filipinos massed in Malate. To control the situation, the Minnesotans were ordered to set up barricades in every street in the suburb to guard against the Filipinos; this only succeeded in irritating them. Tension further mounted as both sides began to taunt the other. The Filipinos, upset over being excluded, threatened and yelled constant insults across the lines, with the Americans responding in kind. The Americans blamed the Filipinos for unnecessarily starting the day's battle, and were irritated by the unnecessary deaths amongst the ranks.[46]

With the situation almost ready to explode in Malate, General Anderson of Merritt's staff, contacted Aguinaldo. He told the Philippine leader in a wire, "[S]erious trouble threatening between our forces. Try and prevent it. Your forces should not try to force themselves into the city until we have received the full surrender. Then we will negotiate with you."

To which Aguinaldo replied; "I have given orders to my chiefs that they preserve strict respect to American forces and aid them if attacked by a common enemy. I do not doubt that the good relations and friendship which unite us will be continued if your soldiers correspond to the conduct imposed upon mine."[47]

By quick and easy communication, the trouble in Malate subsided, and both sides returned to their previously held positions, avoiding the bizarre situation of two victorious allies turning their arms against each other. Even with the situation defused, this was still a ticking bomb.

With the Americans upset with the Filipinos over the fact that not a single soldier had to die, the news that would reach Manila a few days later should have been even more disheartening. Back in May, once Dewey had defeated the Spanish navy in Manila Harbor, he severed the cable connection between Manila and Hong Kong so that the Spaniards would be cut off from the outside world. This move not only isolated Spain's forces, but it also cut off the Americans from what was going on, which would have had ramifications on not only the day's events but events taking place over the next few years. For, while on August 13, when the battle of Manila was in full swing, American and Spanish leaders, due to a peace protocol that was signed on August 12, had actually ended the war one day before. The negotiated sham battle that took the lives of Americans, Filipinos, and Spaniards need never have been played out for the war was already over.

Not knowing how things were developing internationally, Americans concluded the war as quickly as possible. With the fighting over, the city of Manila was deluged with refugees, some who had left before the fighting started, while others were just looking for a place to live. These hundreds of thousands of refugees compounded the city's already monumental problems. With the city under siege for months, the food supply had been exhausted, garbage collection had lapsed completely as had other public utilities, business was at a standstill, the streets were littered, and the water supply had been shut off for at least two months.[48]

Although the city was a disaster, once the Americans took possession, many businesses and daily activities within the city attempted to start up again. By the very next day, August 14, many Filipino shops were again open for business, as were banks, custom houses, and newspapers. Even the cable between

Manila and Hong Kong was repaired, bringing, two days later, the news that the war was actually over.[49]

With the cable repaired, General Merritt's first order of business was to get clarification of what his orders were. Did McKinley want a joint occupation with their Filipino allies in Manila, or did he want them to ". . . submit to the authority of the United States?" McKinley swiftly responded; "[T]he President directs that there must be no joint occupation with the insurgents. . . . Use whatever means in your judgment are necessary to this end."[50]

The tension between these two groups, which quickly abated in Malate the night of the thirteenth, manifested itself again the next day. For the men of the Thirteenth, not knowing what was going on with their leaders' policies, saw the Filipinos as an annoying lot. Most could not understand why the natives were causing such a ruckus. Had not the Americans just saved them from Spanish tyranny? Private Kahlert described how both the American and Filipinos felt about the situation in his diary three days later: "The natives are occupying the trenches of the spaniards [sic]. I guess we will have to whip them. They say now Americanos [and] Filipino's [sic] are not friends. They are beginning to hate us . . ."[51]

On August 18, the St. Paul Pioneer Press, reported on the relations between the Americans and the Filipinos. In a page one story, they explained that the "insurgents," on August 14, had "entered some Spanish trenches on the outskirts of the city, but were repulsed." Not clarifying if they had been removed militarily or not, the story went on to claim that, "Gen[eral] Merritt notified them that they will not be permitted to come inside the city. It is probable that the Americans will now deal with the insurgents unless an amicable arrangement is arrived at soon."[52]

An agreement was exactly what Aguinaldo and most of his men wanted,

but for the Americans this was a much more difficult task. With Washington not having completely developed their policies toward the Philippines, America's leaders continued to send ambiguous orders to the commanders in the field on how to handle situations as they arose. This left military leaders in Manila in no position to settle or to agree on anything with the Filipinos.

One area on which the Filipinos did want an agreement and did talk about with their American counterparts was the name with which they found themselves tagged. They asked the Americans to refrain from calling them "insurgents," the name the Spaniards had called them every since they began to rebel against Spain. Since they believed that the Americans did not officially own them, they were not then rebelling against American rule. Indicative of how relations would take place in the future, most Americans refused to stop the use of this term.

With Merritt's dual orders to control the city without Filipino cooperation and to keep the peace, he needed to establish a Provost Guard (a military policing unit) within the city to accomplish both of these tasks. For him the decision was an easy one, for not only had he seen the Thirteenth Minnesota Volunteers conduct drills flawlessly in San Francisco, but he was also aware of their role in the attack on Manila. With that in mind, on August 20, 1898, Merritt made the Thirteenth Minnesota the Provost Guard of Manila. Colonel Reeve was made chief of police, with his staff taking up various positions in and around the city.

Within a few short days the Minnesotans took off their hats as soldiers and put on the ones of local police. Most were aware by now that any chances they might have had for glory had probably come and gone. Although many had not had a chance to prove their bravery, most, knowing how other units had fared in this sham battle, felt proud about what they had accomplished. Finding out a few days after the battle that it was a staged event never deterred a single Minnesotan from ever speaking out about it. They had come to the Philippines to defeat the Spaniards, vanquish the ghosts of the Civil War, and to earn honor for themselves, their unit, and their state, sentiments that were not missed by the people back home.

With news that not only had the Thirteenth fought the Spaniards but played a key role in their defeat, the Minnesota newspapers were filled with excitement. Both the *Pioneer Press* and the *Tribune* ran articles in which they exalted the Thirteenth for what they had accomplished. The *Pioneer Press* wrote, ". . . the people of the state must feel a thrill of pride that their boys have had their full measure of the glory of war." The *Tribune* added the next day an article entitled "THEIR FATHERS AT GETTYSBURG," which told its readers that the "[T]hirteenth Minnesota Volunteers at Manila Show Gallantry Hardly Surpassed by That of the Old First Minnesota." With this, the men of the Thirteenth Minnesota hoped the Civil War ghosts had been exorcised and that there could no longer be any question of the bravery and manhood of their generation. Believing there was nothing left to do in the islands, it was now time to sit and wait for the ships to come pick them up and bring them home . . . or so they thought.[53]

NOTES

[1]John Bowe, *With the 13th Minnesota: in the Phillippines* (Minneapolis: A.B. Franham Printing and Stationary Co. 1905), p. 28.

[2]Ibid., p. 29.

[3]Martin E. Tew, *Official History of the Operation of the 13th Minnesota Infantry, U.S.V. in the Campaign in the Philippine Islands* (S.I.: S.N., 1899), p. 9.

[4]Lewis Burlingham to his Mother, August 21, 1898. Burlingham, Lewis Preston, 1879-1951. Papers. Minnesota Historical Society, St. Paul, Minnesota.

[5]Leon Wolff, *Little Brown Brother; How The United States Purchased and Pacified the Philippine Islands at the Century's Turn* (Garden City, New York: Doubleday, 1961), p. 104.

[6]William Thaddeus Sexton, *Soldiers in the Sun; an Adventure in Imperialism* (Harrisburg, Pennsylvania: The Military Service Publishing Co., c1939), p. 34.

[7]Karl Faust, *Campaigning in the Philippines* (New York: Arno Press, 1970 [c1898]), p. 86

[8]Burlingham, letter to Mother, August 21, 1898.

[9]Bowe, *With the 13th Minnesota*, p. 30.

[10]Stuart Creighton Miller, *Benevolent Assimilation: The American Conquest of the Philippines, 1899-1903* (New Haven: Yale University Press, 1982), p. 31.

[11]Miller, *Benevolent Assimilation*, p. 42. Stanley Karnow, *In Our Image: America's Empire in the Philippines* (New York: Random House, Inc., 1990), p. 122.

[12]Karnow, *In Our Image*, pp. 122-123.

[13]Mouraine Baker, ed., *Dear Folks at Home: Wright County's View of the Spanish-American War*, George W. Kurtz, Co. I, p. 9.

[14]*Red Wing Republican*, September 12, 1898, p. 1.

[15]Alexander Kahlert. Diary, August 1898. Minnesota Historical Society, St. Paul, Minnesota.

[16]Karnow, *In Our Image*, p. 123. Graham Cosmos, *An Army for Empire; The United States Army in the Spanish-American War* (Columbia: University of Missouri Press, 1971), p. 240.

[17]Wolff, *Little Brown Brother*, p. 119.

[18]*Minneapolis Tribune*, September 10, 1898, p. 13.

[19]*Stillwater Gazette,* September 27, 1898, p. 3.

[20]Carl L. Stone, Letter to My Dear Folks, August 12, 1898. Stone Carl L., 1890-1920. Letters. Minnesota Historical Society, St. Paul, Minnesota.

[21]Bowe, *With the 13th Minnesota,* p. 33.

[22]Faust, *Campaigning in the Philippines,* p. 98.

[23]William C. Fitch and General C. McC. Reeve, *13th Minnesota Vols.: Historical Record in the War with Spain* (Minneapolis: Price Bros. Printing Co., 1900), p. 24.

[24]Kenneth M. Davies, *To The Last Man: The Chronicle of the 135th Infantry Regiment of Minnesota* (St. Paul: The Ramsey County Historical Society, 1982), p. 58.

[25]Gen. Arthur MacArthur's son, Douglas, would go on some thirty years later to gain his own military fame in the Philippines defending them against Japan.

[26]Fitch, *13th Minnesota Vols.,* p. 24.

[27]Wolff, *Little Brown Brother,* p. 127.

[28]Trumball White, *Our New Possessions* (Minneapolis: Creore and Nickerson Publishing, Co., 1898), p. 94.

[29]Tew, *Official History of the Operation of the 13th Minnesota Infantry,* p. 10.

[30]Charles Metz to Julius Heilbron, October 3, 1898. Heilbron, Julius, 1860-1940. Papers. Minnesota Historical Society, St. Paul, Minnesota.

[31]Faust, *Campaigning in the Philippines,* p. 73.

[32]Fitch, *13th Minnesota Vols.,* p. 25.

[33]Bowe, *With the 13th Minnesota,* p. 34.

[34]James Rankin Young, *Reminiscences and Thrilling Stories of the War* (Chicago: World Bible House, 1899), p. 356.

[35]Ibid., p. 357.

[36]*Stillwater Gazette,* September 27, 1898, p. 3.

[37]Fitch, *13th Minnesota Vols.,* p. 26.

[38]Allen Keller, *The Spanish-American War: A Compact History* (New York: Hawthorn Books, 1969), p. 234.

[39]Ibid., p. 234.

[40]*Stillwater Gazette,* September 28, 1898, p. 3.

[41]David Trask, *The Spanish-American War* (New York: MacMillan, c1981), p. 419.

[42]Holbrook, *Minnesota in the Spanish-American War and the Philippine Insurrection,* p. 55. Lewis Burlingham to his mother, August 21, 1898. Burlingham, Lewis Preston, 1879-1951. Papers. Minnesota Historical Society, St. Paul, Minnesota.

[43]*Red Wing Republican,* August 22, 1898, p. 1.

[44]Fitch, *13th Minnesota Vols.,* pp. 26-28.

[45]Ibid., p. 26.

[46]Sexton, *Soldiers in the Sun,* p. 46.

[47]Ibid., pp. 46-47.

[48]Ibid., p. 50.

[49]Wolff, *Little Brown Brother,* p. 136.

[50]Miller, *Benevolent Assimilation,* p. 44.

[51]Alexander Kahlert Diary, August 16, 1898. Kahlert, Alexander J., 1898. Diary. Minnesota Historical Society, St. Paul, Minnesota.

[52]*St. Paul Pioneer Press,* August 18, 1898, p.1.

[53]*St. Paul Pioneer Press,* August 19, 1898, p. 1. *Minneapolis Tribune,* August 20, 1898, p. 1.

Chapter 5

"Be Courteous in Your Contact . . ."

After having viewed themselves as heroes who had defeated Spaniards, most of the Minnesotans were less than thrilled with their assignment as Manila's provost guard. Having seen what Malate alone looked like and knowing how many of the Filipinos felt about them, they knew this job would not be exciting or easy.

With the Spaniards' defeat, the Americans quickly took over control of Manila and its surrounding suburbs. The first order of business was to assign each company a designated area. They were originally assigned accordingly: Companies E, G, and K were assigned to the Walled City; Company D to Binondo, Company A, Malate; Company I, Quiapo; Company H, Tanduay; Companies C and M, Tondo; Company F, San Miguel; Company B, Sampolac; and Company L, Santa Cruz.

Once stationed, their next task was to set up barracks. "During the first few weeks the men slept on the floor, but later, cots and mosquito nets were provided by the Government." The cooking detail also had a hard time of it since most of the wood and coal had been used up during the siege of the city. To fix the situation, the troops began to tear apart several old

buildings for fuel. This decision only helped continue the soldiers' ever-decreasing popularity with the natives, which came as a surprise to the Americans, since all the Filipinos were reimbursed for their loss by the United States Government.[1]

Next came the general orders from their overall commander, General Arthur MacArthur, who was given charge of all Manila and its suburbs. In his second order (the first established Minnesota as the city's police force), he listed nine rules that the Thirteenth had to obey during their time in the city. While some were

Unidentified volunteer reading a letter from home. (Courtesy of the Minnesota Military Museum, Camp Ripley)

petty orders setting up housekeeping, others told them how to treat the Spaniards and Filipinos, with the rest telling them how, as Americans, they should represent themselves. Examples of these are as follows:

#3. Armed native and Spanish soldiers must be disarmed before being allowed to pass through the gates, either way.

#4. Arrest drunk and disorderly persons.

#5. Spanish officers are allowed to wear their side arms.

#8. Be courteous in your contact with both natives and Spaniards and see that all soldiers of others commands observe this rule.

These orders, signed by Major Ed. S. Bean were to be followed to the letter.[2]

Order Number 8, however, was often ignored so that the soldiers could follow Order Number 3, which usually irritated the Filipinos extremely and helped increase tensions. The situation that culminated in Malate with Americans and Filipinos almost shooting at each other was alleviated but never forgotten. Most Filipinos did not trust the Americans, so they did not wish to surrender their arms. Reverend Charles Cressy observed these Filipino sentiments and explained them to his wife on August 22, 1898: "Monday [two days after the fall of Manila] they [the Filipinos] were threatening in their looks and manners toward us. As they passed they would say 'Americanos, Phillipino, [sic] no

Men of the Thirteenth showing off their unit's flag while on guard detail in the Philippines. (Courtesy of the Goodhue County Historical Society)

Amigo' (IE Americans [and] Philippine are no friends) [and] they would draw their hands across their throats. . . ." This attitude could be easily found on both sides of the trenches.[3]

Even with the threat of reprisals, and the stench that rose up from the cities uncollected garbage, the Minnesotans were able to find some good things about policing. The first was that they received new uniforms. The new regulation uniforms consisted of a white coat and trousers, straw hat, and black shoes (which in Bean's order were to be blackened and shiny at all times). Representing the United States, these policemen were expected to be models of neatness and cleanliness throughout their stay in the Philippines.[4]

The other benefit the volunteer soldiers had during their time in the Philippines was their pay. Although not in comparison to the officers who received 125 dollars per month in gold, the lowly private received $62.40 a month. This was an extremely high wage when converted into the peso and allowed these poor soldiers instantly to gain a temporary affluence with all their new found wealth.[5]

Even with their new uniforms and thick wallets, most Minnesotans, along with other states' volunteers, began to have more and more "problems" in the lull after the battle. As Private Bowe put it, "[T]he soldiers are all more or less sick, yet the men in authority . . . quench what little patriotism is left in the boys by making them do the work of horses." The patriotic

Men of Company I lining up for guard duty. Notice the new, lighter uniforms. (Courtesy of the Minnesota Historical Society)

spirit the volunteers had had just a few months ago, Bowe feared had vanished. "Now when the officers ask for [volunteers] the men put on a blank face, sidestep away, and mutter, 'I volunteered once—.'"[6]

Not uncommon to this war, the privates began to dislike and distrust many of their superiors. From their perspective, they did all the work, and the officers got all the glory. This complaint probably was muttered around campfires again later when, on September 4, Colonel Reeve was promoted to Brigadier General, thereby making Lieutenant Colonel Ames the Regimental Colonel, and Major Friedrichs' promoted to Lieutenant Colonel. This further proved to the men that those with a rank were going to get the prestige, while they got to do all the dirty work.

Although no one ever wrote in this early stage about being upset with the Thirteenth's staff, complaints were mentioned when it came to the VIII Army Corps new commanding officer Major General Ewell S. Otis. Taking the place of General Merritt, who had left for Paris to help conclude the peace treaty, Otis' attention to minute detail and his insistence that every single decision be run by him made many field commanders and privates alike dislike and distrust him.[7]

Arriving in late August, Otis brought with him more infantry, cavalry, and artillery. This brought the total number of troops in the Philippines to 15,559 officers and men. Knowing that peace talks were being held in Paris and that hostilities in the islands between the United States and Spain had ceased days before, the arrivals of these additional troops made the Filipinos extremely suspicious of American intentions in their homeland.[8]

As for the Thirteenth Minnesota, who by now were starting to learn the ropes of policing, these growing suspicions on the part of the Filipinos made an already difficult job even tougher. Along with Aguinaldo's soldiers' attitudes toward the Americans, the Minnesotans also had to contend with a group of defeated Spaniards who, for the most part, were not helpful in turning power over to them. They also had difficulty because they did not know the city and had to try to deal with the wide variety of groups and languages found in and around the capitol.

One of their first orders, along with patrolling, was to clean Manila. This turned out to be a job of immense proportions. Having been under siege since May, the city's "70,000 people were crowded into an area that usually housed about 10,000. Food was scarce, and the revolutionaries had cut off the water supply." Their government was totally disorganized, schools were closed, as was the port.[9]

Along with the population and the mess there were also problems with the city's sewage system, which ran into open drains. From there it "accumulated in the dark privy vaults of private dwellings or, even worse, was deposited in the city streets with the garbage." What was left was washed away by the rain and the natural decay that set in so rapidly in the tropics. Many a Minnesotan complained in letters home about light breezes coming up and blowing the stench in their direction.

The Thirteenth Minnesota's first job was to clean out the sewer system and enforce policies that required the Filipinos to dispose of their excrement in other ways. One way to enforce these new regulations was to fix fines on people who emptied slop out of windows or allowed garbage to accumulate outside of their homes. The rule was that each homeowner had to clean his or her sidewalks and empty privy vaults at least once a week. One Minnesota team was even given the unenviable job of removing the human excrement piled up under houses whose toilets consisted of a hole in the floor, and hauling it to the harbor where boats tried to dispose of it.[10]

Along with disposing of refuse, the Minnesotans also began to rebuild roads, repair street lights, renovate public water hydrants, rebuild bridges, open the public water systems, set up clinics, help with vaccinations and re-open the schools. A handful of Minnesotans even helped teach in these new schools. They usually either taught a subject they knew well, or more commonly, how to speak English.[11]

Of all these functions, none was probably more important then the setting up of clinics and helping with vaccinations. In September, due to a fear of epidemic, a Board of Health was established consisting of experts from both the United States and the Philippines. Their duty was to go around and exam dwellings, markets, slaughter-houses, drug stores, and other businesses connected to community health. They also strictly monitored the port for disease, ran

the city leper hospital, and purchased supplies for the hospitals. Finally, always leery of disease spreading and having heard some of the horror stories about camps in the United States, the board began a vaccination process through which they tried to stamp out smallpox among Filipino children.[12]

After weeks of doing the back-breaking work of cleaning the city, Lewis Burlingham wrote home to his parents on September 30, telling them, "[M]anila isn't such an unhealthy place now as it has all been cleaned up pretty well and got most of the smell out. A person can keep well and healthy here if they only take care of themselves and their surroundings. . . ." Of all that they were asked to do those first few weeks, the vaccinations proved to be the most beneficial for all involved.[13]

With filth and disease virtually gone, the Minnesotans could begin to focus their

Company I posing for a photo in Manila, Philippines. Notice the pet monkey on the man's shoulder (back, right) and on a leash in the front. The small boy in front is unidentified. (Courtesy of the Minnesota Historical Society)

attention on their main mission of policing the city. One of the first things they were ordered to do was to eliminate the gambling that was rampant in the city. As the Thirteenth's historian, Martin Tew, later wrote, "[G]ambling devices of all kinds existed on every street corner, and in almost every conceivable place when the Americans entered the city." It was the duty then of the Minnesotans to put a stop to these illegal activities, which, ironically, many of them confessed to have played at one time or another.

Believing that much of Manila's "undesirables" were involved with these games, it was the intention of the top brass to eliminate them from the back streets. To the pride of the Thirteenth's commanders, these gamblers and their games quickly disappeared from the streets of Manila. It is most likely that the gambling moved from out in the open to the underground rather than, as the Thirteenth's commanders boasted, that in only one month their men had destroyed all gambling in the city.[14]

Gambling was not to be the only thing that the conservative and puritanical American leadership looked down upon within the city. The second of the two major problems facing the Minnesota police force was the women of "ill-repute" who had entered the city. While a handful of Minnesotans were swept off their feet by the local ladies of "respectable" backgrounds, others found themselves in the arms of women who were members of the world's oldest profession. These ladies must have been quite a shock for soldiers who had left conservative Minnesota just a few months previous. Whereas women's fashion in the Gopher State at that time showed as little of the female body as possible, fashions in the Philippines were much more practical for the tropical climate. As one volunteer wrote upon returning to the states, the Filipinas "wore transparent bodices, bright-colored skirts fitted snugly from hips to knees, and red heelless slippers. More shocking then the fact that they were without stockings, the bodices and skirts did not meet."[15]

Minnesota's own Lieutenant Carl Stone also commented in a letter home about the Filipinas he encountered. "The women here have beautiful hair and fairly developed shoulders [and] necks [and] chest [and] their arms are generally perfect. . . ." But for him that was as far as their beauty went, because in his eyes they had a "peculiar walk" caused by the "carrying of stuff on their heads."[16]

While some had genuine feelings for "respectable" Filipina women, a great many other volunteers spent much of their free time at the local houses of ill-repute. At first the Army had the Thirteenth Minnesota Volunteers try to contain this business, but with venereal disease being the number one disease for the soldiers in the islands (approximately twenty-five percent of all cases on sick report were of venereal origins) the high command took another approach to solving this problem. Instead of fighting the problem and trying to close these businesses down, they instead had every prostitute be registered, segregated, and examined weekly by an American doctor. If they were found to be afflicted with any sexually transmitted disease, they had to be hospitalized at their own expense, treated and visited by social workers, who tried to persuade them to find a more moral occupation. Although never putting an end to prostitution in the islands, this policy did help significantly reduce the problem of sexually transmitted diseases.[17]

Lieutenant Stone again wrote home on September 22 explaining to his parents what was happening in Manila. "About a week ago a lot of 'ladies' from Hong Kong came over and started up in business in our district and as there is no city law here to prevent such people from running houses of ill fame, we could not close them up. . . ." But with the new policy toward

66

Harry Lyon of Company C with Filipinos. (Courtesy of the Minnesota Military Museum, Camp Ripley)

ation and get us out of here as quick as possible.[19]

For Private Burlingham, though, and the men who agreed with him, those people who did have some pull were not going to help them. The *Red Wing Republican* article reported on September 8 that the Thirteenth Regiment Auxiliary Association, "[R]esolved, That we deem it unwise and impracticable, at this time, for this organization to take any action to have the Thirteenth Regiment Minnesota Volunteers, mustered out of the United States service." It would take more than just a handful of soldiers bored with military service to get any real action done by the folks at home.[20]

With the possibility of going home extremely small, the men of Thirteenth had to focus attention back on their policing of Manila. Even with their strict control of the city and tensions rising outside the city between the Americans and the Filipinos, the Minnesotans found themselves starting to make friends with a great many of the Filipinos living in their district. For the average volunteer, there were two distinct groups of Filipinos, those educated and well to do in the city and those rebellious "insurgents" who followed Aguinaldo. As Private Harry Luxton, Company D, claimed in a letter published in the *Minneapolis Tribune*, "[T]he natives here are divided into two distinct classes, the one that looks upon our presence in the city as a blessing and the other that views our habitation on the island more in the light of a curse. . . ."[21]

prostitution, Stone found himself helping implement it and dealing with these "ladies." He was ordered to go to the houses of "ill fame" and check to see if their certification was posted in the house. Not sure if he would enjoy this new position, he told his parents, "[W]ont [sic] that be a sweet job for a decent self-respecting soldier who enlisted to gain *honor* [and] glory in his country's defense!"[18]

Even with the "perks" of having excess money, the women, and the prestige of being the Provost Guard, many of the Minnesotans were bored with being soldiers and began to talk about going home. Private Burlingham sent these sentiments home when he told his family that he was upset because Colonel Reeve had told the Regimental Auxiliary that the members of the Thirteenth wanted to stay in the Philippines. He concluded this letter by saying, "I just wish that the people that have anything to do with this regiment both at home and here would have a little consider-

In this same vein of Minnesotan-Filipino relations, General Reeve was to report at the end of the war that, "[I]t was remarkable how the men adapted themselves to their new surroundings. Not only was this the case as far as their duties went, but their pleasures also. The sociability of the natives was met more than half way. Dinner and dances were no uncommon occurrences. . . ."[22]

Two other Minnesotans agreed with such positive views of the Filipinos and their islands. Sergeant Edmund Neill, on September 21, writing a letter to his parents in Red Wing told them, ". . . contrary to the usual run of the boys I like the Philippines and the city of Manila especially. It is all so odd and queer and everything is so different from home." He then added a sentiment heard through the years by soldiers found in almost all wars, "I tell you. I know I shall never be able to be contended [sic] at home again."[23]

Another soldier who felt positively about his stint in the islands was Captain Charles Metz. He wrote home to his friend Julius Heilbron, "[T]his will be a great place to make money if the US conclude to hold these Islands, there is money to be made in almost every line of business. . . ." Although many Minnesotans were able to shed some of their racist attitudes toward people of other cultures, and both they and their Filipino counterparts were able to make friendships during this time of tensions, a great many of America's volunteers were unable to do this.[24]

Even with personal contacts being made and friendships being forged during the hostilities, the tension between Aguinaldo's men and the Americans never completely abated. The Minnesotans on duty were regularly met with taunts, insults, and obscenities to which they replied in kind. The Thirteenth also quickly learned to travel in groups of two or more, for if one went out at night by themselves they became easy prey for angered Filipinos and their bolo knives.[25]

In order to alleviate the tensions between these two groups, General Otis demanded that Aguinaldo's troops be withdrawn from some of the suburbs, thereby keeping contact between the two armies at a minimum and possibly reducing tensions. When Aguinaldo finally acquiesced to these demands, the American leaders patted themselves on the back, believing they were again able to avoid war with the Filipinos.

While the commanders in the islands were avoiding a future war, American officials in Washington and Paris were trying to end another. With the war concluded, McKinley sent a small American diplomatic contingent to Paris to sign the peace treaty. One of these people was the pro-imperialist senator from Minnesota, Cushman K. Davis. In regard to the Philippines, this commission was ordered at first only to request Luzon (the northern island of the Philippines), Guam, and Puerto Rico. This, the administration estimated, would give the United States the geographical possessions needed to support a global fleet, provide communication links, and open the door for trade with China.[26]

Once in Paris, however, the commission found itself besieged with advice to demand the entire Philippine archipelago from the Spaniards. Some of these groups included American naval officers who wanted to build ports in the excellent Philippine harbors. Others were America's business leaders desirous of war in the spring of 1898 and now wanting all of the islands as a source of raw materials, a market for their goods, or a base for trade with China. The final faction that wanted the archipelago were church groups, which wanted to set up missionary enterprises and bring more "sheep into the fold." McKinley, on the other hand, was not as sure as these groups and needed a little more political prodding before he made up his mind. With another presidential campaign looming, he wanted to know that the people were behind him in his endeavors.

In the fall of 1898, the president went on a ten-day campaign swing through the Midwest. What he saw on this tour were enthusiastic crowds cheering wildly every time either Dewey's name or the call for acquisition of the islands was mentioned.

Men of the Thirteenth exploring Manila. (Courtesy of the Minnesota Military Museum, Camp Ripley)

With this in mind, on October 26, he sent new orders to his negotiators in Paris. He now told them that he wanted the Philippines in their entirety. "The cession must be of the whole archipelago or none. The latter is wholly inadmissible, and the former must therefore be required." A policy that had waffled back and forth from the first day when Dewey had defeated the Spaniards now had an established goal—complete control of the Philippines.[27]

Election votes were not the only thing McKinley considered when it came time to decide what to do, he also had to contend with other foreign nations. As the battle for Manila came and went, many foreign powers remained in and around the Philippines, waiting to see what the peace treaty would bring. If the United States were to free the Filipinos and leave, other nations such as England, Germany, and Japan were patiently waiting to make them part of their colonial empires.

If the United States stayed and worked out a joint occupation with one of these nations, McKinley feared war could break out between them. If the United States formed a protectorate, any conflicts that Aguinaldo had might force the hand of the Americans to go in and protect their Filipino allies. From the standpoint of the American leadership, they did the only sensible thing they could; they took the whole of the Philippines.

The Spaniards, for their part, argued that the United States had no claim to these islands for, technically, the war was over before the Battle of Manila. Therefore, the city was not legally controlled by the Americans and still belonged to Spain. To escape this loophole, the American commission was informed by President McKinley to offer Spain $20,000,000 for the entire archipelago. Spain, in economic straits from the war and desirous of quickly re-establishing United States relations, accepted this request. Although all sides were happy with this decision in Paris, the Filipinos were less thrilled.

McKinley was all too aware that by this action the United States was on the path of becoming an imperialist power. This, though, was seen as a good thing by the president and those who adhered to the belief of American "Manifest Destiny." America would not be a conquering nation, after all, but rather a more benevolent one passing on to the peoples of this new nation their economic, political, and religious ways of life, all of which, according to most Americans, were the best in the world.

Of all those pushing for America's expansionism, none was more behind it than President McKinley himself. As he told a gathering in the South during another campaign tour, that since the Philippines were already in American hands, ". . . it was the duty of the army of occupation to announce and proclaim in the most public manner that we have come, not as invaders or conquerors, but as friends to protect the natives in their homes, in their businesses, and in their personal or religious liberty."[28]

While the Paris Peace Commission was negotiating in France and McKinley was proclaiming the benevolence and superiority of America over the Philippines, problems remained on the archipelago. While tensions continued to rise to staggering heights and both sides were still trying to avoid an all-out war, it was the Americans who tried to stall the longest. For the Filipinos, most were pretty sure that the Americans outmatched them militarily and talked of striking before more American troops arrived. The Americans wanted to put off fighting as long as possible. As McKinley told Otis, "[T]ime given the insurgents can not hurt us and must weaken and discourage them. They will come to see our benevolent purpose and recognize that before we can

give their people good government our sovereignty must be complete and unquestioned. Tact and kindness most essential just now."[29]

While leading officials and top brass hammered out peace treaties and tried to avoid another war, the Minnesotans went about the monotonous duty of policing Manila. As the days and weeks since the Battle of Manila passed, the boredom level and lackadaisical efforts had hit new highs. Making an example out of one soldier, the *Minneapolis Tribune* printed a letter from an anonymous soldier on November 7, which told about the "illness" of one of the Thirteenth's own. The article said: "[P]rivate Mitchell, is suffering from a disease that so far baffles the skills of our medical dept., who are unable to find anything wrong with him. The symptoms as they appear to the Co[mpany], are a great disinclination for work and great promptness at mess call."[30]

The only thing that added any spice to their lives was the actual patrolling of the city. With many of Aguinaldo's men living in Manila and with the constant threat of an attack, the Thirteenth was forced to stay on its toes. On the night of November 18, this boredom was replaced by sheer terror for four men of Company E who were out on patrol. On that night, Sergeants Jay C. Price and Tracy H. Hoyt, along with Privates Harry Montgomery and George Mahan were attacked by an enraged Filipino wielding a bolo. It took the strength of all four of the armed Minnesotans to arrest this man, who severely wounded Price and Montgomery and left marks on the two privates. He was subdued only after being shot several times.[31]

After a few days of sitting in the regimental hospital, all four of the men were up and around, just in time for Thanksgiving Day. Remembering how they had been treated in San Francisco, the volunteers from Minnesota invited the First

California for a Thanksgiving feast. Among the combination of military and island delicacies was the menu's (they actually had them printed up) specialty: "Fricasseed Chicken a la Mauser Bullet." After lunch, the rest of the day was spent with the Minnesotans and Californians giving speeches, singing songs, listening to the bands, and story-telling.[32]

The Volunteers found that, much like back in Minnesota, the weeks between Thanksgiving and Christmas flew by. This was especially noticed by the men of the Thirteenth, who by this time, had done their job of policing the city so well that there was literally nothing for them to do. The city's gambling was no longer evident, prostitution was controlled, and most Filipino agitators stayed away for fear of being shot. For most of the men, there seemed little to do but write home and wait for word that they would soon be mustered out.

The promise that all American leaders seem to give their troops and their families during wartime, that the boys will be home for Christmas, was again echoed in the fall of 1898. But, with tensions increasing by the day in the Philippines and the Regular army unable to leave Cuba to relieve the volunteers due to the lack of transports, this promise, as it has so many times, was broken.

As many of those who were born and raised in Minnesota could attest, Christmas in the Philippines was nothing like they had experienced back home. With temperatures in the eighties and nineties, many of the men fondly wrote home about missing snow, ice-skating, hot chocolate, and having Santa Claus come down the chimney. Knowing that not being home would be tough on the volunteers, the Regiment Auxiliary Association had earlier adopted a plan whose purpose was to "remember every officer and enlisted man in the [Thirteen]th with a Christmas box." Undertaking this Herculean feat, the Asso-

ciation was extremely successful; on Christmas Eve, every single soldier, private up to general, received little tin boxes from home.[33]

Thrilled with their presents, most of the soldiers wrote home thanking family and friends, often showing a little homesickness in their letters. One of these was Lieutenant Carl Stone, Company F, who took time to write home and thank those who had sent the gifts. "The handkerchiefs are always useful. . . . [T]he candy and gum did not last long I tell you. The mouth organ will last for quite a while. . . ." He, like a great many others, confessed to having "a hard time believing it was Christmas" and to missing everyone back home.[34]

After the gift opening, most of the soldiers decided to do one of two things. One group did what George D. Montgomery, a member of the Thirteenth's regimental band, did. After dinner, he and some friends went to church and then went to watch Minnesota and Oregon "play ball." The Minnesotans, having played earlier in San Francisco, kept their illustrious sporting tradition alive by losing to the Oregonians fourteen to nine.[35]

The story of the group that did not go to church was captured by Private John Lawson, Company K, when he wrote, ". . . the boys are subject to drunkenism and they come in a room and jump and raise h—l. The foremost drink here is native 'Beno' or gin and if a man gets a few glasses in him the stuff is all off. I have seen as high as a dozen men in the hospital stark crazy from drinking it."[36]

One of the soldiers who belonged to the latter group was Damon Runyon. Runyon, who later gained fame as a journalist and author, was only seventeen when the war broke out. Growing up in Colorado and gaining his father's permission to go fight, he went to join the Colorado regiments, but an officer sent him home saying he was both too young and too small.

Two soldiers from Company G (Identities are unknown) taking a break and reading letters from home. (Courtesy of the Goodhue County Historical Society)

Left behind in California, Runyon had to wait for the fourth expedition to Manila to regroup with Company L. Once in the Philippines, he spent much of his time avoiding work, and the rest of the time he spent in a "house of ill repute," which was conveniently located adjacent to Company L's headquarters. There he met and fell in love with the first love of his life, a young Filipina girl. Having joined the rowdies on Christmas Eve, Runyon, like the rest, spent most of Christmas Day recovering from a severe hangover.[37]

But the headaches the rowdies in the Philippines suffered were nothing compared to what McKinley's administration would later endure after relaying a message to the Philippines discussing America's policy there. With the so-called "Benevolent Assimilation" policy, McKinley informed General Otis that, with the actual signing of the peace treaty, absolute control of the islands became immediately necessary, and the military government, which up to that time just controlled the city and harbor, now must extend itself throughout the entire nation.

He went on to add, "[I]t will be the duty of the commander of the forces of occupation to announce and proclaim in the most public manner that we come, not as invaders or conquerors, but as friends. . . ." In closing he stated,

[F]inally, it should be the earnest and paramount aim of the military administration to win the confidence, respect, and affection of the inhabitants of the Philippines by assuring them in every possible way that full measure of individ-

Ignoring the sergeant's advice, Runyon, snuck back into the Colorado barracks and hopped the train to San Francisco where he wandered around Camp Merritt until one of the sergeants of Company L, Thirteenth Minnesota, said his company needed a bugler. In Company L, Runyon stood out due to his size, a caved-in chest and extreme lack of any kind of musical ability. Company L, looking more like a circus act with Runyon, also had in its ranks one Vern Hanson from International Falls, who at six feet four inches and 230 pounds dwarfed Runyon who was five feet six inches and perhaps 125 pounds.

ual rights and liberties which is the heritage of free people, and by proving to them that the mission of the United States is one of benevolent assimilation, substituting the mild sway of justice and right for arbitrary rule."[38]

Upon receiving this proclamation, Otis decided to censor the parts that bluntly informed the Filipinos that the United States intended to retain and govern the islands. Otis had the censored version posted through Manila and the surrounding area. Filipinos, who were leery of American intentions in the first place, obtained a copy of the original and saw for themselves what America's policy was to be. Otis, trying to avoid further bloodshed, had, by concealing information, made the distrustful Filipinos even more upset when they felt that he was purposely trying to keep them in the dark over America's intentions.[39]

With full knowledge of what the American government intended, there was nothing left in the Filipinos' mind but to continue their struggle for freedom. They now looked upon the Americans as they had the Spanish, just another colonial master trying to gain control of their nation.

With leaders in Washington slowly changing policies as the days progressed, the volunteer soldier, usually kept out of any decision that might have affected him anyway, was now given additional burdens to carry. With this new policy, McKinley's administration not only expected this army to set up a colonial government, but they also wanted the soldiers to continue to police, put down any uprisings and become the transmitters of America's culture and values.[40]

Although tensions were growing between the United States and Filipino leaders, most of the common foot soldiers were oblivious to what was taking place. Life in Manila had become a monotonous routine. With no visible hope of gaining glory in war,

the men began to mutter out loud that they did not come all the way around the world to be policemen. If that was all they were going to do, then it was time, in their minds, to go home.

These desires to go home were fueled not only by bad cases of homesickness and boredom but also because disease was beginning to take the life of a great number of the volunteers in the islands. The complaint became that if they were not going to die in glory on the battlefield, then they wanted to get out of the Philippines before they died otherwise.

Ralph Morgan, a nineteen-year-old private in Company I, wrote home on December 29, 1898, describing this situation: "The deadly diseases and fevers which are thinning out our ranks daily is what causes the clamor of voices amongst the soldiers all saying '[W]hen are we going home?'" Morgan concluded with the statement that, "[W]e do not care to do garrison duty in a hot and foreign land, it being the peace work of the regulars."[41]

Private John Bowe later observed in his diary how many of the soldiers were possibly being afflicted by these diseases. He wrote; "S[ergeant Clarence] Carleton [Company A] first 'Protestant' allowed to be buried in Manila. Some boys from the Kansas Reg[iment] came down and took some skulls away for souvenirs and contracted smallpox, so now a guard is placed at the cemetery." He ended by adding sarcastically, "[C]ompany A, guarding graveyards; Company B, guarding prostitutes. One the grave, the other the way to it."[42]

Monotony was again briefly alleviated with the New Year's Eve Day celebration held for the volunteers. Although the band played, people gave speeches, and the crowds sang, what everyone really came to see were the sporting events being held on the Luneta at Manila. At the games the boys of Company A made quite an impressive showing. Private George Riebeth took first at the 100-yard dash, Private Byron

Volunteers competing in a foot race, probably on New Year's Day, 1899. (Courtesy of the Minnesota Military Museum, Camp Ripley)

Elliot took first in the running broad jump, and Privates Walter Lafans and E. R. Smith captured first place in the shot put.

To top off the day, there was even a football game held between the Tenth Pennsylvanians and the Thirteenth Minne-

Young Filipino boy saluting Lieutenant Mellinger in the Philippines. These good relations between the Americans and Filipinos would quickly disappear. (Courtesy of the Goodhue County Historical Society)

sota. Unfortunately no one recorded the final score, but the Thirteenth's official historian, Martin Tew, reassured future generations that the Minnesotans did have a "strong football team."[43]

With the holiday season finally over, the Minnesotans were all too aware that there would be no more breaks from their tedious job. Also, after the first of the year, the rumor mill started up again spreading word that they were either going to go home soon or begin fighting the Filipinos. On January 3, 1899, Corporal August Anderson, a thirty-two-year-old, Swedish-born immigrant wrote home to his brother explaining the situation at hand. "We shall be able to come home in March, but tonight's newspaper says we won't be home until we have corrected what the Spaniards have done."[44]

Since the day they left the *City of Para*, a great many of the Minnesotans held the belief that, before they were to go home, they would have to fight Aguinaldo and his people. At this point of their soldiering most of the volunteers did not mind which path their government took just as long as they were able to do something.

They had done their duty as policemen with such skill and precision that crime all but came to an end in that spring of 1899. By 7:00 P.M. all natives were safe and secure in their homes knowing that the saloons, houses of ill repute, and gambling had either been eliminated or held in check. However, for the Minnesotans who had served as police, this was not the heroic and glorified duty they had wanted. Instead of charging up a hill or defending a position until its last as their forefathers had in the Civil War, the Thirteenth found itself breaking up fights, handing out fines, defending prostitutes, and trying to kill time in a far off land. At this juncture their desires were clear: either let them go home, or let them fight. Either way, the Thirteenth was ready for the change that was soon to come.

NOTES

[1]Martin E. Tew, *Official History of the Operation of the 13th Minnesota Infantry, U.S.V. in the Campaign in the Philippine Islands* (S.I.:, 1899), p. 16.

[2]Murat Halstead, *The Story of the Philippines* (Chicago: Our Possessions Publishing, Co., 1899), p. 193.

[3]Reverend Charles Cressy to Wife, August 22, 1898. Cressy, Charles A., 1861-1916. Papers. Minnesota Historical Society, St. Paul, Minnesota.

[4]Tew, *Official History of the Operation of the 13th Minnesota Infantry,* p. 17.

[5]Franklin F. Holbrook, *Minnesota in the Spanish-American War and the Philippine Insurrection, Vol. I* (St. Paul: The Riverside Press, 1923), p. 59.

[6]John Bowe, *With the 13th Minnesota: In the Philippines* (Minneapolis: A. B. Franham Printing and Stationary Co., 1905), pp. 41-42.

[7]William Thaddeus Sexton, *Soldiers in the Sun; an Adventure in Imperialism* (Harrisburg, Pennsylvania: The Military Service Publishing Co., c1939), p. 63.

[8]Leon Wolff, *Little Brown Brother; How the United States Purchased and Pacified the Philippine Islands at the Century's Turn* (Garden City, New York: Doubleday, 1961), p. 143.

[9]John Morgan Gates, *Schoolbooks and Krags: The United States Army in the Philippines, 1898-1902* (Westport, Connecticut: Greenwood Press Inc., 1973), p. 54

[10]Gates, *Schoolbooks and Krags,* p. 60.

[11]Stanley Karnow, *In Our Image: America's Empire in the Philippines* (New York: Random House, Inc., 1990), p. 131. Gates, *Schoolbooks and Krags,* p. 62.

[12]Gates, *Schoolbooks and Krags,* p. 58.

[13]Lewis Burlingham letter home, September 30, 1898. Burlingham, Lewis Preston, 1879-1951. Papers. Minnesota Historical Society, St. Paul, Minnesota.

[14]Tew, *Official History of the Operation of the 13th Minesota Infantry,* p. 16-17.

[15]Russell Roth, *Muddy Glory: America's "Indian Wars" in the Philippines 1899-1935* (West Hanover, Massachusetts: Christopher Publishing House, c1981), p. 41.

[16]Carl Stone letter home, August 23, 1898. Stone, Carl L., 1890-1920. Letters. Minnesota Historical Society, St. Paul, Minnesota.

[17]Sexton, *Soldiers in the Sun,* p. 57.

[18]Carl Stone letter to parents, September 22, 1898. Stone, Carl L., 1890-1920. Letters. Minnesota Historical Society, St. Paul, Minnesota.

[19]Lewis Burlingham to parents, October 16, 1898. Burlingham, Lewis Preston, 1879-1951. Papers. Minnesota Historical Society, St. Paul, Minnesota.

[20]*Red Wing Republican,* September 8, 1898, p. 1.

[21]*Minneapolis Tribune,* October 18, 1898, p. 3.

[22]Ibid., October 8, 1899, p. 8.

[23]Ed Neill letter to Father and Mother, September 21, 1898. Neill, Edmund P., 1898-1899. Letters. Minnesota Historical Society, St. Paul, Minnesota.

[24]Charles Metz to Julius Heilbron, October 3, 1898. Heilbron, Julius, 1860-1940. Papers. Minnesota Historical Society, St. Paul, Minnesota.

[25]John Walsh, *The Philippine Insurrection, 1899-1902; America's Only Try for an Overseas Empire* (New York: Watts, 1973), p. 29.

[26]Stuart Creighton Miller, *Benevolent Assimilation: The American Conquest of the Philippines, 1899-1903* (New Haven: Yale University Press, 1982), p. 20.

[27]Karnow, *In Our Image,* p. 129.

[28]Miller, *Benevolent Assimilation,* p. 25.

[29]Brian McAllister Linn, *The United States Army and Counterinsurgency in the Philippine War, 1899-1901* (Chapel Hill: University of North Carolina Press, 1989), p. 11.

[30]*Minneapolis Tribune,* November 7, 1898, p. 3.

[31]Roth, *Muddy Glory,* p. 43.

[32]Tew *Official History of the Operation of the 13th Minnesota Infantry,* p. 18.

[33]Ibid., p. 18.

[34]Carl Stone letter home, December 24, 1898. Stone, Carl L., 1890-1920. Letters. Minnesota Historical Society, St. Paul, Minnesota.

[35]*St. Paul Pioneer Press,* February 24, 1899, p. 7.

[36]John Lawson to Brother Adolph, December 24, 1898. Lawson, John E., 1898-1899. Papers. Minnesota Historical Society, St. Paul, Minnesota.

[37]Jimmy Breslin, *Damon Runyon* (New York: Ticknor and Fields, 1991), p. 52. Runyon is probably most noted for his work *Guys and Dolls.*

[38]Walter Millis, *The Martial Spirit; a Study of Our War with Spain* (New York: Houghton Mifflin Co., 1931), p. 396.

[39]Jerry Cooper, *Citizens as Soldiers: A History of the North Dakota National Guard* (Fargo: The North Dakota Institute for Regional Studies, 1986), p. 66.

[40]Gates, *Schoolbooks and Krags,* p. 78.

[41]Mouraine Baker, ed., *Dear Folks at Home: Wright County's View of the Spanish-American War*, Ralph Morgan, Co. I, p. 13.

[42]Bowe, *With the 13th Minnesota,* p. 61.

[43]Tew, *Official History of the Operation of the 13th Minnesota Infantry,* p. 19.

[44]August Anderson letter to brother, January 3, 1899. Anderson, August, 1859-1918. Correspondences. Minnesota Historical Society, St. Paul, Minnesota.

Chapter 6

"... Have at Last Opened the Ball"

With boredom and open hostilities rising between the Filipinos and the Americans, attitudes on both sides began to take an ugly turn. Filipinos, knowing what American intentions were in their homeland, began to prepare for another long, drawn-out battle with a foreign aggressor. As for the American volunteers, they found themselves somewhere between longing to leave the islands for home and fighting another quick battle with the natives in order to kill their boredom and gain more glory.

During the first month of 1899, these tensions rose to new heights. With both sides facing each other with weapons drawn, and with an ignorance of each other's cultures and motivations, high anxiety was the norm of the day. The Filipinos complained about how they were treated by American soldiers. Many told about the practice of the Americans knocking down natives with the butt of their Springfield rifles merely for "seeming disrespectful."[1]

Both sides required passes to go through their lines. Many Americans and Filipinos began to complain that they were not searched as they entered each other's lines but rather robbed. Both sides also used any pretext to shoot at each other.

After the war, one story even suggested that a member of the Thirteenth Minnesota, who was out on sentry duty, killed a civilian just for "looking suspicious."[2]

The crisis that was developing between these two camps was not missed by the common foot soldiers. On February 3, 1899, Second Lieutenant Carl Stone wrote home, complaining about this very situation with the Filipinos. "It has got so now that they hold up our people whenever they have a chance. The condition of affairs is becoming intolerable generally, and there is soon going to be a fight."[3]

Stone was not the only one who noticed that tensions were brewing in late January and early February. On the same day that Lieutenant Stone was writing to his family in Rochester, General Otis was writing to Admiral Dewey, who was still in the islands, concerning the problems occurring just outside of Manila. "There has been a great deal of friction along the lines the past two days, and we will be unable to tamely submit to the insulting conduct and threatening demonstrations of these insurgents much longer." Everyone from the generals down to the lowliest private knew they were sitting on a tinderbox just waiting to explode.[4]

77

Barricade put up by members of the Thirteenth Minnesota. (Courtesy of the Goodhue County Historical Society)

On February 4, 1899 that tinderbox finally found its fuse. A few weeks earlier, General Otis had moved a Nebraska unit further forward into an established neutral area between the Americans and the Filipinos. During the night of the fourth Private William Grayson and Orville Miller were sent out on a routine patrol. When they reached a bridge spanning the San Juan River, they were met by a patrol of four Filipinos. Grayson hollered, "Halt," to the four, who yelled back, "Alto!" to the two Americans. After a brief verbal bantering, Grayson raised his gun and fired, killing one of the Filipinos. Immediately Grayson and Miller ran back to their lines yelling about an imminent Filipino attack. Along a ten-mile front, the Americans and Filipinos met each other in what became the first battle of the Philippine-American War.

Since neither side had prepared for an attack, both found this battle to be a confused and haphazard event. Many of the American units fanned out from the city in wild charges un-orchestrated by their commanders. Often they attacked without orders from their superiors. Having been bridled for too long, most of these volunteers wanted a chance to get into the fray.[5]

With most of the action taking place to the north of Manila, the Minnesotans, held up in the city and its suburbs, still were not completely out of the action. The

78

St. Cloud men of Company M on the night of February 4 found themselves held up in an old church. The "[M]en stationed themselves in the belfry and in advantageous positions in the old church and kept a close watch [on the Filipinos]." Although not suffering an all out attack Company M was able to save the church ". . . from the black devils who had evidently planned to burn the church and the Americans within it."[6]

Most of the rest of the Thirteenth Volunteers, who were patrolling the streets in their respective districts, did have some excitement that evening. They discovered that some of the Filipinos within the city were signaling those outside of it with lights from rooftops. The Minnesotans took it upon themselves to shoot down this make-shift signal corps before any real damage could be done in the city.

By 4:00 A.M. on the morning of February 5, the navy opened fire on the Filipinos' lines with devastating accuracy. To the chagrin of the volunteers, this bombardment did such an excellent job that the Filipinos fled to re-organize, not giving many of the Minnesotans a chance to fight Aguinaldo and his men, or so they thought.[7]

Three hours after the bombardment, patrols from Company C found themselves engaged with about 150 Filipinos carrying bolos and machetes. With blades not being much of a match for the long distance accuracy of the Americans' Springfields,

Members of the Thirteenth guarding a railroad-mounted cannon. (Courtesy of the Minnesota Military Museum, Camp Ripley)

79

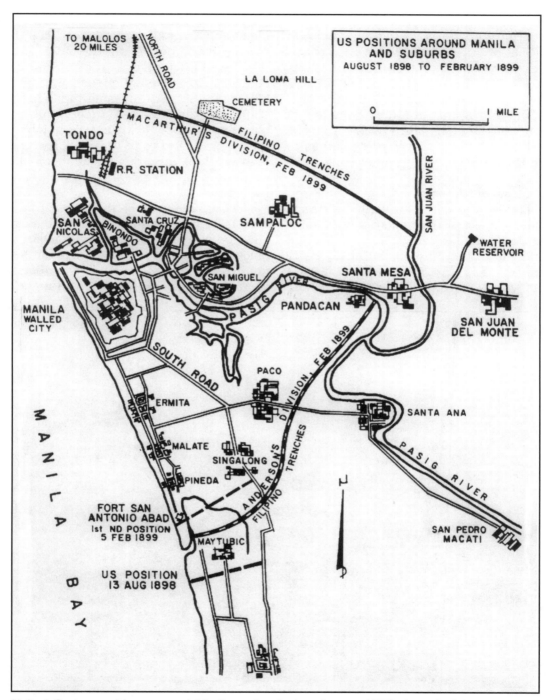

United States positions around Manila and suburbs, August 1898 through February 1899. (Reprinted with permission of the North Dakota Institute for Regional Studies, North Dakota State University)

Company C was able to disperse their attackers. Killing six, capturing thirty-one, and being unable to count the number wounded, Company C considered this "the only serious trouble encountered by our regiment to date." After Captain Noyes Robinson's men of Company C pushed the Filipinos back, the only other official maneuver conducted by the Thirteenth in this fight was to put Company M in another church in the Tondo district, just outside of Manila.[8]

Although a handful of Americans got their chance at some limited skirmishing, those stuck on patrol were too far away from the action and were extremely upset over having to stay put. Not being strict regular army, many of these volunteers still went to the front by taking what they called, "French leave." With gun and ammunition belts these soldiers wanted to fight, but they knew all too well that they had to be back at camp for both roll call and retreat, or suffer the consequences.

As Martin Tew would later write about this incident on February 5, "... Minnesota men were in every regiment and participated in every charge that was made. Some companies found it necessary to place guards at the doors to prevent members from making their escape." This was not all that effective since many of the men still escaped through windows and passageways to join in the fighting.[9]

Having been informed that Minnesotans were shirking their duty to go to the front, Colonel Ames issued an order instructing the arrest of all Minnesota men found on the firing line. Those who were found were to be arrested, court-martialed and fined.[10]

Once the order came down, it was up to men such as St. Cloud's First Sergeant Iver Ingebretson to go out and get his men. In a letter home, he explained, "[I]n the Kansas lines I picked up about [forty] Minnesota men who were out there without permission—the majority of them from

Company M. . . ." Instead of scolding them and marching them back to camp, however, Ingebretson, with orders from a Kansas captain, formed these men into a company and marched them into the line. With the Kansans leading the charge, this rogue bunch of warriors joined in. This impromptu action by the men from Company M came with the penalty of two of their own receiving wounds in the battle.[11]

Behavior like this, to the consternation of the officers, won cheers from the other enlisted men. As John Bowe wrote, "[T]hese soldiers . . . when they fought without their officers and without orders they were court-martialed. The better the company, the more men in disgrace. One day Co[mpany] H had thirty-five lined up in column of fours, and marched up to the summary court to be dealt with by the officers."[12]

Ingebretson, who escaped charges, wrote that Colonel Ames had brought charges on those who were AWOL (away without leave). Of these "[N]ineteen of the boys from the St. Cloud company went through the ordeal. Another company in the regiment had forty-six cases." In all, some 150 men were tried for leaving their posts. Fortunately for those who were tried, the judge was extremely lenient since in the end they showed more courage in battle than disobedience to orders.[13]

In the battle on February 4 and 5, the Filipinos suffered anywhere from 500 to 5,000 casualties, while the Americans only lost fifty-nine killed and 278 wounded. While both sides were caught unprepared for this battle, it would be the Filipinos who found themselves reeling over the loss. They quickly understood that they had terribly underestimated the fighting qualities of the Americans.[14]

The volunteers' hopes for action had finally been answered; they were going to get their war with the Filipinos. As Carl Stone said in a letter written three days

81

after the battle: "[A]s you must know by this time the ins[urgents] have at last opened the ball. Last Saturday they began firing on our out posts and for the next twenty-four hours there was a steady roll of musketry punctuated by an occasional shot from the ships. . . ." He went on to say that he hoped they could get out and fight too, but General Hughes told them that they were too valuable as Provost Guards. Hughes argued that if any other regiment took their place there would be civil unrest in Manila. Stone concluded that neither he nor most of the men believed what the general said, "but we have to stay just the same."[15]

Sergeant Ingebretson, who had escaped the court-martial process, saw this fighting from a different angle. As he put it in a letter published in the *St. Cloud Times*, "I suppose that this trouble will delay our coming home. . . ." The only way this fighting was not going to delay his homecoming to St. Cloud would have been if the commanders of both armies could have worked something out. The initiative to do this fell into the hands of Aguinaldo.[16]

Sending Judge Florentino Torres of Manila to make peace overtures to the Americans, Aguinaldo hoped to put an end to the fighting, especially since he had seen the carnage left by the Americans. On Sunday evening February 5, Torres was received by General Otis at his headquarters. Torres tried to explain to Otis and his staff that the fighting had started accidentally and that Aguinaldo was willing to end it. The Filipinos believed an armistice, along with the establishment of a neutral zone between the two armies while peace negotiations were being negotiated, would be beneficial.

Among General Otis' staff that day was Minnesota's General Reeve, who was given the duty of replying to the questions placed before the Americans. To these questions General Reeve, "sternly replied

that the fighting having once begun must go on to the grim end." Tired of the constant verbal and physical fighting going on between the Filipinos and Americans on the front lines, and being assured that they could easily defeat their adversaries, Otis decided to push on with this war until its bitter end. This decision had ramifications not only for the soldiers who were in the islands then, but also for the thousands who would have to come later.[17]

While bloody fighting was raging in the Philippines, thousands of miles away another fight was ensuing, but this time instead of bullets, rhetoric was used to make their point. In the halls of Congress, senators were debating the controversial Peace Treaty that Senator Davis and the commission brought with them from Paris. The controversy swirled around the issue of what to do with the Philippines. A great many Americans began to argue that not only did they want the volunteers to be brought home, but that the United States should get out of the islands all together. McKinley and his administration had swung a deal with the Spaniards in which they paid twenty million dollars to gain possession of the archipelago. Not wanting to look weak internationally, and trying to appease those in his party with imperialistic notions, under no circumstances was the president going to give up the Philippines.

As the debate heated up in the Senate early that February, it was not clear to anyone which way the voting would go until the battle between the Americans and the Filipinos broke out. Many senators, refusing to look as if they were not backing up their soldiers, decided to vote with the president, thereby making America an official colonial power. With a vote of fifty-seven to twenty-seven, the treaty attained its necessary two-thirds majority vote, but only by one vote.[18]

Back in the islands, news of the ratification had not yet arrived, but for those fighting the war it did not matter. When news leaked that a Kansas regiment was about to make an ordered advance and drive the Filipinos back, it found itself overrun with would-be Minnesota mercenaries who wanted a piece of the action. Private Bowe later recalled; "[A]bout twenty of the Minnesota boys had heard of the contemplated movement, so when Co[mpany] C [Kansas unit] lined up it was one of the largest companies in the Eighth Army Corp." Obviously the light fines that these soldiers were receiving were not enough to dissuade them from future actions.[19]

After three more days of fighting the Thirteenth's leadership found itself continually trying to round up its men. As Charles Flannigan, Company I Musician, calculated in a letter dated February 8, 1899: "[A]bout 750 of our boys are waiting court-martial [sic] for running to the front and leaving their company but they won't do anything because they would have to court-martial [sic] the whole regiment." These men were safe as long as nothing happened in the city of Manila while they were out on their little adventures.[20]

On February 9, this fear was given more credibility when a document from General Antonio Luna, a member of Aguinaldo's staff, was discovered and brought to the attention of the Provost Marshal of Manila. This document described how those Filipinos in Manila, who supported Aguinaldo and his cause against the Americans (known as the Sandatahan) were to help in overthrowing the Americans.

The plan was that once an attack commenced from outside the city, those loyal Filipinos inside Manila were to start an uprising. More specifically they were to ". . . liberate all prisoners, arming them in the most practical manner." Also, "Filipino servants were to burn American masters' homes." Those loyal to the cause were also instructed to spare all Filipinos, "with the

exception of those who have been pointed out as traitors." Anyone who was not of Filipino descent was to be exterminated.[21]

This specific information helped the American military prepare for this attack, even though not knowing its exact date. Having literally stumbled across this document on February 9, the volunteers did not have too long to wait until the Filipinos acted upon these orders.

At 8:00 P.M. on the night of February 22, a fire was spotted in the Santa Cruz district of Manila. Prepared for just such an emergency, the Manila fire department and members of Company L went immediately to help put it out. Once there, they quickly discovered two things. The first was that the materials the Filipinos used to build their homes, such as bamboo, went up in flames quickly, and the fire could spread with the slightest breeze. Unfortunately for those trying to put out the fires that night, there was a hefty wind to help push the fire onward.

The second thing that these fire fighters discovered was that these fires were the work of Filipino arsonists. What the Minnesotans could not figure out was why they would want to torch their own homes. Three hours after the fire broke out, the fire department and the men of the Thirteenth had it well under control with no help from the local Filipinos, who were either getting in the way of the Americans or were actually trying to cut the water hoses. The latter scenario usually earned the Filipino an arrest or a cracked skull from the butt of a rifle.[22]

Why the Filipinos had set their homes on fire was becoming painfully clear to the rest of the Thirteenth, for they quickly discovered that Manila was under attack. When taps was played that night, Tondo, Manila's most northern suburb, was as quiet as a country village, but, shortly after midnight, much like Santa Cruz, fire sprang up in at least a dozen different places. The fire department was again called upon to put out the fires, but this time Filipinos began to shoot at the Americans.[23]

Major Francisco Roman, his Philippine troops numbering 500, had made their way around MacArthur's lines in the north, through the swampy waters and mudflats, and then infiltrated the city and barricaded themselves in Tondo. When the fires began, Roman's troops sprang up from the barricades and began attacking the American soldiers. Unfortunately for Companies C and M, it was their post in Tondo that met the brunt of this attack. When the word came that the city was under siege, Captain Noyes Robinson of Company C ordered First Lieutenant John Snow to keep nineteen men to protect the barracks, while the rest went into the dark streets of Tondo to meet their adversaries. Ordering his men out the front gate in double time, Robinson attempted to rush these men to the hot spots and repulse the Filipinos. For Company C, though, the hot spot would be right in front of them, for as soon as a handful of men stepped outside the gate, they were met with a hot fire from Filipinos waiting in ambush.[24]

With a Remington bullet tearing his upper lip, Captain Robinson was still able to order his men to take a defensive position. After a few more minutes of firing at each other, Company C was finally able to push their enemy away from their barracks, giving themselves time to regroup before they headed toward the fires. Although no one was killed, the St. Paul men did suffer a handful of wounded in this engagement, some lightly while others were more serious.

With their first goal of capturing the Tondo police station a failure, the Filipinos turned their attention to their next objective, the Tondo Cathedral, which was also used as a police station. With the Minnesotans out fighting fires, Aguinaldo's men captured the church without any incident. Here, using better protection, they were able to hold their ground against the Minnesotans inside until the early hours of February 23, when the Kansas Regiment arrived. The Minnesotans and Kansans then began chasing the Filipinos down the Caloocan Road. After fleeing for a few minutes, the Filipinos finally stopped and made a gallant last stand until they were finally overcome by the volunteers. The entire battle cost the Filipinos dearly, for over one hundred surrendered and seventy more were found dead.[25]

With one police station saved, another under attack, and the city in flames, the Americans decided to culminate their effort and drive out those Filipinos still remaining in the city. With two companies from the First Oregon in assistance, Captain Robinson, still smarting from his earlier wound, and Captain James McKelvy of Company M, formed a skirmish line with their left flank ending on the beach. In this long line, the Americans slowly advanced toward the northern suburbs, shooting at any flash from the Filipinos' Mauser or Remington rifles that they encountered. Once fired upon, the units held up, poured a deadly accurate fire into the Filipinos lines, by now divided into small bands, then continued to move forward. To add to the excitement, both sides had to fight each other while the city of Tondo was burning around them. Slowly advancing and hiding behind stone barricades Companies C and M, along with the men from the First Oregon, were able to flush the Filipinos from their positions, thereby making them easy targets as they ran away.[26]

While the general push against the Filipinos was taking place, the nineteen men of Company C under Lieutenant Snow found their barracks again under siege. With only a handful of men, Lieutenant Snow was still able to repulse the attack of over 100 Filipinos. After a hot skirmish, the nineteen men of Company C went into the courtyard and discovered their action had inflicted much damage on their attackers.[27]

Still trying to defend the city against invasion, the Thirteenth Minnesota Volunteers were unable to assist in putting out the fires that had engulfed much of Tondo. Now knowing the Filipino's strategy or why they had cut the hoses in Santa Cruz, the Americans quickly changed from just trying to disperse those bothering them to shooting anyone interfering with the work of the fire department. With this new strategy, at least one of the problems the volunteers were having quickly disappeared.

With the fires almost out in Santa Cruz and the battle still raging in Tondo, the rest of the Thirteenth found themselves on edge waiting to see what would happen next. By 2:30 A.M. on February 23, that mystery was solved. Company D, stationed in the district of Binondo, one of Manila's business districts, soon found their area under attack from Aguinaldo's men.

Binondo, not only being a primary business area, also had large numbers of army supplies stored there, making it a strategic place to defend. With word of the new fires, those who had been working in Santa Cruz quickly dropped their rescue efforts and moved to the more important site of Binondo. Again, the Americans found themselves fighting both fires and the Filipinos, who were shooting at them from rooftops and alleyways. By 7:00 A.M. on the morning of February 23, the Americans had both the fires and the Filipinos under control.[28]

With the efforts of Roman's forces to advance into Binondo thwarted, all of the Thirteenth was given a quick rest before six companies were sent to drive what was left of Aguinaldo's forces out of the northern suburbs of Manila. Having had the whole night to prepare, most Filipinos were well dug in. With time to prepare, Aguinaldo's troops built line after line of barricades early in the morning of February 23. It took the Americans all day to clear the Filipinos out of their positions. Sadly, most Filipinos who stayed and fought were caught in a hopeless situation and were killed because they refused to surrender.[29]

With the battle in Santa Cruz completely under control and mopping up tak-

Postcard of the fires in and around the Tondo district, February 23, 1899. (From Neely's Color Photos of America's New Possessions)

ing place in Tondo and Binondo, the six Minnesota companies that had earlier formed a line to push the Filipinos out of Tondo now had the Filipinos on the outskirts of the city at the Tondo bridge. Knowing that their attack was completely falling apart, the Filipinos decided to stiffen their resolve and make a stand. Two hundred and fifty of Aguinaldo's army had built five trenches across the road and

Picture postcard of the destruction done to the Tondo district. (From *Neely's Color Photos of America's New Possessions*)

Tondo district. Result of the Filipinos attempted invasion of Manila. (From *Neely's Color Photos of America's New Possessions*)

taken possession of the bridge during the night (thereby cutting the line of communication with MacArthur's forces in the front) and were now ready to meet the Americans head on.

When the two forces met, they both encountered some of the heaviest fighting this war had seen. Having dug in and making one last effort to halt the Americans, the Filipinos put up a stubborn resistance, but in the end had to give up their positions to larger numbers and superior shooting ability. Much like the rest of the previous two days' battle, the engagement was costly for the Filipinos who lost another twenty men killed and wounded, whereas the Americans had only seven wounded—six privates and again Minnesota's Captain Noyes Robinson.[30]

Although not as fierce a battle as the volunteers would later recall, the battle at the Tondo bridge did help conclude the most serious battle that the Americans and Filipinos had to date. It was with that desire to be remembered for their heroism that caused a number of Minnesotans to write letters home exaggerating how many of the battles were fought.

With the Filipinos finally expelled from the northern suburbs, and Manila safe again, it was time for the Americans to look around and see what was left. While much of Santa Cruz had been saved, both Binondo and Tondo were different stories. Binondo lost approximately six to seven hundred residential homes and businesses to fire. Hundreds of homeless natives amassed in the streets, making patrolling the city that much harder. In Tondo, Lieutenant Snow and his small band of defenders saved both Company C's barracks and the massive Tondo Church, but little else survived. With much of Manila's northern suburbs laid to waste, the plans of the Filipinos also rested in ashes. Aguinaldo had hoped for a larger civilian uprising and less American

accuracy with their guns, but within twenty-four hours, his plans to expel the Americans from the islands, much like the city of Tondo, lay in ruins.[31]

General Antonio Luna's plan to take a group of 500 Filipino soldiers and push the Americans out to sea failed, but his message that he and his people would fight to the end for their freedom was a point well made to the Americans. For this reason and this reason alone Luna chose February 22, Washington's birthday, as the day to launch his attack. He wanted the Americans to know that, just like their hero George Washington, his people, too, were fighting for the freedom from a new and oppressive colonial power.[32]

With 150 Filipinos dead and many more captured, the battle was a rout. Especially when compared to the casualty list of the Thirteenth Minnesota Volunteers, who were in the heat of the battle. Having only twelve wounded in the regiment that saw the most fighting, the Americans viewed this battle not only as a complete victory, but they also felt it was a sign of what future battles with the Filipinos would be like.

While military commanders were calling it an out-and-out victory, many in the media saw it in a completely different light. In an article a day after the fighting, the *St. Paul Pioneer Press*, referring to one of St. Paul's units, argued that the "Thirteenth Minnesota fared badly yesterday and the preceding day at the hands of the insurgent sharpshooters in the suburbs of Tondo and Binondo. . . ." Going on to give the names of the wounded, the *Pioneer Press* did not paint a rosy picture of what was happening in the Philippines. Articles like this one began to persuade the people back in Minnesota that it was time to bring the Thirteenth home, before any more unnecessary deaths or injuries occurred in what many were beginning to view as a senseless war.[33]

Negative newspaper reports, the frequent stories of deaths from tropical illnesses, and soldiers' requests to come home led the Minnesota Volunteer Auxiliary Association in March to insist that the Thirteenth Regiment be brought home from Manila at once. They forwarded their request to Senator Davis, who personally brought it to the War Department.

Even though the folks at home wanted the Thirteenth Minnesota brought back, this was not necessarily the attitude of those doing the fighting. Having spent months doing nothing, the volunteers were now finally where they wanted to be, right in the thick of things. They were also beginning to feel that they could easily beat the Filipinos, since the Minnesotans so far had not been impressed with their fighting or shooting ability.

In an article in the *Minneapolis Tribune* dated March 12, 1899, these sentiments were spelled out. "As a matter of fact, there are a large number of the Minnesota men who want to stay in the Philippines until a great victory is won and Aguinaldo either surrenders or is cap-

tured. Letters from Major Bean, Colonel Ames and others . . . say that it is the wish of the Thirteenth regiment to stay with Otis and Dewey until the Philippine Campaign ends." This, of course, was based on the preconceived notion that it would be a rather quick war.[34]

Two other members of the Thirteenth Minnesota wrote home about this same time expressing similar feelings. Chaplain Cressy, knowing the war was far from over, wrote his wife, saying, "[T]he hardest part of the fighting with these Insurgents is to come yet—but there can be only one issue: they will be routed, defeated, and the U.S. will be on top."[35]

This belief that it was just a matter of time before Aguinaldo and his men were defeated was also backed up by Red Wing's Ed Neill. In a letter home discussing how boredom had once again found the Thirteenth Volunteers after the attack on Tondo, he told his parents that in the distance he and the rest of Company G could hear the sounds of bat-

A portion of the burnt district of Tondo, February 1899. (From *Neely's Color Photos of America's New Possessions*)

tle. With memories of Civil War stories running through his head, Neill explained to his parents that, whenever any disturbance like that arises, the "boys came out [of their tents] hoping that something has occurred to give them their longed for chance to distinguish themselves."[36]

Even with the battle of Manila and the recent attacks on the northern suburbs, not every soldier from Minnesota felt that he had completely vanquished the memories of the Civil War veterans and attained the necessary amounts of glory for himself or his unit. Believing that the Filipinos were naturally inferior to United States' soldiers, both physically and militarily, most of the Minnesotans, having spent months in the islands, still wanted to stay and gain unquestionable glory before going back to their simple lives.

With a war that broke out as a result of built-up tensions on both sides, and a powder keg exploding over what was actually a minor incident, those glory hungry Minnesotans still had a chance to obtain some before they left for home. Although they felt ready to begin fighting again, they soon discovered that this second war in the islands would be drastically different from the one for which they had signed up a year earlier. The patriotic feelings they had felt back in Minnesota in the spring of 1898 were now changing as rapidly as the policies coming out of Washington. The same policies that defined them as an army of liberation were now slowly beginning to change them into an army of conquest.

NOTES

[1]Stuart Creighton Miller, *Benevolent Assimilation: The American Conquest of the Philippines, 1899-1903* (New Haven: Yale University Press, 1982), p. 58.

[2]Ibid., p. 58. This information was only cited in this book and never mentioned by anyone from the Thirteenth Minnesota Volunteers or their historians.

[3]Minnesota War Records Commission. "Spanish-American War History Files, 1898-1923." Carl Stone letter home, February 3, 1899. Minnesota Historical Society, St. Paul, Minnesota.

[4]John Morgan Gates, *Schoolbooks and Krags: The United States Army in the Philippines, 1898-1902* (Westport, Connecticut: Greenwood Press Inc., 1973), p. 42.

[5]Stanley Karnow, *In Our Image: America's Empire in the Philippines* (New York: Random House, Inc., 1990), p. 144.

[6]*Minneapolis Tribune,* April 7, 1899, p. 3.

[7]Miller, *Benevolent Assimilation,* p. 67.

[8]Minnesota. Office of the Adjutant General. "Spanish-American War muster rolls, 1898-1899." Record of Events— Trimonthly Field Returns, February 10, 1899. Minnesota Historical Society, St. Paul, Minnesota.

[9]Martin E. Tew, *Official History of the Operation of the 13th Minnesota Infantry, U.S.V. in the Campaign in the Philippine Islands* (S.I.: S.N., 1899), p. 22.

[10]*Minneapolis Tribune,* April 7, 1899, p. 3.

[11]*St. Cloud Times,* March 29, 1899, p. 3.

[12]John Bowe, *With the 13th Minnesota* (Minneapolis: A.B. Franham Printing and Stationary Co., 1905), p. 85.

[13]*St. Cloud Times,* April 12, 1899, p. 6.

[14]Russell Roth, *Muddy Glory: America's "Indian Wars" in the Philippines 1899-1935* (West Hanover, Massachusetts: Christopher Publishing House, 1981), p. 46.

[15]Minnesota. Office of the Adjutant. "Spanish-American War Files, 1898-1923." Carl Stone letter, February 8, 1899. Minnesota Historical Society, St. Paul, Minnesota.

[16]*St. Cloud Times,* March 29, 1899, p. 3.

[17]Leon Wolff, *Little Brown Brother; How the United States Purchased and Pacified the Philippine Islands at the Century's Turn* (Garden City, New York: Doubleday, 1961), p. 232.

[18]William J. Pomeroy, *American Neo-Colonialism: Its Emergence in the Philippines and Asia* (New York: International Publishers, 1970), p. 61.

[19]Bowe, *With the 13th Minnesota,* p. 86.

[20]Mouraine Baker, ed., *Dear Folks at Home: Wright County's View of the Spanish-American War.* Charles Flanigan, February 8, 1899, p. 14.

[21]Robert Ginsburg, "Damn the Insurrectos." *Military Review* (January 1964), p. 61.

[22]William Thaddeus Sexton, *Soldiers in the Sun; an Adventure in Imperialism* (Harrisburg, Pennsylvania: The Military Service Publishing Co., c1939), p. 101.

[23]Hiram David Frankel, *Company 'C,' First Infantry Minnesota National Guard: Its History and Development* (Brown, Treacy and Speary, Co.), p. 40.

[24]Sexton, *Soldiers in the Sun,* p. 101. Frankel, *Company 'C', p.* 40.

[25]Edwin Wildman, *Aguinaldo; A Narrative of Filipino Ambitions* (Boston: Lothrop Publishing Co., 1901), p. 214.

[26]Oregon. Adjutant-General's Office. "The Official Records of the Oregon Volunteers in the Spanish-American and Philippine Insurrection," p. 56. Minnesota Historical Society, St. Paul, Minnesota.

[27]Tew, *Official History of Operation of the 13th Minnesota Infantry,* p. 24.

[28]Sexton, *Soldiers in the Sun,* p. 101.

[29]Ibid., p. 101.

[30]Karl Faust, *Campaigning in the Philippines* (New York: Arno Press, 1970), p. 146.

[31]Murat Halstead, *The Story of the Philippines* (Chicago: Our Possessions Publishing Co., 1898), p. 504. Sexton, *Soldiers in the Sun,* p. 101.

[33]Carlos Quirnos, *Filipino's at War: The Fight for Freedom from Mactan to Bessang Pass* (Philippines: Vera-Reyes, Inc., 1981), p. 150.

[33]*St. Paul Pioneer Press,* February 25, 1899, p. 1.

[34]*Minneapolis Tribune,* March 12, 1899, p. 1.

[35]Charles Cressy letter to dearest wife Lizzie, March 12, 1899. Cressy, Charles A., 1861-1916. Papers. Minnesota Historical Society, St. Paul, Minnesota.

[36]*Red Wing Republican,* April 1, 1899, p. 8.

Chapter 7

"... The Rebellion Is Anywhere Near Put Down"

merican military strategists of the day viewed warfare differently than many of their European counterparts, especially the Spanish. With their series of trenches and blockhouses surrounding Manila, Spanish military leaders believed defensive measures were a much safer and wiser tactic in fighting the Filipinos than offensive maneuvers. Since many of America's military leaders had fought in the Civil War and Cavalry-Indian Wars, they argued that only an offensive campaign would end the current war with the Filipinos.

While sitting in Manila watching the Filipinos attack his complacent troops, General Otis decided that they would not stay on the defensive as had the Spaniards, but rather he wanted to take the war to the "Insurgents," destroying what he believed to be a weak and small band of Filipinos hiding out in the countryside. To do this, the general had to once again call on his volunteers since the Regular army had yet arrived to replace these citizen-soldiers.

Nearly four weeks had gone by since the Minnesotans had found themselves defending the city of Manila from General Luna's attack. In that time since the battle, their monotonous routine redeveloped,

compounded with the knowledge that units from other states were fighting at the front. As they had back at Camp Merritt, the Thirteenth believed that less worthy units were again gaining the glory that they felt belonged to them and them alone.

Just as morale was hitting an all time low, the Minnesotans were saved. On March 17, 1899, word came down from the brass that they were to be ordered out of the city and into the field. As Private John Bowe wrote in his diary on that same day, this news was cause for an additional celebration. "Today we had a double celebration. The boys were celebrating the 17th of Ireland (St. Patrick's Day) when Maj[or] Diggles came along and said we had been relieved from police duty and were to go to the front." Bowe went on to say that "pandemonium broke loose" and all the boys, the Irish contingent and "all the rest of the Norwegians, Swedes, and Dutchmen" celebrated in one boisterous party. For many who had not been in serious action, it would be now or never for them to do something gallant—to prove their bravery—to themselves, their regiment, and their state.[1]

Before they left on this great adventure, General Otis reorganized his divi-

Men of the Thirteenth Minnesota overlooking a piece of artillery. (Courtesy of the Minnesota Military Museum, Camp Ripley)

sions. This revamping of the VIII Army Corp put the Thirteenth again under the command of General MacArthur and moved new units away from the city to protect other strategic interests. There they were supposed to keep the enemy occupied, not allowing them to either rest or mount an attack on Manila.[2]

On March 18, the Thirteenth was relieved of its policing duty by the Twentieth Regulars and ordered to camp out on the Luneta. With their role as Provost Guard over, and after having spent the last seven months in and around Manila, the Thirteenth found they had made a good many friends. When it came time to leave, "[S]hops, and windows in private residences were closed as an evidence of the people's grief at the departure of the volunteers who . . . had protected their persons and their homes."[3]

After two days of camping on the Luneta, the regiment was finally ordered to march due East toward the water pumping station. This was considered a strategic position since the Filipinos had cut off the water supply here during their siege of Manila. The Americans, afraid that they might try it again, sent the Thirteenth to protect it. Although picket duty around the pumping station was by no means a pleasure, for most Minnesotans it was still better than policing the city.

Otis' plan to leave Manila and press the fighting toward the Filipinos led many to believe that the war would soon end. In his letter of March 21, Lewis Burlingham commented that, "I don't think this war will last very long as the Americans are pushing the nigers[4] further back all the time and are capturing them by the hundreds and they are also surrendering

Men of Company D, Third Regiment, posing for a picture before their campaign into the jungle. (Courtesy of the Goodhue County Historical Society)

themselves quietly for want of food." Since the fighting had commenced on February 4, the Americans had only seen the Filipinos defeated in battle after battle. Although the war was only in its earliest stages, it would have been easy to see why many of the volunteers felt they could quickly end this war and go home.[5]

Not only a commentary on how Burlingham perceived the situation, this letter also shows how many Minnesotans also had started to view the Filipinos. With a complete lack of understanding of the local culture, and with life inside the city dragging on, many members of the Thirteenth showed some signs of disrespect toward certain Filipinos. Once the Minnesotans got out into the field, however, and had to face the Filipinos continuously in battle, this disrespect slowly turned into a pure hatred of Aguinaldo's men at first, and then the population at large.

The Third Battalion was stationed directly at the reservoir, the Second was posted along the Mariquina Road, which ran from the city to the pumping station, and the First Battalion was to take the Santalan Road between the reservoir and the pumping station. After suffering through numerous Filipino-American skirmishes along these lines, the American leadership decided to follow Otis' orders and take the war to the Filipinos.[6]

At 3:00 A.M. on the morning of March 25 the entire regiment was ordered to move into positions along the Mariquina Road. With reports of Aguinaldo's troops being nearby, the Thirteenth received orders to "execute a flank movement on the extreme right of General MacArthur's division." The Thirteenth had planned on a long day's fight for, as reported by Ed Neill in the *Red Wing Republican*, "[O]nce in line, forty additional rounds were issued

93

and a day's ration of corned beef and hard tack, making 150 rounds we carried into battle." Neill went on to explain what transpired between then and the firing of the first shot:

> For an hour we marched down toward the mountains, in column[s] of squads, sometimes halting and often stopping for a few seconds only. After advancing for several hundred yards through the cane brakes and rice fields and crossing a rocky and torturous stream suddenly there was the sharp spit of a Mauser and through the bamboo brake came a ball tearing everything in its way. Then all along the front spurted the little tongues of fire and battle was on.

At 5:15 after only proceeding approximately 300 yards, the entire regiment encountered heavy fire from entrenched Filipinos.[7]

In the darkness of early morning, the Minnesotans could only locate where the Filipinos were hiding once they fired, for the Mausers they were using showed "lightning-sparks" that gave away their positions. By 5:30 A.M., while still marching through the jungle in a nearly straight line, the Americans closed in on the Filipinos. With fire from the invisible Filipinos increasing, the Minnesotans began to advance more rapidly. In order to try and overcome their enemy, the Volunteers, at every 150 to 200 yards, would stop, drop to the ground on their bellies, fire three quick rounds, get up and again rush forward toward their objective.[8]

After a few minutes, the Americans were able to deduce that most of the Filipinos were on a ridge firing down from this advantageous position. Rapidly advancing, the Thirteenth was able to finally reach the base of the ridge. Still intact and suffering from serious fatigue from their jungle sprint, the Thirteenth Volunteers mustered the last of their strength and rushed up the hill. Surprised by such a rapid attack, the Filipinos withdrew from their positions. They then found themselves shot at by the volunteers, who did not give up the chase until every entrenchment was deserted.[9]

With the main attack clearing out the protected ridge, the Minnesotans pursued the Filipinos for another mile or two toward the north. Unable to catch up to Aguinaldo's men, who could run through the jungle easier than the Americans, they halted and awaited orders. That night, while camping where they had stopped, the First Battalion was attacked by a regrouped and even larger force of Filipinos, who were determined to turn the right of the American line, anchored by the Thirteenth. This battle was waged for a little more than half an hour and was hotly contested on both sides, but with the Minnesotans entrenched and refusing to give any ground, the result was that the Filipinos were repelled.[10]

Having pushed Aquinaldo's troops farther into the interior, the Americans left their conquered ground to re-establish themselves at the posts they had held before the battle at Mariquina Road. The Thirteenth, without the services of twelve members wounded during the battle, were again back doing the all-too-familiar guard duty.

With little or no fear of another attack against the pumping station, the Thirteenth Minnesota was ordered on March 28 to march back from their positions into the city of Manila. From there they were to head north toward the town of Caloocan. This march would prove torturous for the volunteers.

What made this journey so brutal was that the Americans were not prepared for what they had to encounter. First, it turned out to be a fifteen-mile hike in heavy marching order between seven and eleven at night. Second, these soldiers from the North Star State were quickly discovered that, just because a Filipino map said a road existed, it did not necessarily indicate the same kind of road they might find back in Minnesota. Most of the march north out of Manila followed a Philippine "road" covered with thickets of tropical growth that barely could have permitted Filipinos to move carts hauled by water buffalo, let alone a full division of American troops.[11]

After a long and tiresome trip, the men set up camp in the church plaza of Caloocan. Since the commissary stores had not yet arrived, many members of the individual companies were given the duty to forage for food. For the next two days, the Minnesotan's would dine ". . . on chicken and such other provisions as the country yielded."[12]

With barely any rest, the Thirteenth was again ordered north, but this time they were given a break. With a railroad line running from Caloocan to their final destination of Marilao, the Minnesotans were given the opportunity to hop onto flatcars headed that way. Once in Marilao, the Thirteenth was to join up with Brigadier General Lloyd Wheaton's Third Brigade, of the First Division.[13]

MacArthur's troops were removed from east of Manila to the north to capture the city of Malalos. Malalos was seen as a key objective because it had been reported to be Aguinaldo's new capital. Besides the symbolism of destroying the Filipinos' capital, Malalos also had become a war depot and contained a large quantity of rifles and ammunition. Having sent out scouting parties and interrogating Filipino soldiers captured in earlier battles, America's leadership was almost positive they were on to something.[14]

Otis believed "that with the capture of the enemy capital and the scattering of its political functionaries, Aguinaldo would see the hopelessness of opposition and the rebellion would be over." Otis, still fighting the Civil War, believed that with one mighty swoop this war would be over and the Americans could go home. Although

The church in Caloocan where members of the Thirteenth set up camp in the plaza. (From Neely's Color Photos of America's New Possessions, 1899)

this strategy had worked in America's past, it was not in the plans for Aguinaldo or his followers.[15]

The elaborate plans to encircle Aguinaldo and bring the war to a rapid conclusion quickly fell apart. With three brigades marching on Malalos, the victory was expected to be swift. Unfortunately for the Americans, their pincer movement failed due to Philippine geography. General Hale's brigade on the left had to travel, much like the Thirteenth, on a road that was supposed to exist but was covered with tropical growth. His drastically slow advance left an escape route through which the Filipinos fled.[16]

With their advance into Malalos uninterrupted, and the Filipinos fleeing before them, the Americans were able to capture the city with few incidents or injuries. Although it did not conclude the war, Otis counted it as an American victory. As the rest of American's columns advanced on the city, other troops, including the Thirteenth Minnesota, were called upon to return to their picket duty and guard both the conquered territory and the railroad line that traveled through that area.

Constantly on the run from a very large contingent of American soldiers, the Filipinos were also running into the problem of low ammunition reserves and disorder within their ranks. Fearing that things might only get worse, Aguinaldo, in early April, requested a truce from General Otis. This he hoped would give him and his men the necessary time to reorganize and to restock the supplies so desperately needed. Not wanting to deal with the Filipinos, especially since he had them on the run, Otis refused this armistice and pushed on with the war.[17]

Meanwhile the Thirteenth was ordered to guard the railroad track and bridges for a distance of nearly ten miles and patrol the countryside from one to three miles on either side of the tracks. The companies were dispersed as follows. Company D, the first bridge just past Marilao; Company C, Santa Maria and the railroad bridge; Company E, Bigaa and the railroad bridge; Companies K, G, L, and M, the village of Bigaa; and Companies A, B, F, I, and H, the vicinity of Guiguinto.[18]

With American troops taking the war to the Filipinos, the sentiment of many Americans continued in the belief that the war would soon be over. As reported in the *Minneapolis Tribune*, "[M]ost of the Americans are becoming convinced that the backbone of the insurgent opposition is broken. There are numerous rumors pointing to an early collapse of the insurrection." With the Filipino's unable to mount a serious attack, and always looking as if they were running from the Americans, it was believed that they did not have the military might needed to defeat the United States.[19]

For all of the Americans' wishful thinking, many Spaniards, who had fought the Filipinos for years, saw the war in a different light. Another article from the *Minneapolis Tribune* said:

"[T]he Spaniards, reasoning from their experience [dealing with] the natives, refused to believe that the rebellion is anywhere near put down. On the contrary, the Spaniards predicted that the insurgents would hover near the American lines, bothering them as much as possible, and when attacked in force dissolve, only to reappear at other points.

"This sort of tactic—the Spaniards say—will be followed until the wet season compels the Americans to be housed in barracks and then the Filipinos will return and re-occupy such towns as the United States troops did not garrison."[20]

The author of this article laughed at this, since the Spaniards, who could never beat the Filipinos, did not have the military might of United States. Therefore, he believed, the Americans would not make the same mistakes the Spaniards had. Before long, however, it would be the Spaniards who were laughing, for the Americans would make the exact same mistakes Spain had.

While newspapers back home were debating when the war would be over, the men of the Thirteenth did not have time to

Two members of the Thirteenth in their huts, trying to get some protection from the hot Philippine sun. (Courtesy of the Minnesota Military Museum, Camp Ripley)

join in such arguments. With a large force of Americans encamped in Malalos, the role of the Thirteenth became vital to their survival. The only way to get supplies to this expedition, and for it to retreat back to Manila if necessary, was to follow the narrow corridor the Americans had blazed with their advance toward the north, the same stretch of land given to the Thirteenth to guard. Aquinaldo and his men also recognized that this was an extremely important stretch of land. Feeling they could quickly turn the tables on the Americans, on April 10 Aguinaldo attacked.

With the Thirteenth Regiment spread thinly over a ten-mile stretch, their outpost duty became perilous. In order to keep contact with the other companies, and to keep an eye out for Filipinos, every night four privates and a corporal from each company would leave camp. Traveling between 500 to 1000 yards toward the enemy, they would then take up a position for the night in the underbrush, where they remained until daybreak. If trouble started, this small group would be trapped, for they could not escape, nor could anyone get to them in time to ward off an attack.

The *St. Paul Pioneer Press* was able to capture the significance of the Thirteenth's duty in an article discussing their situation along these railroad tracks. The article explained that the men of the Thirteenth did their guard duty "with the knowledge that the loss of the railroad meant the stranding of the whole army in and about Malalos, cutting it off from the base of supplies. . . ."[21]

In an attempt to both sever the expedition from its base of supplies in Manila, and to surround the Americans at Malalos, a large group of Filipinos, personally led by Aguinaldo, decided to attack the railroad lines. Starting at 11:30 P.M., the primary object of the Filipinos was to destroy the bridge at Bocaue. Company C found itself in some of the heaviest fighting of the war,

Private William G. Compton (who took many of the pictures in this book) wrote on the back of this picture: "A jungle in the woods near Bocaue. Our outpost of three men [was] at the spot marked by the man in the picture. When the first shot was fired we made our way through the little opening seen in the background and joined the other outpost." (Courtesy of the Minnesota Military Museum, Camp Ripley)

since the duty of guarding this bridge was theirs.[22]

With a concerted attack all along Minnesota's line, Company C, being only twelve miles from the Filipino army's headquarters, was the first to be assaulted. Filipinos swarmed toward them in the pitch-black night. The Minnesotans were able to protect themselves by entrenching themselves behind the railroad. They soon discovered that they needed this excellent position since they were under a heavy fire for several hours. Knowing they themselves could not thwart the Filipinos' advance, Lieutenant Snow, Company C, called for reinforcements from the Oregon men stationed not far off.[23]

The Oregonians showed up with forty men under a lieutenant, which helped but did not immediately change the flow of this battle. Shooting from "an old white house" which had an excellent view of the camp, the Filipinos were able to pour a hot fire into Company C. Being pinned down by the storm of bullets, Lieutenant Snow ordered his men to slowly retreat back to their base camp, where they could wait until more help arrived.[24]

The help so desperately needed finally came in the form of Company E, which had been stationed just to the north of Company C on the tracks. Captain Spear, along with twenty-five of his men, was able to save the day for the men of Company C. With their arrival, the two Minnesota companies, along with two others from an Oregon detachment, were able to protect the bridge from being destroyed and to drive the Filipinos back.[25]

While the attack on Company C still raged, a half mile down the track another fight was developing. Company D, stationed the farthest from the rest of the regiment, and in an area not clearly visible by the rest, also found itself under heavy attack from a large force of Filipinos. Caught completely off guard, Company D was not able to defend its position on the tracks and had to retreat.

With the city of Malalos under attack and Company C also besieged, Company D

Private Compton wrote: "The bridge at Bocaue guarded by Co[mpany] C [Thirteenth] Minn[esota] Vol[unteers]. The company was camped across the river on the left. On the right o[n] April 10th the insurgents made an unsuccessfull [sic] attempt to capture this bridge from us during which engagement we lost one man killed and several wounded. The wooden bridge seen in the foreground was built in the latter part of March by the Auxillary engineers for the crossing of heavily loaded supply wagons for the American troops in the advance on Malalos." (Courtesy of the Minnesota Military Museum, Camp Ripley)

Company C in camp at Bocaue, Luzon, 1899. (Courtesy of the Minnesota Military Museum, Camp Ripley)

could not rely on anyone to come and save them as Company C had. Captain Metz's men had to try to withhold an onslaught of Filipinos, who attacked them "shooting, yelling, blowing blood-curdling bugles and sending rockets into the air," as they assaulted Company D's position.

Knowing he was outnumbered, Captain Metz began to rotate his company in a way that he hoped would make the invaders think they were going up against a much larger battalion. Not completely falling for this trick, many of the Filipinos actually made it directly into Company D's camp where they quickly began to scavenge through the Americans' equipment

"Guard of Co[mpany] C at Bocaue bridge," wrote Private Comptom. (Courtesy of the Minnesota Military Museum, Camp Ripley)

trying to find usable materiel. Believing that the situation was desperate, Lieutenant Charles N. Clark and fifteen men from Company F, the only troops able to come to Company D's aid in one of those moments reminiscent of the Civil War days, made a gallant charge back into the camp, killing or chasing off the Filipinos.[26]

With Company F's help, Company D pushed the Filipinos out and regained its lost territory. Upon re-entering their entrenchments, Company D was forced to hold on and continue to fight the Filipinos through the night. Dawn brought the exhausted men little chance to rest, for as soon as the sun broke over the Philippine jungle, both Companies C and D took the offensive and began to push the Filipinos back.

While Companies D and C were fighting for their lives early that morning of April 11, they sent word to General Wheaton asking for assistance in driving the Filipinos back. Knowing the situation was desperate, at 3:45 A.M., General Wheaton, on foot, left his command post and started toward the fight. He took with him a detachment of twenty-five men of the Fourth Cavalry (dismounted) under the command of Lieutenant Charles Boyd. Realizing this would not be enough to decide the battle, Wheaton stopped along the way to gather more help.[27]

When he neared Malalos around 4:00 A.M., Wheaton took immediate command of the situation. While making his hike down the railroad line, he first encountered Companies A, B, H, and I of the Thirteenth Minnesota Volunteers. He ordered this battalion to take up Company C's position down the railroad. He then told Companies F and B to head as fast as humanly possible, not in the direction of Company D, but instead toward the village of Guiguinto. What must have seemed an odd order to the men would actually turn out to be a brilliant tactical move by the general. For Wheaton knew that what was in Guiguinto would give the advantage back to the Americans faster than just sending these troops to the aid of Companies C and D.[28]

Surviving an ambush just outside the village, the men of Company F and B got into the village and quickly found what Wheaton valued so much—a train with an armored car with mounted Gatling guns hooked on to it. Finding the train, the company commanders gave the engineer

Wheaton's orders to head down the tracks. Both companies helped fire up the engines as quickly as possible, for, having fought most of the night, they knew that the Filipinos, though pushed back, had not completely lost the initiative early that April 11 morning and were not about to break off this important fight.

The train, with its Minnesota escort riding on the cars, began heading south on the tracks. After a few tense moments, it finally pulled into full view of the Filipinos.

Aguinaldo's men, having attacked numerous other supply trains, believed it was a harmless ammunition car and decided to leave their positions and attack the train. They felt that, by destroying the Americans' supplies, they could regain the momentum of the battle. Shooting as they approached, the Filipinos noticed that the men on top of the train cars were not firing back. The reason for this was that the Minnesotans were under strict orders to wait until the Filipinos were at an ex-

Cartoon from the *Minneapolis Journal* on March 27, 1899. The caption reads "Closing in on Him."

100

tremely close range before the Gatling guns were to return fire.

Once the Americans felt the enemy was close enough, the order came for them to open fire. The rifle fire of the Minnesotans was probably not necessary as the Gatlings on the armored car opened up, shooting Filipinos at close range with deadly accuracy. Retreating helter-skelter into the woods with what was left of their unit, the Filipinos tried to recuperate and regroup before deciding their next move.[29]

While an extremely deadly battle for Aguinaldo and his men, the Americans, too, for the first time, also lost enough men for them to take notice. For the Thirteenth, they were to lose two killed with twelve wounded, some severely. In his end of the month report, Major Bean also reported that the Minnesotans had killed at least forty "rebels." Many more had been killed and wounded but not counted in this total because the Filipinos usually tried to carry off most of their fallen comrades.[30]

Though having the tactical advantages of surprise, knowing the territory, and vastly outnumbering the Americans, the Filipinos continued to lose battle after battle and had devastatingly large losses of men and supplies. For Aguinaldo's army, this would have to continue to be the story, not because the Filipino was less of a soldier, but more for technical reasons.

One reason the Filipinos lost so many battles was that they believed that the rear sights on their guns got in the way of their concentration on the front sight and, therefore, many of Aguinaldo's men mistakenly took them off. This helps explain why so many Minnesotans in their letters home mentioned bullets "whizzing" over their heads. Without back sights, many of the Filipinos' shots consistently went high.[31]

Another reason for their lack of success in battle was that the Filipinos had neither the guns nor the ammunition nor

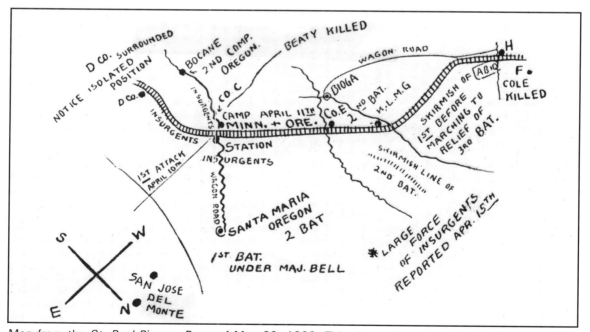

Map from the *St. Paul Pioneer Press* of May 20, 1899. This shows the placement of the men of the Thirteenth Minnesota along the railroad tracks. Notice the special marking for the spot where Private Cole's body was found.

The key to victory for the Thirteenth Minnesota against the attack by Aguinaldo and his men. It was most likely this Gatling gun that turned the tide of battle in favor of the Americans. (Courtesy of the Minnesota Military Museum, Camp Ripley)

the time for target practice. Target shooting would have been an extreme waste of bullets, especially since many Filipinos went into battle with few bullets, and some even without a rifle. These rifleless warriors were ordered to carry their bolo knives into battle until a comrade was shot down, then pick up the gun and continue the fight.[32]

With the Filipinos disorganized, defeated, and on the run, American commanders decided again to press on with the war and try to end it. Knowing the Filipinos were retreating toward the city of Santa Maria, General Wheaton ordered the Thirteenth Minnesota and two Battalions of the Oregon Regiment, to attack. At 6:30 A.M. on April 12, this unit marched on Santa Maria. Tired and disor-

ganized, the Filipinos knew that this was not the time to make a stand and fight. Instead, they retreated to the north and east with the Minnesotans hot on their heels for the next two miles.

With Aguinaldo's army routed from the area, the Oregonians and Minnesotans began marching back through Santa Maria. When they reached the outskirts of this town, they saw that it was in flames. Still unknown is whether the advancing Americans, the departing Filipinos, or just an accident of war started this blaze.[33]

What was for certain, though, was the attitudes both sides started to formulate about each other from this point on. While Filipinos began to blame the Americans for burning villages and terrorizing innocent citizens, the Americans

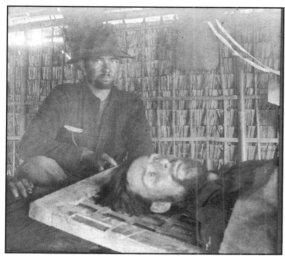

Private Compton wrote, "Dead body of Beatty Co[mpany] C killed on night of April 10 by insurgents at Bocaue." (Courtesy of the Minnesota Military Museum, Camp Ripley)

began to accuse all Filipinos of being treacherous. This belief was present in the ranks of the Thirteenth Minnesota, due primarily to one incident.

A day after the battles for the railroad, Private Jesse Cole, Company F, went looking for food by himself. He was ordered to go barter with the locals to get food but not to steal it since that was

against army regulations. When Cole did not return after a while, a handful of men were sent to look for him. After a few minutes of searching, they came across Cole just 500 yards from the camp. As the *Pioneer Press* reported it, he was found, ". . . mutilated and dead, evidently murdered by the niggers."[34]

The article went on to describe the situation from the soldiers' standpoint. "[W]e all knew him as a faithful, good, hard-working man. His condition is too horrible to describe, but suffice it to say that his throat was cut and a bloody hatchet found near him. The news brought forth some unpublishable remarks from the members of the [Thirteenth] Minnesota concerning the rebels, the 'amigos' and the island in general."[35] (See map on page 101.)

Cole's company mate, Corporal Myron Hingeley, an eighteen-year old from Minneapolis, sent a letter home that was published in the *Minneapolis Tribune.* In it he recalled Cole's death this way. "Co[mpany] F and the whole [Thirteenth] regiment was completely upset April 10 by the finding of the horribly mutilated body of Private Jesse Cole. . . ." Cole was described as having had his skull ". . . crushed in by an ax, which lay partially

Company C on a "firing line" during the campaign against the Filipinos. (Courtesy of the Minnesota Military Museum, Camp Ripley)

Members of Company A at Guiguinto. After a few weeks of being on maneuvers against Aguinaldo and his men, the members of the Thirteenth look nothing like they did while acting as provost guards in Manila. (Courtesy of the Minnesota Historical Society)

under him, the jugular vein was severed and a number of knife wounds were found in the back." He went on to conclude that "[Company] F is all wrought up over the affair, and will show no mercy to Filipinos who may come in contact with them." In a letter published the very next day, Hingeley ominously wrote, "[Y]ou ought to see the change in the company now."[36]

With the death of Private Cole and the knowledge that they too could easily die in this far away land, many volunteers became frightened. Many, from this point on, began to turn their fears into outright hatred of all Filipinos. Rarely, after this incident, was there ever a distinction between a good Filipino and a bad one. In the eyes of the members of the Thirteenth Minnesota they were all becoming "niggers."

These sentiments were heard for the first time back in Minnesota by Private John N. Roberts, who had returned earlier that year from the Philippines. Speaking to a crowd anxious to hear any stories about what was happening in the Pacific, Roberts laid it all on the line and boldly told his audience: "[O]ur boys are fighting more for revenge now than anything else. They want to get back at the niggers who have killed their friends and companions." Displaying the anger that many of the volunteers felt that spring, Roberts, in a plea which might have satisfied many of his comrades back in the jungle, stated that, "[E]very member of the regiment wants to get home as soon as possible."[37]

Even though the men at the front were beginning to complain about their situa-

104

tion, for many, especially those left behind, the real glory was still to be found at the front. After a few weeks of policing Manila soon after arrival, the Thirteenth's sick list hit a high of 133 enlisted men and four officers by the end of December 1898. This stayed about the same until February 1899 when the fighting with the Filipinos began; then many found themselves well enough to fight. When the men were ordered to the front, this number dropped severely to a low of only ten enlisted men and three officers. With the knowledge that there might be glory found in mounting an attack against the Filipinos, many of those who were "deathly ill" during policing, miraculously found a cure to what ailed them.[38]

In a related item, the *Stillwater Gazette* published a letter written home by Company C's Private Arthur Rank. Knowing about the debate going on back in Minnesota over whether the Thirteenth should be returned or not, Rank believed that ". . . the men were discontented . . . but it was not because they wanted to sail for home and leave their comrades to put down the insurrection; it was because they wanted to go out where they could do some fighting and share the *glory of victory*" (italics added).[39]

By the end of April, many of Aguinaldo's men wanted to call a truce with General Otis and the Americans. Fearing that they were just stalling in order to regroup and re-organize, Otis refused this peace initiative and decided to continue to press on with the war, hoping to crush the Filipinos before the rainy season.

Members of Minnesota's Thirteenth had mixed emotions about what was transpiring. Having fought a couple of battles since the attack on the railroad, they, along with the other state volunteers, knew that they could defeat the Filipinos simply because they were routing them in every battle. On the other hand, their lives were becoming miserable because of the constant fear of being ambushed, the heat and difficult travel in the jungle, rampant disease, the sometimes scarcity of their food supply, and, worst of all, some of them were dying.

Still, no matter what adversities they had to face, in the back of their minds many believed they had to stay and fight, if not for their country then just for the simple fact that they did not want to be seen as cowards by the people back home. Many feared that leaving just as the war was getting started would label them cowards and prove to many that the Civil War generation was actually a braver lot. With this in mind, few, if any, were desirous of being returned home. For most were still looking for or wanted that elusive glory which might possibly be just around the corner in one great charge against the Filipinos. With Wheaton's campaign over, the Thirteenth Minnesota was assigned to another campaign against the Filipinos. It was to be here, they assured themselves, that they would be able to prove themselves in battle and then go home as guaranteed heroes. Or so they thought.

Notes

[1] John Bowe, *With the 13th Minnesota: In the Philippines* (Minneapolis: A.B. Franham Printing and Stationary Co., 1905), pp. 94-95.

[2] Karl Faust, *Campaigning in the Philippines* (New York: Arno Press, 1970 [c1898]), p. 156.

[3] Martin E. Tew, *Official History of the Operation of the 13th Minnesota Infantry, U.S.V. in the Campaign in the Philippine Islands* (S.I.: S.N., 1899), p. 25.

[4] Lacking any new or original racial epitaphs, the Western Volunteers took the one used to degrade African-Americans and used it on Filipinos.

[5]Lewis Burlingham letter to parents, March 21, 1899. Burlingham, Lewis Preston, 1879-1951. Papers. Minnesota Historical Society, St. Paul, Minnesota.

[6]Minnesota, Office of the Adjutant General, "Spanish-American War Muster Rolls, 1898-1899," Report of Events-March 31, 1899 (Mariquina Road), Minnesota Historical Society, St. Paul, Minnesota.

[7]*Red Wing Republican,* March 25, 1899, p. 8.

[8]Tew, *Official History of the Operation of the 13th Minnesota Infantry,* p. 27.

[9]Ibid., p. 27.

[10]Ibid., p. 27.

[11]Franklin F. Holbrook, *Minnesota in the Spanish-American War and the Philippine Insurrection, Vol. I* (St. Paul: The Riverside Press, 1923), p. 62.

[12]Hiram David Frankel, *Company "C," First Infantry Minnesota National Guard: Its History and Development* (Brown, Treacy and Speary Co.), p. 55.

[13]Kenneth M. Davies, *To the Last Man: The Chronicle of the 135th Infantry Regiment of Minnesota* (St. Paul: The Ramsey County Historical Society, 1982), p. 63.

[14]William Thaddeus Sexton, *Soldiers in the Sun; an Adventure in Imperialism* (Harrisburg, Pennsylvania: The Military Service Publishing Co., c1939), p. 108.

[15]Richard E. Welch, *Response to Imperialism: The United States and the Philippine-American War, 1899-1902* (Chapel Hill: University of North Carolina Press, 1979), p. 26.

[16]Sexton, *Soldiers in the Sun,* p. 111.

[17]John Morgan Gates, *Schoolbooks and Krags: The United States Army in the Philippines, 1898-1902* (Westport, Connecticut: Greenwood Press Inc., 1973), p. 96.

[18]Minnesota, Office of the Adjutant General, "Spanish-American War Muster Rolls, 1898-1899," Record of Events-March 31, 1899, Minnesota Historical Society, St. Paul, Minnesota.

[19]*Minneapolis Tribune,* April 3, 1899, p. 1.

[20]*Minneapolis Tribune,* April 3, 1899, p. 1.

[21]*St. Paul Pioneer Press,* May 20, 1899, p. 3.

[22]*Minneapolis Tribune,* May 20, 1899, p. 12.

[23]Holbrook, *Minnesota in the Spanish-American War and the Philippine Insurrection,* p. 63.

[24]*St. Paul Pioneer Press,* May 20, 1899, p. 3.

[25]Ibid., p. 3.

[26]Tew, *Official History of the Operation of the 13th Minnesota Infantry,* p. 28.

[27]Faust, *Campaigning in the Philippines,* p. 175.

[28]*Minneapolis Tribune,* May 20, 1899, p. 12.

[29]Ibid., p. 12.

[30]Minnesota, Office of the Adjutant General, "Spanish-American War Muster Roles, 1898-1899," Record of Events-April 10, 1899, Minnesota Historical Society, St. Paul, Minnesota.

[31]Stuart Creighton Miller, *Benevolent Assimilation: The American Conquest of the Philippines, 1899-1903* (New Haven: Yale University Press, 1982), p. 68.

[32]Ibid., p. 68.

[33]Tew, *Official History of the Operation of the 13th Minnesota Infantry,* p. 30.

[34]*St. Paul Pioneer Press,* May 20, 1899, p. 3.

[35]Ibid., p. 3.

[36]*Minneapolis Tribune,* May 20, 1899, p. 12; Ibid., May 21, 1899, p. 12.

[37]*Minneapolis Tribune,* June 20, 1899, p. 1.

[38]Minnesota, Office of the Adjutant General, "Spanish-American War Muster Rolls, 1898-1899," Trimonthly Field Returns—sick list, Minnesota Historical Society, St. Paul, Minnesota.

[39]*Stillwater Gazette,* May 5, 1899, p. 2.

Chapter 8

"... They Were a Rough-Looking Crowd ..."

What had started out as a great adventure for the Minnesotans slowly began to turn into an all-out war. Still wanting to gain the prestige of having fought gallantly in battle, the soldiers of the Thirteenth were thrilled with the idea of pursuing the Filipinos into northern Luzon. After holding off the Filipinos' charge against the railroad and doing their part in Wheaton's campaign, one would have thought that all desires for glory would have been satisfied. While for a handful this was true, but the great majority of Minnesotans still looked for that one decisive battle both to end the war and put their names in the history books. At the end of April 1899, they were to be given that chance, but what was to develop in a Luzon jungle was not what any of them expected.

After their tour of duty with Wheaton, the Thirteenth Minnesota Volunteers were assigned to General Henry W. Lawton's "flying column." Of the entire regiment, only the Second Battalion; consisting of Companies K, L, M, and G under Captain Masterman, and the Third Battalion, made up of Companies C, D, E, and H under Captain C. T. Spear, was called into service. The First Battalion, made up of Companies A, B, F, and I were assigned the guarding of another railroad just outside Manila.

On April 22, the Second and Third Battalions, under the command of Major Arthur Diggles, were ordered to assemble at the Bocaue Bridge. Their orders would tell them which way they were to go, their objectives, and when they were to hook up with General Lawton. Not only were the men excited about heading out with this column, but they[1] were also thrilled with the idea of being led by General Lawton. By this time, most of the men had heard about Lawton, who, at the age of fifty-six, was seen as a bold, and sometimes reckless, figure. Striking at six feet tall and with a commanding presence and field record, he was revered by almost every man who ever served under him. He had won the Congressional Medal of Honor in the Civil War, fought in the Indian Wars, and helped capture the legendary Geronimo. Finally, and most recently, was his record in Cuba, where his victories had made him a hero.[2]

Otis' plan to take the war to the Filipinos was to begin during the last week in April 1899. Knowing that most of the rebellious Filipinos were concentrated north of Manila, he devised a plan to trap

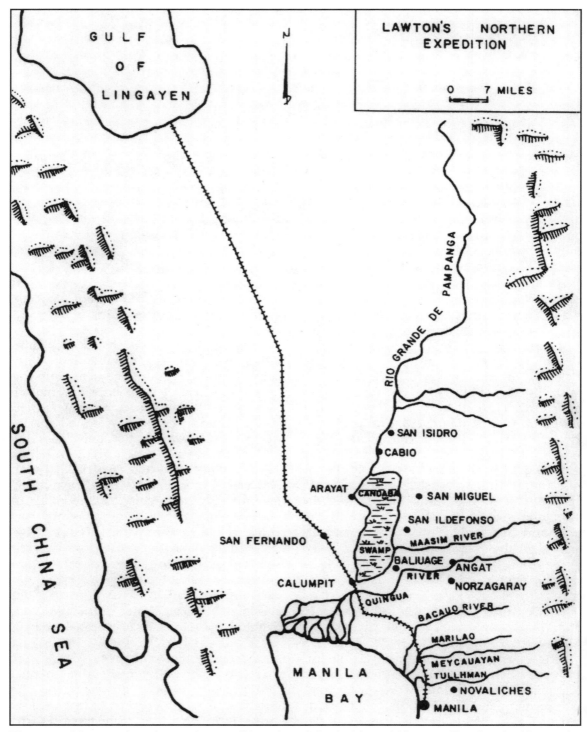

The area of Luzon where Lawton's expedition chased Aguinaldo and his men. (Reprinted with permission of the North Dakota Institute for Regional Studies, North Dakota State University)

them where they lived. Planning a pincers movement, he ordered General MacArthur and his division to move toward the Filipinos from the left, taking a northwest route to the city of San Isidro. Lawton and his division were given a northeast route and were supposed to meet MacArthur a few days later and crush the Filipino army between them.

This campaign, the most serious American military movement in the islands, was supposed to accomplish two objectives. The first was to crush the main body of the Filipino army under the command of General Luna. In order to do this, the Americans would find themselves having to recapture the city of Malalos, since it was Otis' policy to not occupy captured territory. The second objective was to locate and destroy any supplies used by the "insurgents" in fighting the war.[3]

Entering enemy territory, Lawton's "flying column" was to consist of lightly supplied units, which could move out at a moment's notice. Along with the Thirteenth Minnesota, Lawton's Division also consisted of the Twenty-second Infantry, First North Dakota, one squadron of the Fourth United States Cavalry (unmounted), six mountain and two field guns from Battery D of the Sixth United States Artillery, two battalions of the Second Oregon Volunteers, and the Fourth United States Cavalry. All were to meet at the La Loma church just outside Manila and, from there, head to the city of Bocaue on April 23.[4]

Lawton's "flying columns," whose objective was to move fast, "w[ere] equipped in the lightest possible marching order compatible with an expedition of the duration contemplated for this. Ten days' field rations were taken in carts drawn by carabao or water buffalo, as was also a reserve of 100 rounds per man of ammunition." While the supply train packed field

Members of the Thirteenth preparing to head back towards the front. (Courtesy of the Minnesota Military Museum, Camp Ripley)

rations for ten days, for the men, it was quite different. As Martin Tew later recalled; "[E]ach man carried 150 rounds of ammunition, a blanket, poncho, and a change of underclothing besides haversack, canteen, belt, and rifle."[5]

This division of motley units had a strength of 116 officers and 4,473 men. The brigade to which the Minnesotans found themselves attached was under the direct command of Colonel Summers of the First Oregon Volunteers. Not only would they have to take orders from an Oregonian, but they also found themselves doing much of their fighting during this expedition alongside these men from the West Coast. This was all right with the Minnesotans since they had already fought with them at Tondo and during the attack on the railroad.[6]

Even though Lawton knew he was taking the war to the Filipinos, he still fought under the belief that war had rules that needed to be followed. Before his division departed, he sent orders to the men regarding their behavior while under his command. He explained that in order to pacify the Philippines, "we should impress the inhabitants with the idea of our good intentions and destroy the idea that we are barbarians or anything of that sort." The men's conduct was not to impede what the United States policy makers were trying to accomplish, and these rules were enforced, with infractions punished swiftly.[7]

At 5:15 A.M. on April 23, the command was started on road leading to the city of Norazagaray. Barely had they taken off on their march into the "unknown" in the extremely hot Philippine jungle when trouble arose. After less than five hours of travel toward their first destination, the city of Norazgaray, they encountered armed Filipinos. Coming under fire, Colonel Summers ordered the two Minnesota battalions forward to assault and capture the village. Meeting little resistance from the fleeing Filipinos, Captain Masterman and his men occupied the city in a few hours.[8]

Camping there for the night, the men of the Thirteenth awoke the next morning to orders from Captain Spear for the Third Battalion to make a reconnaissance that afternoon of the next village on the map, Angat. Nearing the village, Spear and the Third Battalion found themselves fired upon by Aguinaldo's troops. With orders not to engage, Spear and his men broke off their reconnaissance mission and returned toward Norazagaray.[9]

With Spear and the Third Battalion on scouting duty, the Second Battalion found itself, while still encamped at Norazagaray, under attack from Filipinos. Having used the jungle to avoid discovery, the Filipinos, with the river as a buffer zone, began to rain a fire down upon the American's encampment. Company's K, L, and M were quickly deployed along the bank of the river to disburse the attackers. Because the Filipinos were well entrenched, this battle took the greater part of the day before it finally ended when the Minnesotans pushed their enemy back away from their base. Fortunately for the Minnesotans, there were no wounded, but their marksmanship did inflicting injury and death upon their attackers.[10]

With the return of the reconnaissance party later that afternoon, Spear immediately went to his commanders and reported his findings. Spear's report and the futile attack by the Filipinos that afternoon, led the Americans to believe they had a good idea of what the military situation would be like at Angat. The order to advance toward Angat on the morning of April 25 was given.

The Third Battalion, Minnesota Volunteers, and one Battalion of the Oregon Volunteers were ordered at 5:50 A.M. on the morning of April 25, to take a field piece and move southwest over a plateau that overlooked the village of

Angat. There they were to be the eyes of the division that was on its way to the village. Once in position though, the commanders of these volunteers, not seeing any opposition, decided to march on Angat themselves.

Their observation was correct, for upon entering the village the Americans encountered no opposition. With no sign of danger, they traveled all the way through Angat, where on the other side of the village lay a river. Within a few yards of this river the Americans were surprised, for the Filipinos were hiding on the other side in ambush. From the rather steep banks of the river's opposite side, the Filipinos had found an excellent natural fortification, and began firing at the advancing Americans. The soldiers, having no protection, knelt and began to shoot at the white puffs of smoke left by the Filipinos' weapons.[11]

After an intense forty-minute fight, the Americans were able to force the Filipinos to retreat. With only one Minnesotan injured, the soldiers turned around and began heading back toward Angat. With these two battalions approaching from the east and the rest of the division heading west, both groups noticed that dense smoke was rising from the valley where Angat lay. The rest of the division, which had just arrived, discovered that Angat had already been captured, occupied, and was already burning. This left the Minnesotans to wonder if the fire had been started by their comrades, by accident, or fleeing Filipinos.[12]

After their victory in Angat, the Minnesotans and Oregonians were ordered back to camp at Norazagaray. Since Lawton would not arrive until the next day, these orders came straight from Otis, who insisted that every decision (even those that occurred after Lawton's arrival) be approved by him. This might have been the worst mistake of this campaign and probably the war for the Americans. Otis'

ego refused to allow even minute decisions to be made without his signature. His style of leadership clashed with that of the romantic and bold Lawton whose vigor and dynamism were in complete contrast to his precise, austere, and aloof superior officer.[13]

Although tension was always present between these two, Otis was in charge, and he constantly let Lawton know it. Otis, insisting that he also be kept aware of what his troops were doing in the field, stayed in touch with them by using a telegraph system. Although beneficial to Otis, this system became a nuisance to Lawton and his men since the advancing soldiers were forced to continuously build or repair the telegraphs as they traveled through the jungle. No matter what problems this caused for the men, this was Otis' way of keeping complete control of his men and the situation, and it was through this system that he passed on his next orders. He sent Lawton's division toward the village of Baliuag, where it was estimated a strong force of 3,000 Filipinos had assembled.

On April 27 the division headed in the direction of Baliuag but found obstacles along their way, the first being a very brief skirmish. After this, the entire division moved in and occupied the village of Marunco. Here, Lawton ordered his troops to set up camp for the night and prepare for the next day's march. Camping in Marunco for the night actually proved a more difficult task than fighting the Filipinos for control of it. The Minnesotans spent the night trying to ignore the intense heat and humidity that refused to moderate. Their tents, pitched in an open field, offered little shelter from the intense Philippine heat.[14]

With orders to stay in camp until April 29, the Minnesotans did what they could to keep themselves busy. Toward evening, the Minnesotans thought their ordeal was over when rain clouds began to hover over them. When the rain started to

Men of the Thirteenth crossing one of many rivers during Lawton's campaign. (Courtesy of the Minnesota Military Museum, Camp Ripley)

fall, most had to feel a sense of relief, that is until they discovered that they had been spared from one torturous weather problem only to end up in another. In a matter of minutes, the tents, supply carts, trenches, and the men themselves were soaked while the camp flooded with water. This left the men to scramble to the vacant huts in the village, which were too few and did not provide complete protection from the violent rainstorm.[15]

Awaking on the morning of April 29 soaking wet and with little sleep for two days, the men were ordered to ford a river and make "a most wearisome march . . . along winding footpaths, over ravines and gulleys, through woods and jungles, until San Rafael was sighted." Only a few days into their campaign, the men of the Thirteenth found themselves hungry, wet, and tired of chasing an army of soldiers who refused to stand up and fight as the Minnesotans had been trained to do. In a matter of hours, the men's morale began to sink into depths never before seen by their leaders, or themselves.[16]

The objective, San Rafael, was captured without resistance since the Filipinos had already deserted the city. Having made some decisions without Otis' approval since he had moved ahead of the telegraphic communication system, Law-

ton was reeled in by his superior. Arguing that he was moving too fast for his supplies, on April 29, Otis ordered Lawton to return all the way to Angat until he could be re-supplied. Having too few men to spare to defend what they gained, Lawton was forced to withdraw his troops from San Rafael and return to Angat where they camped for three days awaiting Otis' supplies.[17]

After re-supplying and resting, Lawton was again ordered to take the village of Baliuag. Starting out from Angat, the division retraced its steps down the Quinqua River. This time, though, the Minnesotans brought with them the supply train, ambulance, and all necessary equipment. While the Minnesotans and Oregonians forded the river and proceed down the east bank, the rest of the column continued along the west side.[18]

When the Americans approached within a few hundred yards of San Rafael, some 1,000 Filipinos, who had occupied the town after Lawton's withdrawal, offered stiff resistance. With a group of scouts engaging the Filipinos just one and one-half miles north of the village, the Minnesotans and Oregonians began to drive their enemy through the city where they retreated across another river to make another stand. When other members of Lawton's Division carried out a flanking maneuver, the Filipinos were flushed from their positions and quickly fled from the battlefield.[19]

For this battle to re-capture a once-held city, the Minnesotans lost four wounded along with Private Frank C. Lewis of Company F, who was killed in the short-lived battle. With all else going wrong, the realization of their own mortality and what could happen while on this campaign hit a great many of the men of the Thirteenth.

To add insult to injury many of the Minnesotans believed the death of Private Lewis was senseless since they had already captured the village once and, in essence, were just retaking what they already held. At this point, many of the men began to question not only the military decision-making but also what they, and their country, were doing in the Philippines.

That night they buried Private Lewis "at the foot of the tower of a great stone church. . . ." This was done very carefully in order to conceal the grave because many of the soldiers had seen or heard that, "the insurgents had made it their practice to mutilate the bodies they found. . . ."[20]

Once San Rafael was captured, the next objective for these weary soldiers was the city of Baliuag. At about noon, the division was deployed to start marching toward this destination. Having his division still split by the river, the commands on both sides of the river left their bivouacs of the night before and continued down the river. Nearing Baliuag, the expedition came across citizens deserting the city in great confusion along the road to the north. Since a vast majority of the fleeing people were women, children, and wounded carried on litters, the Americans did no shooting, and a flag of truce was sent out "hoping we might assure them of their safety."[21]

By the time the Americans reached Baliuag, almost the entire population of 30,000 inhabitants had fled. But by nightfall, several hundred had returned looking for food. Having discovered 30,000 bushels of rice stored in the city, the Americans, instead of destroying it as orders had told them to do, distributed it to the refugees, allowing them to carry as much as they could.[22]

Sergeant Ed Neill later summarized the actions of that day:

> As we were about to eat our dinner, orders came to march and extended as skirmishers we made our way to the front and moved along the line to the extreme front one and a half miles away where we

were moved up the skirmish line. The American line was then over five miles long, surrounding the city in a semicircle. Just before we were placed the insurgents had raised a white flag but when Gen[eral] Lawton sent out a party to treat with them they were treacherously fired upon. . . . So at command we began to close on the city.

After what Neill termed a "muddy fight," they were able to capture the city along with a number of Filipinos.[23]

With a couple of days of rest, Neill again found time to jot down a few lines to send to the *Red Wing Republican*. Describing what life had been like out in the jungle, Neill said; "[I]f it were not for such rests as we are enjoying now, it would be impossible to stand this campaign, in sun and heat and always wet through either from rain or perspiration, sleeping in damp clothes in all sorts of places and with the heavy load which must be carried on every march and in every skirmish." He further noted that soldiers had been dropping out every day and going to the supply carts to rest. After a day or two of rejuvenating themselves, they would then reappear.[24]

After two days of resting the entire division, General Lawton ordered them to move out again. This time they were to head toward San Miguel, through the thick jungle and small villages, both held by Aguinaldo's men. The first of their obstacles was the town of Maasin. Departing at 7:00 a.m., the Minnesotans again were ordered to take the lead, with the Twenty-second United States Infantry and the North Dakotans, Oregonians, and an artillery unit following close behind.[25]

Within about seven miles of Baliuag, on the road to San Miguel and situated on both banks of a small river, lay the village of Maasin. About three-fourths of a mile outside the village, the American scouts were suddenly and fiercely attacked by

Filipinos. In response to this, the Thirteenth's Second Battalion, under Acting Major Masterman, "was quickly deployed and made a rapid advance toward the enemy, while the [Thi]rd Battalion, under Acting Major Spear followed closely in reserve."[26]

Finding unusually heavy enemy fire from the 400 entrenched Filipinos, the Minnesotans of Companies H and E, who were placed on the firing line, decided to advance rapidly toward them. Taking a page out of their Civil War history books, the Minnesotans decided to charge wildly into the jungle while keeping up a spirited yell. With the help of the Utah field piece, the charge by the Minnesotans was able to dislodge the Filipinos, who were routed in about forty minutes.[27]

While another military success, the heavy firing from Aguinaldo's soldiers did cause some problems for the Americans. Private James Barrett, Company H, was slightly wounded in the right shoulder. Another casualty was Private Fred Buckendorf, Company L, who was "fatally wounded in the abdomen" and died a couple of days later in the hospital.

Although a relatively easy battle for the Thirteenth, Sergeant Neill told his readers how this battle could have turned out a great deal worse for the Americans. As he claimed, "[H]ad the insurgents awaited our troops and allowed them to come up within 500 yards before firing our loss would have been heavy, but they preferred to fight at long range and run. . . ." Knowing they neither had the manpower nor the supplies to defeat the Americans in a traditional battle, from here on out the Filipinos resorted to fighting the war with the guerrilla tactics of hit and run which they had been using for the past few weeks.[28]

With Lawton's army rolling through the Luzon countryside, Otis, always the jittery leader, again halted this campaign. With rumors floating that a Filipino army as large as 5,000 strong waited to attack

Lawton from the rear, the ever cautious Otis decided to consolidate his forces. Lawton, annoyed with his orders and wanting to finish the Filipinos off, began to send out reconnoitering parties to locate the enemy.

One of these reconnoitering parties was sent in the direction of the village of San Ildefenso. The men from Stillwater were ordered to accompany this brigade. Major Diggles, probably bored with sitting around camp, decided to go along and observe. Ordered to find the enemy so that they could get an accurate idea as to where their positions were, these scouts found themselves coming out of the jungle within 800 to 900 yards of the entrenched Filipinos.

While the scouts jumped out almost on top of the Filipinos, Major Diggles was standing on a hill overlooking the entire area. Surprised by the Americans, the Filipinos began firing and, in typical Filipino fashion, were shooting too high, which turned out to be deadly for one Minnesotan. When the skirmish began, one of these random Mauser bullets flew over the heads of the scouts and struck Major Diggles. The bullet, ". . . pierced the upper part of his forehead and made its exit near the crown of the head." Holding on to life for a few days, Diggles finally passed away in his sleep on May 26.[29]

Of all the events that happened to the men of the Thirteenth, this was one of few that made a big impact not only on those in the field but also for those back home. Few, if any, newspapers, soldiers' letters home, official reports, or the histories written about the regiment after the war failed to mention the death of Major Diggles. Much like the death of Private Lewis, this single event helped change how people viewed the war. For the soldier in the field, the loss of such a popular commander kept their morale spiraling down, while for those at home this death proved that none were safe in this new war in the Philippines.

A group of Minnesotans posing by a *nipa* hut in Luzon. (Courtesy of the Minnesota Military Museum, Camp Ripley)

Portrait of Major Arthur M. Diggles. (Reprinted from *Campaigning in the Philippines* by Karl Irving Faust, 1899)

General Otis' decision to consolidate forces meant that Lawton's expedition could rest and reconnoiter from May 6 until May 12, 1899. With time to reflect on what was transpiring around him, Private Gerald G. Groves, Company I, wrote home explaining what he felt was going to happen in the islands. "These natives are indeed a strange people . . . I do not believe they will ever come in a body and surrender. They will carry on a sort of guerrilla warfare for, say, two or three years. . . ." He then wishfully added, ". . . but the 'Regulars' can easily take care of that."[30]

These sentiments were also captured in a letter from Company K's, Captain James McKelvy to his friend John P. Bernich.

> We are having a hard old time of it here and we all wish we were back home. With our hard times, hard fighting, hard matches and worse food we are a sorry looking lot. Fighting is of a daily occurrence with us and of course loose [sic] a good many men which makes us ugly and we pay it back, with interest.
>
> A soldier's life is like a game of cards you are lucky one game and unlucky the next and so it goes if I am lucky in this game of cards and get home again to those that are dear to me I will never leave them again. You are a lucky man that you did not come along for there is only turmoil, toil and strife. War is

> h— and no mistake, my company has been in fourteen engagements and have seen enough. . . .

He concluded by voicing the thought so many volunteers had on the tips of their tongues but dared not speak. He told Bernich, ". . . the country [Philippines] is no good and I don't see what our Uncle Samuel is fighting for."[31]

Corporal James P. Koll of Company A, reinforced this sentiment when his letter home was published in the *Minneapolis Tribune*. In it he told the people at home, "[G]en[eral] Lawton's expeditionary force has seen much hard work, fighting and long marches, and the men have suffered terribly in the intense heat. Not a day passes that an ambulance wagon train does not bring in scores of men from the front, suffering from sunstroke, heat exhaustion, dysentery, fever, sore and blistered feet. . . ." Then after long and trying days, he reported that the men lie down to rest on the ground and are completely soaked by the night dews or heavy rains.[32]

As Lawton's expedition progressed, the newspapers in Minnesota closely followed what was happening. On almost every front page would be the "official" story sent out over the wires and passed on by the military leaders. Then, a few pages further back, there would almost inevitably be a letter from one of the soldiers describing the horrors of life on the campaign. These letters, combined with the section on the front page that gave the daily death/injury reports, began to make a great many in Minnesota, and around the nation, question why the volunteers were still fighting in the Philippines. Had

Cartoons from the *Minneapolis Journal*, March 21, 1899, and (opposite) April 6, 1899. Both depict the racial stereotypes many of the men from Minnesota brought with them to the Philippines. They also show how many Americans misunderstood what was actually happening on the other side of the world. The caption for the cartoons read, "'Twixt the Devil and the Deep Sea" (above) and "Wonder if He Can See the Point?" (opposite).

not the Spanish-American War ended months ago? What was the United States trying to accomplish by conquering the Filipinos, the very people to whom they had gone to bring liberty in the first place? Questions like these began to turn some Americans against this war.

Back on the campaign in Northern Luzon, while the rest of the company was still resting, Company D captured the city of San Ildefonso. Captain Metz, and one company of the Second Oregon, who captured the city, had been sent on a reconnoitering mission toward San Ildefonso on May 12. Attacking Aguinaldo's men in the city, these two companies were to push them through the town. Unlike other battles, though, the Filipinos put up an excel-

117

lent defense, forcing the pursuing Americans to fight from hut to hut before taking the town.

Once pushed out of the city limits, the Filipinos began to flee toward the city of San Miguel, Lawton's next objective. Knowing Lawton's expedition was heading there anyway, Metz and Summers ordered their troops to continue on the heels of Aguinaldo's men. Following them in hot pursuit, the Americans did not stop until they were within three miles of that city. Covering twelve miles that day, the small band of Americans held up and awaited the rest of the column, which soon arrived.[33]

With the objective of San Miguel only three miles away, and believing the Filipinos had to be tired after having been chased by the scouting party, Lawton decided to move on the city the next day. Used to being in the front, the Minnesotans were surprised to find out that seven of their companies, now under the command of Captain J. P. Masterman, were ordered to form to the rear of the column and wait as a reserve. One unit, Company H, was given yet other instructions.

Under the command of Captain Bjornstad, Company H, along with one company of the Second Oregon, was sent northward toward San Miguel and ordered to support a small group of scouts already in that area. Repeating their successful flanking tactics, these scouts routed the Filipinos from their trenches into the open where Company H chased them beyond the city limits.[34]

By 12:30 P.M., the town of San Miguel was taken, and, by all official reports, an army of almost 500 Filipinos was routed by fewer than 100 Americans. Suffering only one seriously wounded man, the Thirteenth moved into the city by 5:00 P.M. and set up camp.

Again ordered by General Otis to take a two-day rest, Lawton and the men in his command were getting extremely tired of how this war was being fought. In their estimation, the war would come to a quick and successful ending if Otis would let Lawton run the war the way he wanted. Tired of the delays, Lawton asked and received permission to move his men on May 15. Leaving one battalion to garrison Baliuag, Lawton moved the rest toward the important objective of San Isidro, designated as Aguinaldo's "national capital." Otis believed that not only would this be a great symbolic victory, but with rumors that there was an ammunition factory there, he also hoped it would be the battle that would bring this war to a close.[35]

By 3:00 P.M. on May 15, Colonel Summers with the Second Oregon and the Thirteenth Minnesota, accompanied by a section of artillery, moved out of San Miguel and proceeded north toward San Isidro. Only three miles out on their march, they were met with heavy fire from a strongly entrenched group of Filipinos. Forcing Aguinaldo's men from their dugouts, the Americans drove them across a stream about a mile and one-half closer to their objective.[36]

When the Filipinos made a stand on the other side of the stream, the Thirteenth Minnesota quickly deployed Company K to the front, with Companies G and M taking the right and Company L sent to the left. With the rest of the division in reserve, the Minnesotans were forced to take action. While having little or no cover, Captain Masterman decided to make a headlong attack into the Filipino defenses. With the Minnesota sholdiers shooting and screaming their way toward them, Aguinaldo's men held their ground until the last possible moment. Under increasing pressure, the Filipinos finally broke and ran, only to have many of their comrades shot down by the pursuing Minnesotans.[37]

Making such a bold charge, the Minnesotans fortunately had only one man injured among their ranks, while the Filipinos, as far as the Minnesotans could tell, had lost eleven as prisoners of war, nineteen killed, and several wounded.[38]

While all these smaller battles were taking place along the expedition, there was still the bigger picture of the overall campaign objectives of both Lawton and MacArthur. While running into similar circumstances with his men to the west of Lawton, MacArthur was also gaining on the town of San Miguel, where the two were to meet and destroy Aguinaldo's resistance once and for all.

Lawton, outraged with Otis' lack of military skills, requested a rapid move by his men on San Isidro. Knowing that MacArthur was struggling with the Filipinos not far from the city, Lawton hoped that a quick movement on his part might yield victory. The general argued that he could turn west and trap those Filipinos resisting MacArthur's advance but only if Otis quickly gave him the order. Giving in to the field commander's request, Otis finally ordered Lawton to make his move.[39]

After two minor skirmishes with Filipinos at Baluarte and San Rogue on May 16, Lawton's expedition finally stood in front of the city of San Isidro, where most felt the war would be brought to its conclusion.

With the North Dakotans, Oregonians, and the Twenty-second United States Infantry taking the lead, the Minnesotans, to their chagrin, were ordered into reserve. Still, they needed to be ready to fill in any gap that might open up in the lines. Upon advancing on the city, the Americans again received another hot fire from the entrenched Filipinos. But the basic outline of battles with the Filipinos followed a familiar pattern. The Filipinos fled, and the "important" city of San Isidro was taken after only a few minutes. For the men of the Thirteenth Minnesota, and for American military leaders as well, San Isidro proved neither the major objective that they had been led to believe it was nor a source of battle glory.[40]

With hopes again raised high, the Third Battalion, Thirteenth Minnesota, along with one battalion of the First Oregon, were sent to the village of Gapan, to which it was believed the Filipinos had fled and which contained, they believed, a huge supply of stores.

Organizing rapidly, the Americans headed out toward Gapan the afternoon of May 17 and, they hoped, toward fulfillment of their destiny. In their minds, it was all too fitting that the Thirteenth Minnesota Volunteers be the ones to bring this war to its successful conclusion. Quickly traveling over three miles up the river, they soon sighted their objective. Charging into the village, the men were not surprised at what they saw. Typical of this campaign and the war itself, they found the city deserted. Their hopes and dreams of being the unit to end this war were quickly destroyed when they looked around at all the empty huts surrounding them. Realizing that there was not going to be a fight and that this war was not going to be over any time soon, the men set up camp for the night.[41]

On May 18, they reunited with the rest of the expedition in San Isidro. That afternoon, with their mission accomplished, the division was ordered back to Manila. Of all their orders since joining the army, this was by far the best one any of the Minnesotans had heard. This march, which consisted of traveling through the dense jungle, fording rivers, and occasionally skirmishing with Aguinaldo's troops, did not seem as trying for the men as it had before. They knew that they had survived this expedition, and if they and the people back at home began to push hard, they might soon be returned to Minnesota. It was at this point that many of the soldiers, who had earlier wrote letters to their hometown newspapers glorifying the war

Members of Company C on a firing line during Lawton's expedition. (Courtesy of the Minnesota Military Museum, Camp Ripley)

and themselves, began to write letters telling of the horrors of war and why they wanted to leave the Philippines.

After retracing their steps back through the jungle, on May 21 they reached the city of Candaba and there, instead of at Manila, Lawton's expedition was disbanded. On May 23, while relieving them of duty from the expedition, Lawton thanked the men of the Thirteenth by stating in his report, "[T]he commanding general in relieving this regiment, desires to express his appreciation of the efficiency, courage, and uncomplaining endurance constantly shown by its officers and men while on this expedition." With that, their front-line duty ended.[42]

Having survived thirty-three days of almost daily battles with Filipinos, covering 120 miles, capturing twenty-eight towns, traveling through dense jungle, dealing with uncooperative weather and a variety of diseases, the Minnesotans were happy to be sent back to the mundane job of policing. In order to reunite the entire regiment, the Second and Third Battalions were sent to rejoin the First Battalion, which guarded the railroad between Caloocan and Guigunto.[43]

When they took their place along the railroad line, the appearance of the men indicated the severity of what they had just been through. "Thin, hardened, ragged, bearded, they were a rough-looking crowd, and it took many weeks for them to get back to their former condition. Only the strongest constitution could stand it, and quite a number of the men were sent home before final orders for the regiment came."[44]

With the expedition over, and with less success than the Americans had hoped, the Otis-Lawton feud continued. With the rainy season about to begin, and the volunteers clamoring to be sent back to the states, Lawton was ordered back to Manila and his forces brought with him. From Lawton's standpoint, and that of many of his men, this was a huge mistake. They believed that their expedition was a complete waste unless they fortified these captured towns with American troops. The Filipinos easily could come back in and re-capture them later. These words surely had to resonate through Lawton's mind when, a few months later, he was sent to fight his way back into San Isidro.[45]

Back on guard duty, the men had time to write letters home and could let their friends and families know what they felt about what was happening in the islands. In a lengthy and bitter letter home, the recovering Private Burlingham summed up to his parents what his, and a great many other Minnesotans', view on this war:

"From letters and newspaper talk it appears to me as if our people thought we had an inferior class of people to fight against. . . ." After chasing them through the Luzon jungles, Burlingham knew bet-ter, and he wanted the people back home to understand it also. "If you people think there is glory in [chasing after the Filipinos] please send one of your worst enemies to take my place and I will will-ingly exchange with him."

"Why did the [United States] go into war with spain [sic] why did she take this white elephant on her hands and pay $20,000,000 to get it. Then she turns around and does what Spain was doing when we entered. All done for greed, greed that will cause insanity. . . ."

"This war here is nothing more than a damn political and religious affair and has caused the lives of 2,000 good American

The Thirteenth Minnesota Volunteers returning from the front. (Courtesy of the Minnesota Historical Society)

men to be laid away forever or else crippled for life. . . ."

He concluded by discussing the men's desires to gain glory during the war, the one thing all the soldiers wanted.

"It was all right to talk about the glory your sons were getting fighting with spain [sic] but now it is different we are now forced to fight and kept here against our will because Gen[eral] Otis (the ——) cables home that all volunteers want to stay here."

"Father and Mother and the people of the U[nited States] you are all in the dark, you are blindfolded, you think you know all that is going on here, you think your sons are fighting for a good cause—but no[,] you are wrong you know nothing, absolutely nothing."[46]

Although only seventeen years old, Burlingham's anger was indicative of how the rest of the volunteers felt about what was happening in the Philippines. Realizing that this war was not as much fun as the stories they had heard told of the Civil War, the men wanted to return to the safe confines of their home states.

With bitterness fermenting among the volunteers as well as among many people in the states, McKinley realized he had to bring the soldiers home as soon as possible. Caught between the popular opposition to this war and the need for the volunteers in the islands, McKinley began to recall the troops that summer. The Minnesotans, however, would have to wait until they completed their current assignment before they too sailed for America.[47]

Members of the Thirteenth boarding trains to take them back to Manila after Lawton's campaign. (Courtesy of the Minnesota Military Museum, Camp Ripley)

Knowing their fighting days were behind them, many of the men began to reflect on what their legacy would be from this war. Summing up what probably most of the soldiers felt, Private George W. Kurtz, Company I, wrote, "[W]e have been through a hard battle and seen some soldiering. We got what we have been praying for a long time and we found that it was not as much fun as we expected."[48]

NOTES

[1]Franklin F. Holbrook, *Minnesota in the Spanish-American War and the Philippine Insurrection, Vol. 1* (St. Paul: The Riverside Press, 1923), p. 64.

[2]Stuart Creighton Miller, *Benevolent Assimilation: The American Conquest of the Philippines, 1899-1903* (New Haven: Yale University Press, 1982), p. 70. Stanley Karnow, *In Our Image: America's Empire in*

Private Compton wrote this on the back of the photo: "A bit of country around San Fernando where the American forces rested during the rainy season of [18]99. The mountain seen in the background [too faded over time to see now] is Mt. Aryat, a lone mountain towering above the many foothills in the interior. We marched with General Lawton in his campaign through the interior, all sides of this mountain until at last we came to the very foot of it at the Rio Grande de Pampanga River, which we crossed by means of canoes and continued our march skirting the foot of the mountain, which ended our campaign. One month in which time we marched one hundred and thirty miles and had [twenty-three] engagements." (Courtesy of the Minnesota Military Museum, Camp Ripley)

the Philippines (New York: Random House, Inc., 1990), pp. 148-149.

[3]Leon Wolff, Little Brown Brother; How the United States Purchased and Pacified the Philippine Islands at the Century's Turn (Garden City, New York: Doubleday, 1961), p. 240.

[4]William Thaddeus Sexton, Soldiers in the Sun; an Adventure in Imperialism (Harrisburg, Pennsylvania: The Military Service Publishing Co., c1939), p. 130.

[5]Karl Faust, Campaigning in the Philippines (New York: Arno Press, 1970 [c1898]), p. 228. Martin E. Tew, Official History of the Operation of the 13th Minnesota Infantry, U.S.V. in the Campaign in the Philippine Islands (S.I.: S.N., 1899), p. 32.

[6]Sexton, Soldiers in the Sun, p. 131.

[7]John Morgan Gates, Schoolbooks and Krags: The United States Army in the Philippines, 1898-1902 (Westport, Connecticut: Greenwood Press, Inc., 1973), p. 83.

[8]Hiram David Frankel, Company "C," First Infantry Minnesota National Guard: Its History and Development (Brown, Treacy and Co.), p. 57. Kenneth M. Davies, To The Last Man: The Chronicle of the 135th Infantry Regiment of Minneota (St. Paul: The Ramsey County Historical Society, 1982), p. 64.

[9]Minnesota, Office of the Adjutant General, "Spanish-American War Military Service Records, 1898-1900," Report from Masterman to Col. Summers—May 27, 1899, Minnesota Historical Society, St. Paul, Minnesota.

[10]Ibid.

[11]Oregon, Adjutant-General's Office, "The Official Records of the Oregon Volunteers in the Spanish-American and Philippine Insurrection," p. 85, Minnesota Historical Society, St. Paul, Minnesota.

[12]Tew, Official History of the Operation of the 13th Minnesota Infantry, p. 34.

[13]Thomas Burdett, "The Memorable March of the 3rd Infantry from San Miguel to Balinag," Military Collector & Historian (Fall 1974), p. 83.

[14]Oregon, Adjutant-General's Office, "The Official Records of the Oregon Volunteers in the Spanish-American and Philippine Insurrection," p. 85, Minnesota Historical Society, St. Paul, Minnesota.

[15]Ibid., p. 85.

[16]Tew, Official History of the Operations of the 13th Minnesota Infantry, p. 34.

[17]Sexton, Soldiers in the Sun, p. 132.

[18]Ibid., p. 132. Tew, Official History of the Operation of the 13th Minnesota Infantry, p. 34.

[19]Faust, Campaigning in the Philippines, p. 215.

[20]Frankel, Company "C," p. 58.

[21]Faust, Campaigning in the Philippines, p. 216.

[22]Ibid., p. 217.

[23]Red Wing Republican, June 24, 1899, p. 8.

[24]Ibid., June 30, 1899, p. 8.

[25]Ibid., July 6, 1899, p. 8.

[26]Tew, Official History of the Operations of the 13th Minnesota Infantry, p. 36.

[27]Ibid., p. 36.

[28]Red Wing, Republican, July 6, 1899, p. 8.

[29]Tew, Official History of the Operations of the 13th Minnesota Infantry, p. 36.

[30]Mouraine Baker, ed., Dear Folks at Home: Wright County's View of the Spanish-American War, Gerald G. Groves, May 10, 1899, p. 22.

[31]James McKelvy letter to John P. Bernich, May 11, 1899, McKelvy, James E., 1898, Letters, Stearns County Historical Society, St. Cloud, Minnesota.

[32]Minneapolis Tribune, June 17, 1899, p. 11.

[33]Holbrook, Minnesota in the Spanish-American War and the Philippine Insurrection, p. 67.

[34]Ibid., p. 67.

[35]Sexton, Soldiers in the Sun, p. 136.

[36]Faust, Campaigning in the Philippines, p. 226.

[37]Tew, Official History of the Operations of

the 13th Minnesota Infantry, p. 38.

[38]Ibid., p. 38.

[39]Jerry M. Cooper, *Citizens as Soldiers: A History of the North Dakota National Guard* (Fargo: The North Dakota Institute for Regional Studies, 1986), p. 100.

[40]Tew, *Official History of the Operations of rhe 13th Minnesota Infantry,* pp. 38-39.

[41]Faust, *Campaigning in the Philippines,* p. 229.

[42]Minnesota, Office of the Adjutant General, "State Report, 1900," Volume II, p. 867, Minnesota Historical Society, St. Paul, Minnesota.

[43]Holbrook, *Minnesota in the Spanish-American War and the Philippine Insurrection,* p. 68.

[44]Fitch, *13th Minnesota Vols.,* p. 40.

[45]Sexton, *Soldiers in the Sun,* p. 140.

[46]Lewis Burlingham letter to parents, June 1, 1899, Burlingham, Lewis Preston, 1879-1951, Papers, Minnesota Historical Society, St. Paul, Minnesota.

[47]Daniel Shirmer, *Republic or Empire; American Resistance to the Philippine War* (Cambridge, Massachusetts: Schenkman Publishing Co., 1972), pp. 149, 151.

[48]Baker, *Dear Folks at Home,* George W. Kurtz, p. 18-19.

Chapter 9

"... Each One Dropped from the Ranks ..."

Those who survived Lawton's expedition into the jungle never complained about their new assignment of guard duty around Manila. After spending months of grumbling about having to be either policemen or doing guard duty, the experience in the front lines made them painfully aware that war was dangerous, and picket duty was usually a lot safer. They also were aware that just doing guard duty would give them the opportunity to write letters home, pleading with

Private Compton wrote: "The camp of Co[mpany] H in Marilao after we returned from the campaign with Gen[eral] Lawton. The shacks were built with more idea for comfort than for beauty with the idea of keeping off the hot sun." (Courtesy of the Minnesota Military Museum, Camp Ripley)

the people of Minnesota and their political leaders to get them out of the Philippines.

The entire regiment was assigned again to the Manila and Dagupan railroad lines, the same area where they had fought the Filipinos just a few weeks earlier, and outpost duty was quite an unpleasant task once the rainy season began. The tremendous rains, that could sometimes last four or five days, forced the men to often stand in water up to their knees. The rain ruined their clothes by either beating them apart or forcing rapid deterioration through moisture and subsequent mildewing. The rains also helped destroy the men's morale, which, after Lawton's expedition, was not hard to do.

With the state volunteers clamoring to be sent home, General Otis found himself in a precarious position. Up to half of his forces in the islands were made up of state volunteers who, under their original agreement to join, were to serve until the Spanish-American War ended. That feat having been accomplished and all the treaties having been signed, the volunteers felt it was time to go home. The departure of the volunteers would have left Otis terribly short of the soldiers needed to conclude this other war. Without replacements for the volunteers, he feared the war would turn into a long affair.[1]

Back in Minnesota, responding to stories of how horrible the war was becoming, many people began to push for the return of the Thirteenth. Those wanting this found an ally in the Minnesota governor's chair. John Lind, a Swedish immigrant, had beaten out the Republican candidate William E. Eustis in that fall's campaign. Clough, who had been a fairly popular leader, was barred from running because he had already held the position for two consecutive terms, and Minnesota law did not allow a third. With the Republicans having to put up a candidate some considered less desirable than Clough, parties such as the Democrats, Populists, and Silverites were able to join forces and unseat the Republicans from the governor's office for the first time since 1858.[2]

Although both sides felt they had serious issues to bring forth in this campaign, what they had to say was often overshadowed in the newspapers by the Spanish-American War. Lind's strategy was to focus his attention on state issues and leave national events alone. Because of Lind and Eustis being very close friends, and with national events stealing the headlines, many came to consider this to be one of Minnesota's most "dull and boring elections."[3]

While Lind had at first vowed to stay out of national affairs, on one issue he could not help himself. When it came to the topic of imperialism, Lind was often quite outspoken. Adamantly against President McKinley's new foreign policies, Lind, in a handful of political speeches given in the fall of 1898, spoke against America's retention of either the Philippines or Puerto Rico. Ironically, Lind was not considered either a pacifist or anti-military, for he had himself signed up and served as a volunteer Quartermaster for the Twelfth Minnesota Volunteers. Many people actually equated his victory in the fall to the fact that not only had he served but that he was immensely popular with the men of both the Twelfth and Fourteenth Minnesota Volunteers.[4]

Lind was inaugurated on January 3, 1899. Although he had occasionally brought up the issue of imperialism, for the most part he stuck to his plans of putting Minnesota first. This worked throughout the first few weeks of his administration; then events out of his control slowly began to force him back into the debate over America's imperialistic policies.

When the United States Senate ratified the treaty between America and Spain, some people became irate. One Minnesota state senator who disliked the treaty's ratification even went so far as to bring a bill before the Minnesota Senate opposing annexation of the Philippines. Although easily defeated, those who believed in this idea found an ally in Governor Lind.[5]

Along with the political leaders trying to either stop the war or get the Thirteenth home were many Minnesota citizens. With newspapers publishing the casualty list, and no end in sight for this war with the Filipinos, many quickly turned against the war. Although no polls existed, it would have been interesting to see how many of these same people who were now adamantly opposed to the war had been cheering as the men went off to war a few months earlier?[6]

The Thirteenth Auxiliary, the official voice of the Thirteenth Minnesota in the state, also began worrying about how to get the men out of the Philippines. They took it upon themselves to literally bombard the War Department and the president with letters pleading for the return of the Thirteenth Minnesota Regiment. When even this failed to grab government leaders' attention, the anti-imperialists of Minnesota turned to Governor Lind.[7]

Lind, still trying to hold to his campaign pledge of not wanting to get involved with national affairs, finally was prompted into action after he received a cablegram from the officers of the Thirteenth Minnesota (including General Reeve). The cablegram simply read: "[T]he regiment must be ordered home and mustered out of service immediately."

With this, along with the pressure from people across the state, Lind finally got deeply involved in helping bring back the men of the Thirteenth. Without delay, along with other state governors who agreed with him, Lind began to petition McKinley for the return of all the state volunteers, even going to the extreme of actually going to Washington to meet with the president and to discuss the issue.

The governor, who himself lived in the camps during the war, wanted the War Department to call back both those lingering in camps in the south as well as those doing service in the Philippines. With this much pressure coming from the states, McKinley and his staff slowly began to change their policy and began calling the volunteers home.[8]

Lind's actions did not meet with universal approval though. He especially irritated his Republican counterparts still smarting from losing the governorship. Some Republicans accused Lind of being "spineless" and of "playing godmother to a few weakling officers." He, and those who agreed with him, also received a reprimand from former Governor Clough. In a *St. Paul Pioneer Press* article, Clough explained that he was ". . . not at all pleased with the conduct of the Thirteenth Minnesota Auxiliary and others who were demanding that the Thirteenth regiment be mustered out." As he said, he felt the president and the War Department were "entirely competent to determine these matters . . ." and those who were less qualified should stay out.[9]

Not everyone who wanted the Thirteenth brought home could be considered an anti-imperialist. Many wanted their fellow Minnesotans brought home but still wanted the United States to control the Philippines. Instead of using the volunteers, these people wanted the Regular Army to do the work. The desire to bring the Thirteenth home, and also quickly end the war, was summarized in an editorial in the *Red Wing Republican* on June 29, 1899. This editorial stated a belief that the United States had involved itself in a war that must end soon. They added, ". . . do not let this insurrection drag on, with all its intended hardships, and all the incidents of prolonged fighting that are hostile to the whole American idea. We believe in fighting like demons when we have to, and then stopping as quickly as possible. Clean out the hornets' nest whatever it may cost, and let us have peace."[10]

Still holding onto some of the excitement that swept the state months before, the *Red Wing Republican* played the dual role of asking for the Thirteenth's return while, at the same time, remaining staunchly behind McKinley and his foreign policies by saying the Thirteenth should be brought home only after the job was finished. As for newspapers across the state, the *Republican* was the lone voice when it came to this belief, for the rest of the state's newspapers either demanded an immediate return of the Thirteenth, an end to the war, or both.

This belief was a fair reflection of most Minnesotans, who wanted to bring the Thirteenth home, end the war, and then go on with things as though the Philippine-American War had never happened. Many Americans wanted to put the war behind them as quickly as possible for it was not the kind of war they had wanted back in the spring of 1898. This fight with the Filipinos was neither going to be a clear and easy victory, nor did it put the Americans in the light of gallant saviors bringing democracy to an oppressed people. Rather, for a great many who agreed with Governor Lind, the war made the United States look more like an imperialistic oppressor. Many Americans began to question their nation's role in a war where it was not completely clear that they were on the morally right side.

With the dream of bringing the Thirteenth home, many people began to raise money to accomplish that goal. To all Minnesotans, no matter what they felt about the war, their soldiers were heroes and deserved a hero's welcome.

One official who took the initiative to bring the troops home was Minneapolis Mayor James Gray. It was his idea to sell pins made of little red, white, and blue ribbon upon which were printed the words, "'I Have, Have You?' The ribbon was evidence that the wearer had paid a dollar—the price for which it was sold—toward bring-

ing the Thirteenth Regiment home." Not to be outdone the *Minneapolis Times* donated $1,000, while many private donors gave liberally. In the end, the money raised from the sale of these ribbons would prove to be more than enough to bring the soldier's home to Minnesota.[11]

Desiring to have the Thirteenth mustered out in their respective hometowns, the five cities that had offered companies were able to raise over $25,000 for the soldiers' return. The rest of the $31,000 was to be picked up by the governor.[12]

Ironically, while the people were preparing to bring the troops home to one of the biggest celebrations the state had ever seen, the men in the Philippines had quite different plans. In an almost unanimous vote, the members of the Thirteenth decided that they preferred to be mustered out in San Francisco. The reason for this was not to snub their fellow Minnesotans but for purely economic reasons. "The choice was determined by the fact that the Federal Government allowed each soldier travel pay from San Francisco to his place of enlistment, besides two months' pay." If they were mustered out in Minneapolis they would lose out on all this pay.[13]

Irritated with news from home about the mustering out plans, Lewis Burlingham wrote his parents, telling them, "[L]et the boys have their say, it was them that did the work and risked their lives for the sake of the country and not those cold-footed ducks that are doing so much talking back there." Caught in the middle of national and state politics, and now with the only wish of being returned to the states, many of the volunteers were getting irritated with the whole system.[14]

With all the other political wrangling going on at this time, it came as no surprise that a compromise would have to be made before this issue was settled. The final deal was that the money raised by the people of Minnesota would be used to buy every soldier a ticket back to the state.

Picture of the Thirteenth's unofficial photographer, Private Compton. He wrote on the back of the print: "Compton with monkey in convent yard." (Courtesy of the Minnesota Military Museum, Camp Ripley)

That way the soldiers could pocket the money from the government and not have to use it to travel back home. For the men of the Thirteenth, this was an excellent idea; they would still be mustered out in San Francisco, plus they could keep their travel pay and be welcomed back home as returning soldiers.

Before any of these plans could be acted upon, though, the Thirteenth had to receive official orders to be sent home. Having watched other states' volunteers leaving since the completion of Lawton's expedition, the Minnesotans felt that they would soon be sent home, too. Until then they had to continue their policing of the railroads, bridges, telegraphic communication lines, and the local citizenry. The return to this monotonous duty, now far away from the fighting, was generally accepted.

The new assignment, although better than chasing after Filipinos in the jungle,

still had a physical and mental affect on the men. As John Bowe remembered in his diary, ". . . sneaking through blind alleys after crooked googoos [racial epitaph against Filipinos], double-timing across country under tropical skies, going hungry several days at a stretch, lying in trenches soaked to the skin, and pushing buffalo carts across country had reduced the companies until there are only from one-fourth to one-half the men doing duty."[15]

With the morale of the Americans in the islands at a record low, the Minnesotans received news that brought their spirits back to a level probably not seen since being mustered in at Camp Ramsey. They were told to prepare to pack their belongings and head for home. With the heartiest voices they could muster, the regiment let forth the exuberant yell, one only known to men who have served, fought, and died together.

By July 31, Companies G, E, D, M, L, and K were relieved by six companies of the Sixteenth United States Infantry and took the train that they had been guarding for the past few weeks into Manila. There they waited for four days until Companies I, A, F, B, H, and C were also relieved of duty and joined them in their scramble to pack and head for home.

In their haste to leave the Philippines, the men did decide to take time out of their schedule to remember those who they were to leave behind. On August 8, 1899, the "regiment formed in columns and marched to the cemetery at Paco, southeast of the Walled City." There, with a service conducted by Reverend Cressy, the Thirteenth ". . . paid its tribute to those of its number who were now on that journey over seas uncharted—a tribute not only to those who rested at Paco but as well to the ones who slept near the little church at San Rafael, at Baliuag, at Honolulu, in the depths of the Pacific, and back in the homeland."[16]

With the memorial services over, the men of the Thirteenth somberly returned to their barracks to continue to prepare for their homeward voyage. Whereas a great many could not wait to see American shores once again, sixty members decided, for various reasons, to remain in the islands and join new regiments. Whether it was for patriotic reasons, the need to find more glory, just a love of military life or the islands, these former members of the Thirteenth joined either the Thirty-sixth, Thirty-seventh Infantry or Eleventh United States Cavalries to help finish what they had started in the Pacific.[17]

With bags packed and emotions running high, the Thirteenth Minnesota Regiment was ordered on board the *Sheridan* for its return trip to the United States. After two days of getting settled on board, the ship set sail on August 12, 1899, while the band played "Home Sweet Home." After spending a little over one year in the islands, these Minnesotans were able to leave with at least some of what had drawn them to enlist—the desire to be seen as heroes and win glory in battle. This, they believed, had been accomplished. Their hopes and dreams were to be verified by the receptions that awaited them back in the United States, especially the one in Minnesota.

The Minnesotans had to share the ship with the troops from South Dakota. The South Dakotans were given the after part of the vessel while the Minnesotans took the forward. Being larger and better outfitted than the *City of Para,* the *Sheridan,* due to the regimental fund, also had the benefit of having better food, causing little sea-sickness for the men, and, best of all, the honor of taking them home.[18]

The return voyage also reflected changes in the volunteers' attitudes toward military life. Knowing that they were just weeks away from being mustered out of the army forever, most no longer took their commanders seriously. While on board ship, John Bowe recalled in his diary that

"orders came down that from that point on they were to drill twice a day and [have] inspection twice a day and had to wear a certain uniform on drill." These orders, which would have been obeyed a year earlier, now were virtually disregarded since most of the men "turned loose and hollered 'rotten' and bawled the officers out to their faces," whenever they were given a command.[19]

Not only was military discipline different on this return trip but so was the ship's route. On August 16, instead of passing the Ladrones, the *Sheridan* went to Japan where it stopped for several days to re-coal. After landing in Nagasaki, many of the Minnesotans received shore leave and became tourists, traveling around the city in rickshaws taking pictures and observing local customs, which all seemed quite bizarre to the Minnesotans.

Setting sail two days later, the soldiers patiently waited to see the United States again. Knowing they would soon reach the states and would probably beat any letters home, most decided to discontinue letter writing or the keeping of diaries until on dry land. The only report of anything on this portion of the trip again comes from John Bowe, who in a diary entry entitled "Aug. 32, 1899" explained, "[T]his is the place where we lose a day. Went to bed last night (Thurs. Night) and woke up Thurs. morning. . . ."[20]

With the exception of the fascination of crossing the International Dateline, the only thing these men anxiously anticipated was landing in San Francisco, which took place on September 8. Remaining on board for a few days prior to disembarking, the Minnesotans found themselves wrapped up in two controversies that had been developing in the states, as well as in Minnesota, for weeks.

Both controversies dealt with two commanders and how they had behaved while in the Philippines. The first one dealt with how General Otis was prosecuting the war. Many Americans felt that this war, in

The Thirteenth Minnesota returning to the United States aboard the *U.S.S. Sheridan*. (Courtesy of the Goodhue County Historical Society)

a more capable commander's hands, would have been over in a few weeks. It seemed obvious that every battle had presented a lop-sided victory for the Americans, leaving to blame Otis' seek-and-destroy methodology as the reason why the war continued. By chasing after the Filipinos and then not fortifying the captured villages allowed Aguinaldo's men easily to recapture these objectives. This forced American military leaders to back track and expend more American lives recapturing those same villages again. This strategy quickly exasperated both the soldiers in the field and the folks back home.

Many newspapers polled volunteers disembarking in San Francisco; nearly to a man, they were all against General Otis. Even some of Minnesota's highest leaders faulted the general's conduct. As General Reeve left the *Sheridan* that bright September day, he told reporters that he faulted Otis for treating the Filipino leaders "as half civilized savages" on some occasions, while on others he "ignored them completely." Reeve, eager to shed light on how he felt Otis had mishandled the war with the Filipinos, held an impromptu press conference on the dock while his men were still disembarking. Reeve went on to criticize Otis for "not adopting the tactics used against the Indians in the West." In essence, Reeve thought that Otis was too tough on the Filipinos during peace time and too lenient with them in war.[21]

A more local and personal issue for the men of the Thirteenth Minnesota was the controversy dealing with Colonel Ames and his conduct during the war. While serving as part of Wheaton's expedition, Colonel Ames, during the heat of battle, told his men that he was suffering from an illness and left the regiment for Manila, passing the command to Major Friedrichs. In Manila, some of the men reported having seen the colonel out and about and not looking the least bit ill. This immediately brought on charges of cowardice by some of the other leaders in the Thirteenth, and soon after by almost all of the print media back in Minnesota.

Due to the dual way in which newspapers received information from the Philippines, it is easy to see how this one-sided view of Ames developed. With the telegraphic services repaired the August before, any official news coming from the American leadership was quickly sent across the Pacific and then picked up by the newspapers through the Associated Press. Either not liking him personally or his easy-going command style, some of his fellow commanders began to send back word about Ames' supposed "cowardice" in battle.

While these reports got back almost immediately to the states, letters written by the common soldiers took anywhere from four to six weeks to get back home. Then if the recipient decided to have it published in the local paper, it would take additional time. With Ames' supporters not given a chance to express their views until June or July, few newspapers back in Minnesota heard their side of the story. Therefore, Ames' backers would not get their say until they were back home.

The controversy peaked just as the Minnesotans were landing in California. Anxious to hear the men's view of this issue, most newspapers sent reporters to welcome the soldiers and to see what they could find out about the Ames controversy. The first to respond was the *Stillwater Gazette*, which noted that "[O]ne of the officers of the regiment is credited with saying that not a commissioned officer would shake hands with Col[onel] Ames and another with remarking that he had better not show his face to the regiment."[22]

After another day, and having a chance to talk to more of the soldiers, the *Minneapolis Tribune* wrote a more cautious story about how the soldiers felt. The newspaper reported that while "all of the

officers and a great majority of the enlisted men are anti-Ames," most of the common soldiers, "are not as bitter, though, as
the officers are." Many common men in the
regiment held "the theory that the colonel
was troubled with dementia while at
Manila and was not responsible for anything that he did out of the way."[23]

To reinforce the *Tribune's* story, John
Bowe later recalled what he and the rest of
the volunteers observed as they left the
ship: "When the boys arrived in camp,
they all flocked to the Colonel's tent and
cheered for Colonel Ames." For the average
soldier, there was no real controversy
here. By the time the Thirteenth reached
Minnesota, this issue had all but disappeared. In what was more than likely a
ploy to sell more copies of their individual
papers, many of the state's news editors
seemed to play up this controversy.[24]

One reason the Colonel Ames controversy quietly died was because of the lack
of interest in the subject due primarily to
the fact that the men were home and anxious to be mustered out of service. Military
squabbles seemed to be part of their past
life, and part of the military they wanted to
forget. As Private Bowe remembered later
in his journal, for the men it was now just
a matter of reuniting with family and
friends and not concerning themselves
with military matters.

Although Bowe mentioned that most
of these reunions were happy, some did
not turn out this way. "Some of the boys
inquired for were in the hospital, others
were disabled for life, and here the meeting
was a mixture of sorrow and gladness
combined. Other folks who had friends
and kindred of boys [buried] in Luzon,
came to hear the boys' friends tell them of
how the poor fellow died." For the family
and friends left behind, the war was finally brought home, and they were forced to
realize its terrible cost.[25]

While the rest of the 13th was greet-
ing family and friends or unpacking the

ship, General Reeve continued with his
press conference, berating General Otis
and the war. When asked by a reporter if
the bloodshed could have been averted by
an intelligent policy of conciliation, Reeve,
in an answer that summed up not only the
war, but also how most of the Thirteenth
felt about it, said:

> Conciliatory methods would have pre-
> vented the war. Now, we all agree to the
> proposition that the insurrection must be
> suppressed, but in the beginning a con-
> ciliatory course was not adopted. General
> Otis' unfortunate proclamation of Janu-
> ary 4 (the changing of the Benevolent
> Assimilation Proclamation) rendered con-
> ciliation almost impossible. He adopted
> the policy of ignoring the natives by treat-
> ing them as half-civilized savages. No
> indication was given to the Filipinos as to
> the future intentions of the government.[26]

Reeve, much like the men of the
Thirteenth, felt all along that the war was
unnecessary, and that if the United States
would have been more sure of its policies
in the Philippines from the very start,
many of the problems that later developed
might have been solved through diplomatic means. But, instead of any solid policies
coming out of Washington, governmental
leaders continued to allow small groups
dictate America's new foreign policies. In
the Philippines that meant letting military
leaders, who are not trained in the art of
diplomatic dealings, conduct America's
foreign policy without consent from political leaders. Being used to giving orders
and having them followed, men like
General Otis were not adept at dealing
with the Filipinos, a group of people that
they considered inferior.

When the men disembarked from the
Sheridan and once again set foot on
American soil, they were met by crowds
from San Francisco, who threw flowers and
cheered the men as they reached their
camp. But, compared to what they had witnessed when they left, the crowds were def-
initely smaller and less enthusiastic. As

noted in the *Minneapolis Tribune*, "[T]he people of San Francisco are tiring of enthusiasm over soldiers and that may have been the reason for the rather quiet time the returning volunteers had along the line of march. . . ." Unable to keep their enthusiasm at a fevered pitch for so many months, many Californians, much like many across the nation, were tired of this war. Not knowing why their government was fighting there still, and having heard thousands of volunteers complain about their role in that war, for many the excitement they showed months earlier had, by the spring of 1899, waned.[27]

A week after they landed, the regiment was honored with a banquet held by Governor Lind and other state dignitaries who traveled to San Francisco to show their respects to the men. After the formal dinner of September 15, the men had to sit and wait until they were mustered out and sent back to their home states. As was the case when they were in San Francisco before, the men found themselves bored with the monotonous camp life. With military discipline being quite lax now, most of the men decided to go into town and stay at hotels rather than in the dusty tents at the Presidio.

Lewis Burlingham, writing home to his father on September 19, explained what life was like in those final weeks of soldiering. "Peddlers of all kinds and descriptions and of both sexes come here all looking for the soldiers money. . . ." After he received his pay, he tried to put the harshness of soldiering behind him. Immediately he went to town and bought, ". . . a good suit . . . underwear and a couple of pairs of socks and then went and got a haircut, shave and a good hot water bath and when I came out I felt like a new man I tell you."[28]

Finding various ways to keep themselves occupied, the men were finally excused from military service on October 3, 1899. The federal government gave each soldier railroad fare back to his place of origin, along with two months' extra pay. Overjoyed with this opportunity that the people back in Minnesota gave them, the members of the Thirteenth pocketed this rail fare and prepared to leave.

Their final journey home began when three trains pulled out of San Francisco on October 5, loaded with a cargo of exuberant soldiers. Heading north, the Minnesotans passed through Portland, Tacoma, Seattle, Spokane, and across Idaho, Montana, and North Dakota. They received huge celebrations, parades, speeches, and dinners at nearly every stop, no matter what time of day they arrived. Then, passing the Red River from Fargo into Moorhead, the men of the Thirteenth finally found themselves back in their home state.

Early in the morning of October 11, after being told they were back on the North Star state's soil, "[E]very passenger shouted himself hoarse and many fired off their army rifles, which, by a special dispensation of the War Department, they had been allowed to carry home for use during the parades in St. Paul and Minneapolis."[29]

With the men knowing they were just a matter of hours away from home, their minds turned to what they were going to do after returning to civilian life. This was something that many back in Minnesota had also considered. While the troops were still traveling across the Pacific to the United States, the *Minneapolis Journal* established an employment bureau as an intermediary between "the disarming veterans from the Philippines," and a "grateful and patriotic public."[30]

When the soldiers had begun to disembark in San Francisco, a representative from the *Journal* passed out employment blanks to the men. While approximately 100 needed employment and were able to use this system, most of the rest either had jobs waiting for them, or were attending the University of Minnesota.[31]

The men of the Thirteenth enjoying one of many banquets held in their honor during their return trip to Minnesota. This banquet was held in Spokane, Washington. (Courtesy of the Minnesota Military Museum, Camp Ripley)

These plans of re-entering civilian life would have to wait for one more day though, for the grandest of all the celebrations which they had witnessed, awaited them in the Twin Cities. Reaching St. Paul early on the morning of October 12, the Thirteenth Regiment formed a parade at 8:00 A.M. near the Union Depot in St. Paul, where they began marching through the city streets to the auditorium; there they were served an elaborate breakfast.

From there they boarded trains into Minneapolis where the main parade formed at noon. The celebration was considered "the most elaborate affair of the kind ever seen in the northwest," starting on twenty-ninth street, then headed down Park Avenue. The parade wound its way through Minneapolis until it came out at Nicollet Avenue where it proceeded toward the Exposition Building.[32]

Being the largest crowd ever gathered that anyone could remember, the spectators were standing "from curb to curb, and even filling the vacant lots and yards outside the street lines, the people crowded until it seemed that another one could not find room; and off to the left and right of the platform as far as the human voice could be heard, there was the same scene of upturned faces."[33]

Joining in the parade, which, due to the sea of humanity, took an hour to pass any given point, were representatives of the state and national military organizations, university cadets, Zouaves and Boys' Brigades, a handful of fraternal organizations, and probably most significantly for the men of the Thirteenth Minnesota Volunteers, a thousand or more Civil War veterans. Showing their support, they symbolically followed the Thirteenth Minnesota Volunteers in the parade. A thought that probably passed through the minds of at least some of the veterans of the Philippine wars—for the first time, the Civil War soldiers walked in their shadows.[34]

On Nicollet Avenue, all members of the parade passed by a reviewing stand that added a special touch to the day's events. With the election approaching, President McKinley had decided to make an appearance in Minneapolis to help welcome back the Thirteenth Minnesota. On the same stand as the president was Secretary of the Navy Long, Mayor Gray, Bishop Joyce, and Governor Lind.

Having arrived in Minnesota earlier, McKinley was neither greeted with a formal reception nor met by Governor Lind. Lind, who had fought with the president both in bringing the troops home and with his imperialistic policies, was not speaking to McKinley that cool October day. The first lady, suffering from a headache, even had to stay at a McKinley supporter's house since state officials had nothing prepared for them.

On the reviewing stand stood President Northrup of the State University, the master of ceremonies. After introducing Bishop Joyce, who gave a benediction, Northrup then asked Mayor Gray to the podium to give a few brief comments welcoming the men home and thanking President McKinley for attending. Gray, in turn, asked Governor Lind to come forward and give a few comments. Lind stood, boldly walked toward the center of the stage and proceeded to give both a welcome-home address to the men as well as a scathing attack on President McKinley's foreign policy.

In his speech, Lind welcomed home the soldiers of the Thirteenth Minnesota and rejoiced over all the happy reunions he had witnessed. He thanked the men for the glory and honor they had brought themselves and the state. He then went on to describe how this was also a solemn event because he hoped that it would bring an end forever of the use of the volunteer soldier in the sphere of national activity. He concluded his speech by stating:

> By our growth and development the mission of the American volunteer soldier has come to an end. For purposes of conquest and subjugation he is unfit, for he carries a conscience as well as a gun. The volunteer soldier has always stood for self-government, liberty, and justice. With your generation he will pass from the stage of our national life. His fame and his example will continue the heritage of our people—the theme of story and song. May the spirit which has actuated him ever guide our people, and temper the strength of the nation which has outgrown him, with the eternal principles for which he has fought and died.[35]

Depending on which newspaper one read the following day, the reaction to this speech varied. Whereas those papers supporting the governor and his comments all noted the applause that followed, others, like the *Minneapolis Tribune,* reported that "[T]here was not a whisper of approval . . ." and that ". . . no one hardly clapped. . . ."[36]

Those few newspaper reporters who heard cheers after Lind's speech were showing their own political bias. President McKinley had stopped in Red Wing earlier that morning and, after a brief speech, it was reported that the people cheered excitedly. Also with campaign swings through the Midwest and the South just weeks earlier, the president was met with huge crowds cheering wildly every time he mentioned the war. One has to assume, then, that the majority of Minnesotans, excited both with the return of the Thirteenth and the presence of the president, were also at a fever pitch that day.

How loudly people cheered for Lind was actually somewhat overshadowed by what happened next, which could only have compounded the tension felt on that stage. Having pre-arranged the speaking order, the last one to speak was to introduce the next. With no foresight as to what might happen between the president and governor, organizers slated McKinley to follow Lind. Lind, aware of this, as well as the fact that McKinley would not be pleased with what he said, refused to introduce the president. Rather, he turned from the podium and briskly walked back to his chair and sat down. With an uneasy silence on stage as well as in the crowd, University President Northrup sprang to his feet and quickly introduced the nation's leader.

McKinley, probably prepared for Lind's remarks, got up and gave a rousing speech on American patriotism and imperialism. In it he said:

> [T]he century has blessed us as a nation. We have had wars with foreign powers, and the unhappy one at home—but all terminated in no loss of prestige or honor or territory, but a gain in all. The increase of our territory has added vastly to our strength and prosperity without changing our republican character. . . . I sometimes think we do not realize what we have, and the mighty trust we have committed to our keeping.

No matter the political ideology of the state's newspapers, it was obvious that McKinley's speech did hit a responsive chord; when he finished speaking, a loud and boisterous cheer went up from all in the crowd.[37]

Not knowing it at the time, the Minnesotans in the crowd were first-hand witnesses to a debate that would, over the next few years, slowly encompass most of the nation. With one side totally against the war and the idea of America becoming an imperialist power, the other, just as adamant in their beliefs, desired nothing more than to expand America's influence around the world. In the end, the group of expansionist would win this political debate but not without a serious fight from the anti-imperialists that would hang on for years.

With the same kind of welcome-home receptions occurring in St. Cloud, Stillwater, and Red Wing for companies M, K, and G, respectively, every returning soldier received his moment in the sun. Thus all the men of the Thirteenth who had gone away in order to gain the same honor and prestige given to the Civil War veterans, finally received theirs. With the speeches and parades over, the men found their families and friends and went back to their everyday lives.

Having left the state a year and one-half earlier, the volunteers had returned with everything they sought, and now it was time to return to their normal, mundane lives, which they had wanted to escape back in the spring of 1898. With the war behind them, the mundane suddenly seemed exciting enough. As Private John Bowe, now plain citizen, commented in his diary for the last time, after the celebration, "each one dropped from the ranks and assumed the interrupted duties of a private citizen." With that, the journey of the Thirteenth Minnesota Volunteers came to an end.[38]

Notes

[1]Stuart Creighton Miller, *Benevolent Assimilation: The American Conquest of the Philippines, 1899-1903* (New Haven: Yale

University Press, 1982), p. 78.

[2]George Stephenson, *John Lind of Minnesota* (Minneapolis, Minnesota: The University of Minnesota Press, 1935), p. 140.

[3]Ibid., pp. 140, 143.

[4]Ibid., p. 138.

[5]Ibid., p. 173.

[6]Ibid., p. 173.

[7]Russell Roth, *Muddy Glory: America's "Indian Wars" in the Philippines 1899-1935* (West Hanover, Massachusetts: Christopher Publishing House, 1981), p. 52; George Stephenson, *John Lind of Minnesota* (Minneapolis, Minnesota: The University of Minnesota Press, 1935), p. 173.

[8]Stephenson, *John Lind of Minnesota,* p. 174; Miller, *Benevolent Assimilation,* pp. 78-79.

[9]Ibid., p. 173. *St. Paul Pioneer Press,* May 18, 1899, p. 6.

[10]*Red Wing Republican,* June 29, 1899, p. 4.

[11]Martin E. Tew, *Official History of the Operation of the 13th Minnesota Infantry, U.S.V. in the Campaign in the Philippine Islands* (S.I.: S.N., 1899), p. 108.

[12]Franklin F. Holbrook, *Minnesota in the Spanish-American War and the Philippine Insurrection, Vol. I* (St. Paul: The Riverside Press, 1923), p. 125.

[13]Tew, *Official History of the Operations of the 13th Minnesota Infantry,* p. 108.

[14]Lewis Burlingham to parents, July 3, 1899, Burlingham, Lewis Preston, 1879-1951, Papers, Minnesota Historical Society, St. Paul, Minnesota.

[15]John Bowe, *With the 13th Minnesota: In the Philippines* (Minneapolis: A.B. Franham Printing and Stationary Co., 1905), p. 142.

[16]Holbrook, *Minnesota in the Spanish-American War and the Philippine Insurrection,* p. 70.

[17]Ibid., p. 71.

[18]William C. Fitch and General C. McReeve, *13th Minnesota Vols.: Historical Record in the War with Spain* (Minneapolis: Price Bros. Printing Co., 1900), p. 42.

[19]Bowe, *With the 13th Minnesota,* p. 168.

[20]Ibid., p. 173.

[21]Miller, *Benevolent Assimilation,* p. 87.

[22]*Stillwater Gazette,* September 8, 1899, p. 3.

[23]*Minneapolis Tribune,* September 9, 1899, p. 6.

[24]Bowe, *With the 13th Minnesota,* p. 184.

[25]Ibid., pp. 181-182.

[26]*Minneapolis Tribune,* September 19, 1899, p. 10.

[27]*Minneapolis Tribune,* September 10, 1899, p. 4.

[28]Lewis Burlingham to Father, September 19, 1899, Burlingham, Lewis Preston, 1879-1951, Papers, Minnesota Historical Society, St. Paul, Minnesota.

[29]Tew, *Official History of the Operations of the 13th Minnesota Infantry,* p. 109.

[30]Holbrook, *Minnesota in the Spanish-American War and the Philippine Insurrection,* p. 126.

[31]Ibid., p. 126.

[32]Tew, *Official History of the Operations of the 13th Minnesota Infantry,* p. 109.

[33]*Minneapolis Tribune,* October 13, 1899, p. 3.

[34]Tew, *Official History of the Operations of the 13th Minnesota Infantry,* p. 109.

[35]Stephenson, *Lind of Minnesota,* p. 175.

[36]*Minneapolis Tribune,* October 13, 1899, p. 3.

[37]Ibid., p. 3.

[38]Bowe, *With the 13th Minnesota,* p. 187.

Chapter 10

"Will Live in History"

As the sun rose on the morning of October 13, 1899, the men of the Thirteenth Minnesota Volunteer Infantry found that they had returned to the normal, seemingly boring, lives they had tried to escape only a year and a half earlier. After eighteen months of service in the United States military and fighting two wars for their government, these mundane lives looked pretty good to them again.

Waking up that morning, many of the men probably reflected on what they had experienced since the day they enlisted to fight in the war against the Spaniards. For most, that spring of 1898 had held much promise. With their government and the newspapers telling them for weeks that a war with Spain would be a relatively quick and easy affair, many signed up so they could do their patriotic duty, prove their manhood and join in what was suppose to be the United States' last great adventure.

Reflecting on what they had happened to them since first enlisting, some undoubtedly had to be amazed at how much their feelings about the fighting in the Philippines, their own country's foreign policies, and even themselves had changed in the last eighteen months.

Enlisting in a frenzy of patriotic fervor, these soldiers, along with most of the nation, had found themselves heading into a war most did not understand. Believing they were going to go and save the Cubans and Filipinos from the Spaniards, the members of the Thirteenth Minnesota went to the Philippines with the understanding that they were off to fight a just and righteous war.

A year and one-half after signing up for this great cause, most soldiers remembered something quite different from their adventure in the Pacific. With political leaders in Washington and military commanders in Manila either waffling or constantly changing their policies toward the Philippines, those who were asked to fight these wars were made to enforce policies that many, at least by the time they left the Philippines, did not support. The men of the Thirteenth Minnesota believed they had signed up for a war to free the Filipinos by defeating their colonial masters, the Spanish. After a relatively easy victory over the Spanish and the signing of a peace treaty, which demanded that the Philippines become American territory, those who volunteered to fight found themselves forced to implement new and very different policies.

Minnesota's volunteer soldiers originally went along with this transformation of being an army of liberation to one of conquest, not because they agreed with what was happening, but because it was their duty and would give them the opportunity to further prove themselves. After listening to the Civil War generation question their patriotism and manhood for years, these men were not going to leave in the middle of a fight, thereby proving the older generation correct.

Reflecting on what they had accomplished in the Philippines, the veterans of the Thirteenth Minnesota believed they had not only earned their manhood but also had gained enough recognition to finally overshadow the Civil War veterans. They believed that after all they had endured, they too could put their names in the history books alongside those Minnesota units that had fought in the Civil War.

Agreeing with this notion, the editor of the *Red Wing Republican* wrote an article entitled "WILL LIVE IN HISTORY," published on October 12, 1899, the same day as the Thirteenth's return to the Twin Cities. The *Republican* told its readers that Minnesota was just as proud of the Thirteenth as they were of the most famous of all the Civil War units, the First Minnesota. The editor claimed that, "Minnesota's name has again been carried to the front of battle and another regiment bearing the name of the state shares the people's pride." Writing what the returning soldiers all wanted to hear, the *Republican* concluded by stating; ". . . they acquitted themselves with honor and glory and added new luster to the honored name of the state. . . ." For those who volunteered eighteen months before, this was not only a vindication of their manhood but a thank-you for the glory and honor they brought not only to themselves but to their state through their actions in the Philippines.[1]

The stirring words of the *Red Wing Republican* proved unprophetic, however. For the men of the Thirteenth, the memory of what they had done all but vanished from the historical landscape by the end of that October. Once the volunteer returned to their everyday lives, Minnesota and the nation at large quickly forgot about them and what they had done.

The fading recognition was due in part to the war in the Philippines, which still raged. With the removal of the volunteers, the Regular Army remained in the islands trying to conclude the war, which had started in February 1899. This conflict, which officially continued until July 4, 1902 (when President Theodore Roosevelt finally declared it over), quickly turned into a cruel and brutal war waged between two sides that shared common misunderstandings and growing hatreds.[2] While the Minnesotans left at a time when animosities were still at a relatively low level, the war turned more violent as the years passed.

With soldiers returning home, supplemented by newspapers recalling the war's events, stories of the brutality developing in the Philippines were heard by all. With knowledge of the brutal acts committed by both sides, and with this war seeming to have no end, many Americans began to question why the United States was so set on the subjugation of the Filipinos.

The birth of groups such as the Anti-Imperialist League, coupled with a national election in 1900, intensified these questions around the nation. After much soul searching, many Americans could not find any reason for America to be in the Philippines except for the notion that the United States was trying to become an imperialist power. If this were true, was America not then just as guilty of being an oppressive nation as the Spaniards had been? This belief intensified when reports came back from the Philippines that

THE THIRTEENTH REGIMENT UNDER FIRE MANY TIMES

The following is an Official List of Engagements the Thirteenth Minnesota Volunteer Infantry participated in.

Battle of Manila	(Regiment)	August 13, 1899.
Uprising and Attack by Insurgents	(Regiment)	February 14, 1899.
Riot in Tondo District	(Company C)	February 5, 1899.
Tondo District Uprising	(Cos. C, M, D, L)	February 22, 1899.
Tondo District Uprising	(Cos. C, M, G)	February 23, 1899.
Battle of Mariquina Road	(Regiment)	March 25, 1899.
Skirmish on Mariquina Road	(Regiment)	March 26, 1899.
Skirmish near Bocave	(Company D)	April 9, 1899.
Skirmish near Santa Maria	(Company C)	April 9, 1899.
The Attack on Railroad Track	(Regiment)	April 10-11, 1899.
Battle of Santa Maria	(Regiment)	April 12, 1899.
Skirmish near Quingua	(Company I)	April 14, 1899.
Skirmish near Guiguinto	(Cos. F, B, A, L, M)	April 14, 1899.
Skirmish near Quingua	(Company I)	April 16, 1889.
Battle of Guiguinto	(Cos. A, B, F)	April 20, 1899.
Battle of Quingua	(Cos. A, B, F, H)	April 21, 1899.
Skirmish near Quingua	(Company I)	April 25, 1899.

With General Lawton's Expedition—Cos. K, L, M, G, C, D, E and H.

Battle of Norzagaray	(Cos. C, D, E. H, K, L, M, G)	April 23-24, 1899.
Skirmish Near Angat	(Cos. C, D, E, H)	April 24, 1899.
Attack on Norzagaray	(Cos. C, D, E, H, K, L, M, G)	April 25, 1899.
Battle at Angat	(Cos. C, D, E, H,)	April 25, 1899.
Battle of Marangco	(Cos. C, D, E, H, K, L, M, G)	April 27, 1899.
Capture of Polo and San Rafael	(Cos. C, D, E, H, K, L, M, G)	April 29, 1899.
Battle of San Rafael	(Cos. C, D, E, H, K, L, M, G)	May 1, 1899.
Battle of Baliaug	(Cos. C, D, E, H, K, L, M, G)	May 2, 1899.
Battle of Maasin	(Cos. C, D, E, H, K, L, M, G)	May 4, 1899.
Skirmish Near San Ildefonso	(Company K,)	May 8, 1899,
Capture of San Ildefonso	(Cos. C, D, E, H, K, L, M, G)	May 12, 1899.
Capture of San Miguel	(Cos. C, D, E, H, K, L, M, G)	May 13, 1899.
Battle of Salacot	(Cos. C, D, E, H, K, L, M, G)	May 15, 1899.
Capture of Baluarte	(Cos. C, D, E, H, K, L, M, G)	May 16, 1899.
Capture of San Roque	(Cos. C, D, E, H, K, L, M, G)	May 16, 1899.
Battle of San Isidro	(Cos. C, D, E, H, K, L, M, G)	May 17, 1899.
Capture of Gapan	(Cos. C, D, E, H,)	May 17, 1899.
Skirmish at San Antonio	(Cos. C, D, E. H, K, L, M, G)	May 20, 1899.
Skirmish Near Arayat	(Cos. C, D, E, H, K, L, M, G)	May 21, 1899.

By Order of **COLONEL AMES,**
Commanding.

E. G. FALK,
1st Lieut. and Adjt. 13th Minn. Vol. Inf'y.

A list of the battles in which the members of the Thirteenth served during their time in the Philippines. (From the *Minneapolis Tribune*, October 8, 1899)

American soldiers were fighting the Filipinos—the very same people Americans had been told only a few months earlier that they had to free from the Spanish so that they could enjoy the same kind of democracy Americans enjoyed.

Remembering the war from their unique vantage point, the Minnesota volunteers had mixed emotions about what continued to transpire in the Philippines. On the one hand, many believed the fighting against the Filipinos was wrong. They agreed with General Charles McC. Reeve that the war need not have been fought had it not been for mistakes made by both American military and political leaders. On the other hand, they had gone off and served their country valiantly, had defeated the Spaniards and, when asked, took up arms against the Filipinos. Although these soldiers may have questioned their role in the wars in the Philippines, none ever lost their sincere patriotism.

The men of the Thirteenth also never lost many of the beliefs they brought with them. Entering the islands with stereotypes and prejudices, many of the Minnesotans sincerely believed that people who did not look or act like them were naturally inferior. These beliefs intensified with the brutal killing of Private Jesse Cole. In the minds of many, this was justification that the natives were not only inferior but also treacherous, which, for many volunteers, gave them and the United States the right to control the islands.

With all the controversy swirling around what should have, or should not have, taken place in the Philippines, many Americans chose to forget completely what had transpired. While the Spanish-American War was always remembered as a "splendid little war," the Philippine-American War would all but disappear from American history books. The Spanish-American War itself only became remembered through slogans that would have made the most ardent jingoist proud.

"Remember the Maine," Teddy Roosevelt's Rough Riders, and the Battle of San Juan Hill are all that are usually recalled by most Americans.

Twenty years after the wars in the Philippines, with the conclusion of World War I, the memory of the War of 1898 and its aftermath was almost completely wiped from America's conscience. With dreams of forever being remembered as brave and gallant soldiers fading, veterans of the Spanish-American War realized their campaign had lost its luster. For now, not only was their war sandwiched in the history books between the Civil War and World War I, but those two wars, in the minds of most Americans, were seen as righteous and justifiable wars, while the war against Spain and the Filipinos was of questionable motivation. Unlike the "glorious causes" of saving the union, freeing the slaves, or making the world safe for democracy, the fighting in 1898 and 1899 was seen by many as the United States forcing its will upon weaker nations such as the Philippines, Cuba, and Puerto Rico.

Fearful of how he felt people would remember those Minnesotans who served during this time, General Charles Reeve later wrote, "[H]istory will record Minnesota's part in the struggle with Spain, whatever of praise or blame should attach to her sons in southern camps and on tropical field, posterity shall judge."[3]

Reeve understood that the controversies that followed the wars in the Philippines might besmirch the good name of the volunteers who had fought in the far-off islands. Reeve and his men wanted it remembered that they had served in an unpopular war, but that when their country called on them they were ready to serve.

Doing their duty by enlisting to fight for their country, the soldiers later believed they were doing their duty when they began to question America's policies toward the Philippines. As Governor Lind had stated in his speech of October 12, 1899, the volunteer soldier not only carried a gun but a conscience as well.

By questioning Washington's policies, these Minnesotans, along with other state's volunteers, were able to force many American citizens, as well as military and political leaders, to look at what was going on in the Philippines. Putting the spotlight on America's new imperialistic policies, these volunteers forced the United States to take a serious look at itself before it completely entered the arena of international affairs.

By questioning their own and their country's role in the Philippines, these Minnesotans can be given the title of "reluctant heroes." Their unquestionable service to their country and bravery on the battlefields helped many to find the necessary emotions to make themselves feel proud of who they were. For others, it was their open questioning of America's imperialistic policies that they felt truly gave them the title of heroes. In the end, it was a combination of the two that made the members of the Thirteenth Minnesota Volunteers heroes. Unfortunately for those men who served, they became heroes that history books have all but forgotten.

NOTES

[1] *Red Wing Republican,* October 12, 1899, p. 7.

[2] Although officially declared over, battles were still fought between the Americans and Filipino's until 1913, which would make this one of America's longest wars ever fought.

[3] William Fitch and General McC. Reeve, *13th Minnesota Vols.: Historical Record in the War with Spain* (Minneapolis: Price Bros. Printing Co., 1900), p. 11.

Appendix 1

Field and Staff Rosters

Field and Staff officers of the Thirteenth Minnesota Infantry

Name	Occupation	Address
Col. Fred W. Ames	Cashier, Post office	Minneapolis
Lieut. Col. John H. Friedrich	Wholesale Grocer	Red Wing
Maj. Edwin S. Bean	Department County Clerk	St. Paul
Maj. Jos. P. Masterman	Ass't County Auditor	Stillwater

Name	Occupation	Address
Maj. Noyes C. Robinson	Real Estate	St. Paul
Capt. and Adjt. Edward G. Falk	Harness Dealer	Minneapolis
1st Lt. & Bat. Adj. Monroe D. Garcelon	Clerk	Minneapolis
1st Lt. & Bat. Adj. Milton S. Mead	Steamship Agent	St. Paul
1st Lt. & Bat. Adj. Hugo O. Hauft	Lawyer	St. Paul
Maj. & Surg. Reynaldo Fitzgerald	Physician	Minneapolis
Capt. & Asst. Surg. Arthur Ayer Law	Physician	Minneapolis
1st Lieut. & Asst. Surg. Harry Ritchie	Physician	St. Paul
Capt. And Chap. Chas. A Cressy	Clergyman	St. Paul Park
1st Lieut. And Q.M.W.H. Hart	Insurance	St. Paul
1st Lieut. & Coms'y Arthur R. DeMuth	Butcher	St. Paul

PROMOTED

Col. C. McC. Reeve	Capitalist	Minneapolis

WOUNDED

Maj. Noyes C. Robinson ......Wounded on upper lip at Tondo District Feb. 22, 1899

DEAD

Maj. Arthur M. Diggles .... Died of wounds received in action May 26, 1899

NON-COMMISSIONED STAFF

Name	Occupation	Address
Sergt. Major Feodor E. Krembs	Bookkeeper	St. Paul
Q.M. Sergt. Herbert A. Leawitt	Commission Merchant	Minneapolis
Coms'y Sergt. Roy C. Davis	Grain Buyer	Minneapolis
Hospital Steward Englehart G. Grau	Student	Minneapolis
Hospital Steward Austin L. Ward	Student	Minneapolis
Hospital Steward Chas. J. Hartman	Druggist	Hutchinson
Bat. Sergt. Maj. John N. Loye	Teacher	Red Wing
Bat. Sergt. Maj. Chas. E. French	Clerk	St. Paul
Bat. Sergt. Maj. Lawrence J. Koerble	Telegraph Operator	Minneapolis
Chief Musician Chas. U. Fowler	Musician	Minneapolis
Principal Musician Arthur W. Riches	Musician	Minneapolis
Principal Musician Jos. E. Grohx	Engraver	St. Paul

DISCHARGED

Principal Musician Robt. P. Smith	Student	Mason City, Iowa
Bat. Sergt. Maj. Harry B. Dyer	Clerk	Minneapolis
Hospital Steward Robt. S. Miles	Student	Glencoe

Appendix 2

Hospital and Band Corps

HOSPITAL CORPS

Minnesota Thirteenth Hospital Corps

NAME	OCCUPATION	ADDRESS
Englehart G. Grau	Student	Minneapolis
Austin L. Ward	Student	Minneapolis
Chas. J. Hartman	Druggist	Minneapolis
Fred E. Andrews	Assayer	St. Paul
Geo. C. Blend	Pharmacist	Minneapolis
Jos. R. Craigue	Pharmacist	Minneapolis
Hermann H. Gehm	Laborer	St. Cloud
Edwin G. Ireland	Student	Appleton
Harry B. Miles	Laborer	Glencoe
Harvey W. Stark	Student	St. Peter
Frank H. Pease	Clerk	St. Paul

DISCHARGED

Acting Hospital Steward John R. Gill	Student	Howard Lake
Jenner P. Chance	Student	Howard Lake
Willard C. Foster	Student	Minneapolis
Christian Gilbertson	Clerk	Red Wing
Gerhart N. Middents	Clerk	St. Paul
Harry Sutton	Student	Minneapolis

THIRTEENTH MINNESOTA BAND

Thirteenth Minnesota Band

NAME	COMPANY	INSTRUMENT
Chas. U. Fowler	Chief Musician	Snare Drum
A. W. Riches	Principal Musician/Director	Solo Cornet
William H. Foster	Co. K and Acting Sergeant	Drum Major
Julius L. Weyand	Company H	B-flat Clarinet
George H. Wilcox	Company B	First Clarinet
Emil Johnson	Company B	First Clarinet
John Sibbits	Company E	Third Clarinet
Henry Freedland	Company G	Soprano Saxaphone
Carl W. Colby	Company F	Soprano Saxaphone
Chas. R. Meacham	Company E	Alto Saxaphone
Henry S. Opsahl	Company L	Tenor Saxaphone
Jos. F. Auger	Company A	Baritone Saxaphone
Frank C. Bradley	Company D	Solo B-flat Cornet
Fred E. Sine	Company L	Solo B-flat Cornet
Charles A. Wendler	Company G	First Cornet
Royal E. Horton	Company D	Third B-flat Cornet
George Pracna	Company M	First B-flat Trumpet
John Henry Brandhorst	Company E	Second B-flat Trumpet
Frank Merrill	Company L	Solo Alto
John W. Ellstrom	Company G	First Alto
Llewellyn W. Vinal	Company A	Second Alto
William Olander	Company A	Third Alto
Merle F. Chapel	Company K	Solo Trombone
Magnus Salinger	Company B	Solo Trombone
William Hager	Company F	Third Trombone
William H. Mahar	Company C	E-flat Bass
George D. Montgomery	Company I	B-flat Bass
James B. Webb	Company G	B-flat Bass
John S. Wilson	Company E	Snare Drum
William H. Lawrence	Company M	Cymbal
George A. Kearney	Company K	Bass Drum

Appendix 3

Officers

FIRST BATTALION

NAME	RANK
Edwin S. Bean	Major
Milton S. Mead	First Lieutenant and Adjutant
Frank T. Carriston	Captain, Co. I
William J. Byrnes	First Lieutenant, Co. I
John F. Chambers	Second Lieutenant, Co. I

Regimental officers of the Thirteenth Minnesota Infantry

FIRST BATTALION CONTINUED

NAME	RANK
William S. McWade	Captain, Co. A
Roy Pearse	First Lieutenant, Co. A
Burt Kenaston	Second Lieutenant, Co. A
William Arthur Carleton	Captain, Co. F
Walter H. Johnson	First Lieutenant, Co. F
Martin E. Tew	Second Lieutenant, Co. F
Frank B. Rowley	Captain, Co. B
Harry L. Keiler	First Lieutenant, Co. B
Don F. Fitzgerald	Second Lieutenant, Co. B

SECOND BATTALION

Joseph P. Masterman	Major
Monroe D. Garcelon	First Lieutenant and Adjutant
Oscar Seebach	Captain, Co. G
Edward S. Mellinger	First Lieutenant, Co. G
Carl A. Anderson	Second Lieutenant, Co. G
Alfred Sully Morgan	Captain, Co. L
Harry D. Lackore	First Lieutenant, Co. L
Hugh R. Scott	Second Lieutenant, Co. L
James E. McKelvy	Captain, Co. M
Leigh D. Bruckart	First Lieutenant, Co. M
Henry J. Limperich	Second Lieutenant, Co. M
Edwin M. Conrad	Captain, Co. K
John J. Walsh	First Lieutenant, Co. K
George Howard Grant	Second Lieutenant, Co. K

THIRD BATTALION

Noyes C. Robinson	Major
Hugo O. Hanft	First Lieutenant and Adjutant
C. Treat Spear	Captain, Co. E
Charles A. Clark	First Lieutenant, Co. E
Russell S. Bunker	Second Lieutenant, Co. E
Charles E. Metz	Captain, Co. D
Milford L. Merrill	First Lieutenant, Co. D
Henry W. Tenvoorde	Second Lieutenant, Co. D
Alfred W. Bjornstad	Captain, Co. H
Frank C. Sauter	First Lieutenant, Co. H
David H. Whitney	Second Lieutenant, Co. H
Clarence Gilford Bunker	Captain, Co. C
John F. Snow	First Lieutenant, Co. C
John M. Smethurst	Second Lieutenant, Co. C

The Companies of the
Thirteenth Minnesota

COMPANY A - FIRST BATTALION

NAME	OCCUPATION	ADDRESS
Wm. S. McWade, Capt.	Clerk	Minneapolis
Roy Pearse, 1st Lieut.	Advance Agent	Minneapolis
Burt Kenaston, 2d Lieut.	Student	Minneapolis
Geo. Christensen, 1st Sergt.	Clerk	Minneapolis
Harry F. Kennedy, Q.M.	Clerk	Minneapolis
Charles E. Thompson, Sergt.	Lumberman	Minneapolis
Fred Bettschen, Sergt.	Miller	Minneapolis
Clarence H. Carleton, Sergt.	Salesman	Minneapolis
Wm. H. Stites, Sergt.	Bookkeeper	Minneapolis
Walter C. Jackson, Corp.	Student	Minneapolis

Name	Occupation	Address
Richard M. Cole, Corp.	Miller	Minneapolis
Holden P. Guilbert, Corp.	Student	Minneapolis
Chester B. Simmons, Corp.	Clerk	Minneapolis
Sevar B. Christopher, Corp.	Clerk	Minneapolis
Charles C. Collins, Corp.	Clerk	Minneapolis
Otis G. Bates, Corp.	Solicitor	Minneapolis
James P. Koll, Corp.	Miller	Minneapolis
Roy G. Roberts, Corp.	Student	Minneapolis
Arthur W. Folsom, Corp.	Pressman	Minneapolis
Alick D. Millar, Corp.	Clerk	Minneapolis
Herman P. Bradish, Corp.	Clerk	Minneapolis
Frank E. Creighton, Cook	Salesman	Minneapolis
Harry C. Raymore, Mus.	Clerk	Minneapolis
Harry C. Anderson, Mus.	Chair Caner	Minneapolis
Geo. P. Hayes, Artificer	Student	Minneapolis

PRIVATES

Archer S. Avery	Printer	Hutchinson
Jos. F. Auger	Machinist	St. Paul
Chas. F. Alderson	Lawyer	Minneapolis
Geo. W. Armstrong	Lawyer	Minneapolis
Philip H. Burgess	Grain Buyer	Northwood, North Dakota
Sydney W. Bagley	Student	State Center, Iowa
Alfred E. Browe	Printer	Minneapolis
Howard R. Baxter	Contractor	Minneapolis
Jorgen H. Birkebak	Watchmaker	Hutchinson
Jos. A. Buckendorf	Salesman	Minneapolis
Chas. H. Craigie	Printer	Minneapolis
John P. Connelly	Harness-maker	Minneapolis
Hal Downey	Student	Minneapolis
Bertram G. Dickinson	Student	Minneapolis
Horace Dean	Student	Minneapolis
Wm. W. Dunn., Jr.	Student	Minneapolis
Byron Elliot	Clerk	Minneapolis
Frank E. Force	Student	Minneapolis
Bjorn B. Gislason	Student	Minneapolis
Wilhelm F. Gerretson	Traveling salesman	Waupon, Wisconsin
Matt. L. Higbee	Student	Minneapolis
James D. Harris	Student	St. Anthony Park
Frank O. Holm	Clerk	Litchfield
Ralph E. Herring	Student	Minneapolis
Eugene Hanscom	Salesman	Minneapolis
Nicholas Hanson	Student	Minneapolis
William Larson	Farmer	Minneapolis

NAME	OCCUPATION	ADDRESS
Leon M. Lane	Student	Minneapolis
Joseph F. Mikulecky	Artist	Hutchinson
Michael J. Moran	Clerk	Minneapolis
Williard B. Mosier	Stenographer	Minneapolis
Carl P. McKusick	Clerk	Minneapolis
William McGann	Clerk	Wayzata
Bertle Nelson	Student	Hutchinson
William Olander	Student	Maynard
John J. O'Loughlin	Hotel-keeper	Litchfield
Carroll W. Peirce	Clerk	Minneapolis
Howard W. Page	Mail-Carrier	Minneapolis
Horace W. Roberts	Student	Minneapolis
Alfred D. Runyon	Reporter	Pueblo, Colorado
Geo. H. Riebeth	Student	Minneapolis
Chas. H. Skillman	Salesman	Minneapolis
Ezra R. Smith	Student	Minneapolis
John B. Streeter	Student	Hutchinson
Fred Stahr	Shoe-cutter	Minneapolis
Edw. W. Turner	Student	Minneapolis
Llewellyn W. Vinal	Bookkeeper	Minneapolis
Alex. S. Williamson	Surveyor	Minneapolis
Fred Williamson	Student	Minneapolis
Chas. E. Waiste	Student	Minneapolis

DISCHARGED

John Donaldson, 2d Lieut.	Salesman	Minneapolis
Richard E. Woodworth, Corp.	Grain Buyer	Minneapolis
Sam'l G. Anderson, Jr.	Student	Hutchinson
John L Barrett	Bookkeeper	Minneapolis
John W. Bates	Salesman	Minneapolis
Herman H. Bates	Shoe Cutter	Minneapolis
Guy D. Boynton	Clerk	Minneapolis
Chas. J. Borncamp	Storekeeper	Minneapolis
Geo. E. Church, Jr.	Log Scaler	Minneapolis
Roscoe A. Day	Salesman	Minneapolis
L. M. Darby	Student	Minneapolis
Geo. W. Evans	Student	Minneapolis
Ernest A. Feis	Laborer	Minneapolis
Wm. W. Hinman	Clerk	Minneapolis
Merton E. Harrison	Student	Minneapois
Geo. S. Johnson	Clerk	Minneapolis
Chas. M. King	Cook	Minneapolis
Walter S. Lafans	Student	Minneapolis
Arthur M. Magoon	Draughtsman	Minneapolis

157

NAME	OCCUPATION	ADDRESS
Andrew Mortenson	Clerk	Minneapolis
Henry Meyers	Laborer	Minneapolis
Geo. C. McKibbin	Traveling Salesman	New York City, New York
Samuel Pickard	Student	Minneapolis
Harry A. Rosie	Printer	Minneapolis
Allen W. Smith	Clerk	Minneapolis
Robt. W. Terry	Student	Minneapolis
Wirt Wilson	Student	Minneapolis
Robt. M. Whyte	Clerk	Minneapolis

TRANSFERRED

Ray C. Davis	Grain Buyer	Minneapolis
Willard C. Foster	Student	Minneapolis
John R. Gill	Student	Minneapolis
W. H. McDonald	Student	Minneapolis
John B. Pattison	Student	Minneapolis
Harvey W. Stark	Student	Minneapolis

DEAD

Harry L. Currier	Died of fever at Manila, P. I., September 19, 1899
C. E. Payson Colwell	Died of fever at Manila, P. I., September 24, 1899
Wm. Flanigan	Died at San Francisco, September 20, 1899
Sidney Pratt	Died of fever at Manila, P. I., August 18, 1899

WOUNDED

Holden P. Gilbert, Corp. . . . . Wounded in left hand at Guiguinto, P.I., April 20, 1899

Harry C. Anderson, Mus. . . . . Wounded in left ear at Guiguinto, P. I., April 20, 1899

Bjorn Gislason . . . . Wounded in head at Guiguinto, P. I., April 20, 1899

Eugene Hanscom . . . . Wounded in left hand at Guiguinto P. I., April 20, 1899

Nicholas Hanson . . . . Wounded in left leg at Guiguinto P. I., April 20, 1899

Andrew Martenson . . Wounded in both feet at Mariquina Road, P.I., March 25, 1899

COMPANY B - FIRST BATTALION

NAME	OCCUPATION	ADDRESS
Frank B. Rowley, Capt.	Dry Goods Buyer	Minneapolis
Harry L. Keiler, 1st Lieut.	Stenographer	Minneapolis
Don F. Fitzgerald, 2d Lieut.	Bank Clerk	Minneapolis
Allen C. Hemphill, 1st Sergt.	Stenographer	Minneapolis
Frank A. Bates, Q.M. Sergt.	Insurance	Minneapolis
Charles H. Law, Sergt.	Salesman	Minneapolis

NAME	OCCUPATION	ADDRESS
Jno. B.W. Corey, Sergt.	Railroad Clerk	Minneapolis
Otto N. Raths, Sergt.	Bank Clerk	Minneapolis
Henry A. Lyngaas, Sergt.	Salesman	Minneapolis
Jno. B. Armstrong, Cook	Plasterer	Minneapolis
George P. Rising, Corp.	Salesman	Minneapolis
Lyndon K. Emery, Corp.	Salesman	Minneapolis
Orrin R. Beals, Corp.	Salesman	Minneapolis
Lindley I. Moses, Corp.	Railroad Clerk	Minneapolis
Andrew H. Smith, Corp.	Salesman	Minneapolis
Wm. H. Salisbury, Corp.	Miller	Minneapolis
Michael P. Shaughnessy, Corp.	Lawyer	Minneapolis
Charles W. Fletcher, Corp.	Student	Minneapolis
Jeremiah L. Manning, Corp.	Clerk	New York City, New York
Jno. E. Newton, Corp.	Ticket Inspector	Minneapolis
Jno. E. Upson, Corp.	Student	Minneapolis
Bernard J. Farnham, Corp.	Farmer	Holloway
Martin E. Smeby, Musician	Window Dresser	Minneapolis
Emery E. Farr, Musician	Shipping Clerk	Minneapolis
James J. Coates, Artificer	Engineer	Lime Springs
Chas. J. Meggison, Wagoner	Mattress-maker	Minneapolis

PRIVATES

Jno. M. Alsdorf	Bookkeeper	Minneapolis
James C. Baker	Railroad Clerk	Chatfield
Henry H. Barrett	Student	Minneapolis
Chas. F. Brackett	Bookkeeper	Minneapolis
Harry R. Blend	Railroad Clerk	Minneapolis
Ludger J. Bedard	Shoemaker	Minneapolis

Name	Occupation	Address
Jno. Bowe	Hotel Keeper	Canby
Sidney Buchanan	Teamster	Appleton
Wm. J. Broberg	Student	Minneapolis
H. Christian Borhus	Bookkeeper	Minneapolis
James W. Brown	Stage Hand	Minneapolis
Oren L. Cole	Engineer	Minneapolis
Frances A. Campbell	Lawyer	Minneapolis
Alva G. Catlin	Printer	Delano
Wm. R. Cochran	Butcher	Buffalo
Herbert H. Cornell	Operator	Mapleton
Harry W. Collins	Salesman	Minneapolis
David E. Ehle	Sign Writer	Minneapolis
Jno. R. Ehlinger	Bill Poster	Minneapolis
Leuie H. Emond	Elevator Man	Minneapolis
Chas. A. Foster	Farmer	Appleton
Jas. M. Farnham	Farmer	Holloway
Thos. P. Graham	Laborer	Virgil, Illinois
Joseph Gross	Electrician	Glencoe
Albert G. Hale	Cook	Minneapolis
Wm. B. Hanscom	Lumberman	Minneapolis
Jno. A. Heenan	Helper	Minneapolis
Francis D. Heenan	Printer	Minneaplis
John A. Huard	Drug Clerk	Minneapolis
Emil Johnson	Musician	Grand Rapids, N.D.
Chas. J. Johnson	Operator	Minneapolis
Geo. B. Knowles	Lumberman	St. Paul
Clarence E. Keatley	Clerk	Minneapolis
Wm. V. Kennedy	Student	Adrian
Frank B. Lufkin	Steam-fitter	Minneapolis
Jno. F. McCarren	Clerk	Minneapolis
Percy L. McClay	Fireman	Minneapolis
Archie McGinnis	Clerk	San Francisco, California
Myron L. McKeever	Student	Worthington
Fred M. Mitchell	Carpenter	Colburn, Wisconsin
Wm. A. Mohr	Laborer	Minneapolis
Milton M. Morgan	Clerk	Minneapolis
Wm. J. Obele	Salesman	Minneapolis
Roy L. Powers	Civil Engineer	Minneapolis
Emel C. Priebe	Steam-fitter	Minneapolis
Wilson L. Robinson	Wood-worker	Minneapolis
Quincy R. Shoemaker	Painter	Minneapolis

Name	Occupation	Address
Horace A. Smith	Student	Minneapolis
Otto Schneider	Bookkeeper	San Francisco, California
Albert E. Snyder	Business Man	San Francisco, California
Magnus Salinger	Electrician	San Francisco, California
Geo. G. Shumway	Farmer	Appleton
Frank Spaulding	Lithographer	Minneapolis
Aldin Sprague	Lumberman	Minneapolis
Thos. F. Thomsen	Printer	Neenah, Wisconsin
Harry J. Thom	Blacksmith	Rushmore
C.A. Van Valkenburg	Painter	Minneapolis
Dirk J. Vos	Iron-worker	Muskegon, Michigan
Martin J. Welch	Clerk	Minneapolis
Wm. A. Wilson	Miller	Minneapolis
Herbert W. Wilson	Student	Minneapolis
Lewis R. Williams	Fireman	Hutchinson
Hugh Worden	Waiter	Paullina, Iowa
Herman Weiss	Baker	Minneapolis
Geo. H. Wilcox	Electrician	Nevada City, California
Wm. E. Wyman	Engineer	Minneapolis

DISCHARGED

Name	Occupation	Address
Jos. C. Strachan, Sergt.	Foreman	Minneapolis
Samuel O. Abrams	Clerk	Minneapolis
Howard P. Budge	Butcher	Minneapolis
Emil Carlson	Printer	Minneapolis
John E. Dallam	Minister	Minneapolis
Henry Foss	Conductor	Manila, Philippines
Joseph M. Hays	Clerk	Minneapolis
Eugene A. Harvey	Machinist	Minneapolis
Charles M. Heck	Laborer	Minneapolis
Albert A. Miles	Surveyor	Minneapolis
Thos. A. Patterson	Lumberman	Manila, Philippines
Jos. M. Scallen	Fireman	Minneapolis
Geo. J. Seymour	Framemaker	Minneapolis
Frank D. Scott	Engineer	Minneapolis
Wallace G. Skidmore	Dentist	Manila, Philippines
Francis H. Varney	Salesman	San Francisco, California

TRANSFERRED

Geo. C. Blend	Druggist	To Hospital Corp, June 26, 1898	Minneapolis
Harry Postel	Barber	To Co. H, May 11, 1898	Minneapolis

DEAD

A.M. Diggles, Maj.	Of wounds received on May 8th at Manila, May 26, 1899
Timothy Enright	Accidentally by electricity at Manila, March 11, 1899
Albert W. Olson	Of smallpox at Manila, January 29, 1899

WOUNDED

Chas. J. Megison, Wagoner . . . Gunshot wound in right shoulder at Guiguinto, April 11, 1899

Chas. F. Brackett . . Gunshot wound in the right hand at Guiguinto, April 11, 1899

Henry Foss . . . . Gunshot wound in right leg at Guiguinto, April 10, 1899

Eugene A. Harvey . . . . . Gunshot wound in right hand at Guiguinto, April 11, 1899

John A. Heenan . . . . . Gunshot wound in left shoulder at Guiguinto, April 11, 1899

Wm. J. Obele . . . . Gunshot wound in left ear at Guiguinto, April 11, 1899

COMPANY C - THIRD BATTALION

NAME	OCCUPATION	ADDRESS
Clarence G. Bunker, Capt.	Bookkeeper	St. Paul
John F. Snow, 1st Lieut.	Railroad Clerk	St. Paul
John M. Smethurst, 2d Lieut.	Asst. Manager	St. Paul
George K. Sheppard, 1st Sergt.	Clerk	St. Paul
James G. Wallace, Q. M. Sergt.	Salesman	St. Paul
Fred C. Robinson, Sergt.	Clerk	St. Paul
John McK. Heffner, Sergt.	Clerk	St. Paul

NAME	OCCUPATION	ADDRESS
John L. Phillips, Sergt.	Electrician	St. Paul
Eugene B. Crandall, Sergt.	Clerk	St. Paul
Walter E. DeLamere, Corp.	Machinist	St. Paul
A. Frank Kavanagh, Corp.	Salesman	St. Paul
Edw. Jungbauer, Corp.	Clerk	St. Paul
Charles T. DeLamare, Corp.	Student	St. Paul
Edwin D. Belden, Corp.	Janitor	St. Paul
Charles D. Crowther, Corp.	Clerk	St. Paul
James H. Fiddes, Corp.	Bookeeper	St. Paul
Bert W. Parsons, Corp.	Clerk	St. Paul
Olin H. Espy, Corp.	Student	St. Paul
Charles W. MacCormack, Corp.	Bookeeper	Rush City
Daniel F. MacCarthy, Corp.	Bookeeper	St. Paul
William M. Dunn, Corp.	Fireman	La Crosse, Wisconsin
Dennis J. McConville, Cook	Salesman	La Crosse, Wisconsin
Robert S. Bouland, Musician	Clerk	St. Paul
Sylvester G. Stark, Artificer	Insurance	St. Paul
Henry H. Tetzlaff, Wagoner	Clerk	St. Paul

PRIVATES

George F. Anderson	Laborer	St. Paul
Victor A. Anderson	Clerk	St. Paul
Arnold Arneson	Clerk	St. Paul
Charles M. Barlow	Clerk	St. Paul
John F. Beasom	Clerk	St. Paul
Harry L. Beckjord	Stenographer	St. Paul
Harry R. Bogart	Engraver	St. Paul
Charles W. Boxer	Clerk	St. Paul
William Brack	Clerk	St. Paul
William C. Brennan	Clerk	St. Paul
William C. Bruce	Clerk	St. Paul
Charles A. Campbell	Mechanic	St. Paul
Williams Cochran	Civil Engineer	St. Paul
Thomas S. Colcord	Student	Langford, South Dakota
Clinton S. Colledge	Railroadman	St. Paul.
Michael D. Collins	Printer	St. Paul
William G. Compton	Student	St. Paul
Robert Cotton	Clerk	St. Paul
John E. Darmody	Barber	St. Paul
Andrew Dickey	Clerk	River Falls, Wisconsin
Mark A. Durham	Telegrapher	St. Paul
Walter S. Elvidge	Electrician	St. Paul
Walter G. Finck	Clerk	St. Paul
Frans W. Fosberg	Student	St. Paul

Name	Occupation	Address
William Frick	Painter	St. Paul
Robert B. Hall	Clerk	St. Paul
R. W. E. Hasenwinkle	Student	St. Paul
Frank J. Kelly	Candymaker	St. Paul
William F. Kern	Clerk	St. Paul
Patrick Knessey	Railway Mail Clerk	St. Paul
Joseph F. Kritta	Clerk	St. Paul
Charles H. Lafever	Molder	St. Paul
C. Wyman Lawrence	Student	St. Paul
L. Lester Lee	Clerk	St. Paul
Miles J. Leppen	Clerk	St. Paul
Henry W. Lyon	Clerk	St. Paul
William H. Mahar	Clerk	San Francisco, California
James J. Mullarky	Binder	St. Paul
Martin Munson	Laborer	St. Paul
Harry H. Oakes	Switchman	St. Paul
Carl I. Overton	Clerk	St. Paul
Oscar J. Pederson	Carpenter	St. Paul
Thomas M. Phelan	Clerk	St. Paul
Harry Pomeroy	Merchant	St. Paul
William J. Ritchie	Carpenter	Marshall
Herbert C. Shannon	Painter	St. Paul
George A. Smith	Stenographer	St. Paul
Ira B. Smith	Laborer	St. Paul
William R. Stephenson	Clerk	St. Paul
Herbert E. Sweeney	Student	St. Paul
Guy H. Thayer	Clerk	St. Paul
Henry M. Wethy	Detective	St. Paul
George Whitty	Canvasser	St. Paul
Edward F. Wolterstorff	Clerk	St. Paul
George S. Wooding	Butcher	St. Paul
Paul I. Zimmerman	Clerk	St. Paul

DISCHARGED

Name	Occupation	Address
Edmund R. Simons, 1st Sergt.	Clerk	St. Paul
Charles B. Gordon, Corp.	Clerk	St. Paul
David H. Kimball, Corp.	Attorney	St. Paul
Paul J. Belber	Collector	St. Paul
Thomas F. Galvin	Boilermaker	St. Paul
George T. Harris	Cook	St. Paul
John H. Henry	Student	St. Paul
Herbert Hughes	Clerk	St. Paul
John J. Kelly	Tailor	St. Paul
Richard I. McKinney	Student	St. Paul

NAME	OCCUPATION	ADDRESS
Russell L. Moore	Student	St. Paul
Peter M. Newgard	Conductor	St. Paul
Arthur C. O'Brien	Student	St. Paul
Arthur W. Rank	Painter	St. Paul
Edw. W. Robinson	Expressman	St. Paul
Claude H. Still	Stenographer	St. Paul
Jas. M.S. Wilmot	Clerk	St. Paul
John J. Young	Moulder	St. Paul

TRANSFERRED

Joseph E. Groh, Musician	Engraver	To N.C. Staff	St. Paul
Fred E. Andrews	Assayer	To Hosp. Corps	St. Paul
James R. Baptie	Telegrapher	To Signal Corps	St. Paul
William E. Gowling	Telegrapher	To Signal Corps	St. Paul

WOUNDED

Clarence G. Bunker, Capt. . . . Wounded in right hand and wrist at Manila, Aug. 13, 1898
Geo. K. Sheppard, 1st Sergt. . . Wounded in right leg at Tondo District, Feb. 23, 1899
Chas. T. De Lamere, Corp. . . . . . Wounded in right knee at Bocaue, April 12, 1899
Bert W. Parsons, Corp. . Wounded in right hand at Mariquina Road, March 25, 1899
Henry H. Tetzlaff, Wagoner . . . . Wounded in thumb at Bocaue, April 12, 1899
Arnold Arneson . . . . Wounded in scalp at Mariquina Road, March 25, 1899
Harry L. Beckjord . . . . Wounded in thumb at Bocaue, April 12, 1899
Thos. F. Galvin . . . . Wounded in left shoulder at Manila, Feb. 23, 1899
Ira B. Smith . . . . .Wounded in left breast at Manila, Feb. 23, 1899
Geo. S. Wooding . . . . Wounded in both thighs at Manila, Feb. 23, 1899
Jno. J. Young . . . . Wounded in face at Bocaue, April 11, 1899

DEAD

Maurice P. Beaty	Killed in action at Bocaue, April 11, 1899
Joseph O. Daley	Smallpox at Manila, Oct. 5, 1898
Jno W. Flynt	Dysentery at sea, May 14, 1899
Herbert L. Keeler	Diphteria at Manila, May 16, 1899
Wm. O. Martinson	Smallpox at Manila, Oct. 9, 1899
Harry G. Watson	Typhoid fever at Cavite, Aug. 29, 1898

COMPANY D - THIRD BATTALION

NAME	OCCUPATION	ADDRESS
Charles E. Metz, Capt.	Merchant	St. Paul
Milford L. Merrill, 1st Lieut.	Merchant	St. Paul
Henry W. Tenvoorde, 2d Lieut.	Salesman	St. Paul
Alex J. Kahlert, 1st Sergt.	Dyer	St. Paul
Christian A. Iltner, Q.M. Sergt.	Clerk	St. Paul
Jno. H. Kich, Sergt.	Letter-carrier	St. Paul
Lewis H. Lawton, Sergt.	Clerk	St. Paul
Geo. C. Jackson, Sergt.	Clerk	St. Paul
Jno. G. Poehler, Sergt.	Clerk	St. Paul
A. W. Henschel, Corp.	Merchant	St. Paul
Lewis C. Miss, Corp.	Clerk	St. Paul
Jackson V. Parker, Corp.	Bookkeeper	St. Paul
Elmer E. Schooley, Corp.	Printer	St. Paul
Jno. C. Bennett, Corp.	Salesman	Davenport, Iowa
Peter J. Dwyer, Corp.	Mail-carrier	St. Paul
Louis M. Delaney, Corp.	Merchant	St. Paul
Charles J. Lark, Corp.	Clerk	Chicago, Illinois
William C. Fitch, Corp.	Printer	St. Paul
Gabriel A. O'Reilly, Corp.	Attorney	St. Paul
Jno. M.C. Johnson, Corp.	Clerk	St. Paul
Henry T. Larkin, Corp.	Clerk	St. Paul
Clarence Hayes, Cook	Barber	St. Paul

NAME	OCCUPATION	ADDRESS
Albert J. Casper, Musician	Clerk	St. Paul
Wirt H. Kelley, Musician	Printer	St. Paul
Abram K. Sleeger, Artificer	Driver	St. Paul
John K. Kenny, Wagoner	Cook	St. Paul

PRIVATES

Percy C. Atkinson	Railroadman	St. Paul
John T. Becker	Bookkeeper	Aberdeen, Washington
George C. Burnell	Traveling Salesman	Cincinnati, Ohio
Frank C. Bradley	Telegrapher	St. Paul
Edward J. Delaney	Plumber	St. Paul
Albert J. Dries	Bookbinder	St. Paul
Samuel A. Engel	Farmer	Alexandria
Edward G. Fetsch	Clerk	St. Paul
Wm. D. Fifield	Bookkeeper	Wahpeton, North Dakota
Jno. J. Flynn	Plumber	St. Paul
Robt. O. Glanville	Clerk	St. Paul
Merton G. Grinnell	Clerk	St. Paul
Harry H. Gealy	Driver	St. Paul
Adolph P. Guerin	Butcher	St. Paul
Henry C. Greenlee	Dentist	St. Paul
Robert Hamp	Bookkeeper	St. Paul
James Hartley	Machinist	St. Paul
John Hartfield	Carpenter	South St. Paul
Isaac. S. Hull	Student	St. Paul
Royal E. Horton	Teacher	St. Paul
Charles A. Henry	Druggist	Minneapolis
Hermann H. Hillman	Insurance Broker	St. Paul
Wm. H. Holmes	Bricklayer	St. Paul
Chas. M. Harrington	Shoemaker	St. Paul
Arthur J. Jerome	Farmer	St. Paul
Jacob A. Kamp	Barber	St. Paul
Wm. B. Klein	Merchant	St. Paul
Henry N. Klein	Student	St. Paul
Chas. H. Lacey	Clerk	St. Paul
Walter E. Lacey	Laundryman	St. Paul
Geo. M. Landon	Clerk	St. Paul
Walter W. Lange	Salesman	St. Paul
Walter Lund	Farmer	Mankato
Joseph E. Malloy	Printer	Red Wing
Frank M. Maruska	Bookbinder	St. Paul
Abner J. Matthews	Teacher	Ortonville

Name	Occupation	Address
Jno. S. McCune	Compositor	St. Paul
Patrick J. McGrath	Painter	St. Paul
Wm. H. Miss	Clerk	St. Paul
Alexander M. Nicoll	Clerk	St. Paul
Christ. Nelson	Painter	La Crosse, Wisconsin
Ingolf J. Offerdahl	Compositor	St. Paul
Walter A. Proctor	Clerk	Fall Rivers, Wisconsin
Fred W. Pederson	Salesman	St. Paul
John B. Price	Butcher	South St. Paul
Frederick M. Schutte	Bookkeeper	St. Paul
Carl J. Seibold	Bookkeeper	St. Paul
Wm. J. Thone	Salesman	St. Paul
Jacob J. Weber	Teamster	St. Paul
Harold W. Whitcomb	Bookkeeper	Alexandria
Frank Wiplinger	Twinemaker	St. Paul
Frank H. Wesenberg	Clerk	St. Paul

DISCHARGED

Name	Occupation	Address
Christian A. Bach, Sergt.	U.S. Army	Manila, P.I.(reenlisted)
Chas. S. Downs, Sergt.	Clerk	Manila, Philippines
Herman E. Heller, Sergt.	Soldier	Manila, Philippines
Chas. E. Nathorst, Corp.	Railroadman	Manila, Philippines
Wm. Woodward, Cook	Farmer	Manila, Philippines
Wm. N. Bish	Clerk	Manila, Philippines
Frank DeA. Burton	Salesman	Manila, Philippines
Chas. E. Banker	Policeman	St. Paul
Chas. C. Conley	Policeman	Manila, Philippines
Benjamin C. Dailey	Student	St. Paul
Arthur R. Demuth	Butcher	St. Paul (reenlisted)
James G. Donnelly, Jr.	Student	St. Paul
Arthur W. De Frate	Soldier	Manila, Philippines
Marvin H. Hanna	Merchant	Manila, Philippines
Wm. E. Harrington	Salesman	St. Paul
James Y. Hamilton	Clerk	Manila, Philippines
Frank C. Keogh	Bookkeeper	St. Paul
Chas. D. Mason	Waiter	St. Paul
Charles McBain	Waiter	St. Paul
Augustus P. Mitchell	Engineer	St. Paul
Wm. L. Murkland	Salesman	St. Paul
Chas. F. Mullen	Printer	St. Paul

NAME	OCCUPATION	ADDRESS
Christopher W. Ney	Attorney	Manila, Philippines
Charles S. Odell	Machinist	St. Paul
Nicholas Remakel	Lather	St. Paul
Conrad H. Rowe	Cook	St. Paul
M. A. Trenham	Salesman	Alexandria
Carl H. Van Hoven	Stenographer	Manila, Philippines
Chas. H. Velie	Waiter	St. Paul

TRANSFERRED

Chas. E. French, Corp.	Salesman	To N.C. Staff
Gerhard N. Middents	Mail-carrier	To U.S. Hosp. Corps.

WOUNDED

Wm. C. Fitch, Corp. . . . . Wounded in left leg at Caloocan, Feb. 11, 1899

Merton G. Grinnell . . . . Wounded in body at Manila, Feb. 22, 1899

James Hartley . . . . Wounded in both legs at Caloocan, Feb. 11, 1899

John Hartfield . . . . Wounded in right side at Manila, Feb. 22, 1899

H.H. Hillman . . . . Wounded in left wrist at Manila, Feb. 22, 1899

M.A. Trenham . . . . Wounded in face near Manila, Aug. 13, 1898

Frank Wiplinger . . . . Wounded in left wrist at Manila, April 24, 1899

Frank H. Wesenberg . . . . Wounded in left hand at Santa Maria, April 5, 1899

DEAD

Gilbert C. Perrine	Smallpox at Manila, Jan. 6, 1899
John S. Wood	Typhoid fever at Manila, Aug. 23, 1898

COMPANY E - THIRD BATTALION

NAME	OCCUPATION	ADDRESS
C. Treat Spear, Capt.	Cashier	St. Paul
Chas. Clark, 1st Lieut.	Traveling Salesman	St. Paul
Russell S. Bunker, 2d Lieut.	Clerk	St. Paul
Thos. C. Fernald Jr., 1st Sergt.	Clerk	St. Paul
Edward E. Good, Q. M. Sergt.	Clerk	St. Paul
Jay C. Price, Sergt.	Clerk	Wauconda, Illinois
Omar C. Humphrey, Sergt.	Clerk	St. Paul
Wm. C. Montgomery, Sergt.	Clerk	St. Paul
Tracy H. Hoyt, Sergt.	Clerk	St. Paul

NAME	OCCUPATION	ADDRESS
Henry E. Williams, Corp.	Clerk	St. Paul
Silas W. Tucker, Corp.	Painter	Hastings
Wm. A. Lenz, Corp.	Clerk	St. Paul
Lindsley Hoyt. Corp.	Machinist	Portland, Oregon
Ralph H. Billingsley, Corp.	Engineer	St. Paul
Wm. H. Eckley, Corp.	Clerk	St. Paul
Lisle D. Tucker, Corp.	Conductor	Hastings
Willard B. Williams, Corp.	Salesman	Muncie, Indiana
Myron R. Gibbs, Corp.	Clerk	St. Paul
Edmond C. Worley, Corp.	Clerk	St. Paul
Karl G. Anderson, Corp.	Draughtsman	St. Paul
Frank L. Haskell, Corp.	Clerk	St. Paul
Joseph H. O'Brien, Lance Corp.	Clerk	St. Paul
Edw. D. Loftus, Cook	Salesman	St. Paul
Fred C. Steele, Musician	Clerk	St. Paul
Chas. H. Baker, Jr., Musician	Clerk	St. Paul
Fred E. Giese, Artificer	Printer	St. Paul
Oscar E. Pearl, Wagoner	Bookkeeper	St. Paul

PRIVATES

Andrew Ahlberg	Clerk	St. Paul
Louis W. Bailey	Printer	St. Paul
Simon Beach	Laborer	St. Paul
Fredk. L. Bogart	Engraver	St. Paul
John H. Brandhorst	Musician	St. Paul

NAME	OCCUPATION	ADDRESS
Edw. E. Carson	Laborer	Hastings
Edw. P. Campbell	Clerk	St. Paul
Jno. D. Canner	Salesman	St. Paul
Frank Carle	Tailor	St. Paul
Frank C. Dekay	Student	Hastings
Albert A. Duenwald	Student	St. Paul
Geo. W. Fernald	Paint Manufacturer	St. Paul
Ben F. Guy	Coachman	No town listed
Alfred G. Hagerty	Clerk	St. Paul
Theo. C. Hamann	Clerk	St. Paul
Sidney C. Johnson	Moulder	Shakopee
David H. Knickerbocker	Hotel-keeper	Annandale
Paul D. Kniss	Student	No town listed
Wm. Kurtn	Butcher	Alma, Wisconsin
Wm. F. Lewis	Traveling Salesman	St. Paul
Chas. H. Lipke	Painter	St. Paul
Gust Lyberg	Shoeworker	St. Paul
Jno. MacArthur	Clerk	St. Paul
Chas. R. Meacham	Clerk	Minneapolis
Ben Moorman	Clerk	St. Paul
Frank Mortenson	Clerk	Hinckley
Francis H. Morgan, Jr.	Clerk	St. Paul
Jas. F. Mullins	Clerk	St. Paul
Robert Nugent	Soldier	St. Paul
August Olsen	Clerk	St. Paul
Magnus Opp	Farmer	Hegbert
Louis Peyer	Painter	St. Paul
Frank Prendergast	Student	St. Paul
Otto H. Raddatz	Bookkeeper	St. Paul
Wm. A. Repke	Painter	St. Paul
Jesse M. Ricks	Barber	St. Paul
John J. Schillo	Clerk	St. Paul
Geo. E. Scoville	Farmer	Red Wing
John Sibbetts	Band Master	Junction City, Oregon
Herbert E. Sperry	Barber	Berville, Michigan
Jno. T. Stapleton	Mechanic	St. Paul
Harry J. Van Keuren	Clerk	Wheeling, West Virginia
Fred P. View	Clerk	Sparta, Wisconsin
Chas. J. Wigley	Ferryman	St. Paul
Allan T. Williams	Clerk	Hastings
Niles L. Williams	Clerk	St. Paul

NAME	OCCUPATION	ADDRESS
Chas. P. Wood	Paint Manufacturer	St. Paul
Chas. M. Woodworth	Clerk	St. Paul
John S. Wilson	Lineman	Mankato

DISCHARGED

NAME	OCCUPATION	ADDRESS
Max C. Schieber, Sergt.	Clerk	St. Paul
Harry L. Hart, Corp.	Clerk	St. Paul
George Mahar, Corp.	Merchant	Hastings
Robt. J. Kelliher, Corp.	Salesman	St. Paul
Jesse C. Furnell, Corp.	Switchman	St. Paul
Thos. H. Larkin, Artificer	Clerk	Manila, Philippines
Harry W. Acheson	Soldier	Manila, Philippines
Alden E. Blood	Machinist	White Bear Lake
Chas. W. Buggert	Farmer	Manila, Philippines
Bert D. Carrier	Engineer	St. Paul
Chester L. Chamberlin	Farmer	Northfield
Leo M. Cutts	Clerk	Manila, Philippines
Harcourt N. Hatton	Clerk	St. Paul
M. L. Hanft	Traveling Salesman	Minneapolis
Wm. D. Hobart	Clerk	Manila, Philippines
Leo W. Hurley	Clerk	St. Paul
Wm. A. Kimball	Salesman	St. Paul
Geo. J. F. Lenz	Clerk	St. Paul
Charles Lund	Soldier	Manila, Philippines
Harry T. Montgomery	Clerk	Manila, Philippines
Alfred Mortenson	Soldier	Manila, Philippines
Clarence P. Rice	Student	St. Paul
Oscar Ross	Fireman	St. Paul
Westley G. Smith	Merchant	Manila, Philippines
Lester P. Sorenson	Mechanic	Newport
George Thiessen	Clerk	Manila, Philippines
Joseph Webb	Conductor	St. Paul

PROMOTED

C. R. Trowbridge, Lieut.	To 1st Lieut., 11th Cav. U.S.V. (military information)
Hugo O. Hanft	To 1st Lieut. and Battalion Adjt., June 26, 1899

TRANSFERRED

NAME	OCCUPATION	ADDRESS
Harry B. Miles	Clerk	To Hosp. Corps
Frank H. Pease	Clerk	To Hosp. Corps

Wounded

Merwin M. Carleton, Sergt. . . . . Wounded in right thigh near Manila, Aug. 13, 1898
Jay C. Price, Sergt. . . . . .Wounded in groin at Manila, Nov. 18, 1898
Wm. C. Montgomery, Sergt. . . Wounded in left breast and arm at Manila, Nov. 18, 1898
Henry E. Williams, Corp. . . Wounded in right shoulder near Manila, Aug. 13, 1898
George Mahar, Corp. . . . . Wounded in breast bone at Manila, Nov. 18, 1898
Robt. J. Kelliher, Corp. . . . . . . Wounded in right leg at Santa Maria, April 12, 1899
Clarence P. Rice . . . Wounded in right thigh and right heal at Manila, Aug. 13, 1898

Dead

Merwin M. Carleton, Sergt. Bullet wound accidentally received at Manila, Dec. 18,
1898
Fredk. Buckland, Musn.   Rheumatism of heart at sea, July 27, 1898
Paul M. Crosby   Consumption at Cavite,   Oct. 4, 1898
Fred C. Fritzon   Typhoid fever at Manila, June 26, 1899
Leslie B. Paden   Typhoid fever at Cavite, Aug. 6, 1899

Company F - First Battalion

Name	Occupation	Address
Wm. C. Carleton, Capt.	Stenographer	Minneapolis
Walter H. Johnson, 1st Lieut.	Druggist	Minneapolis
Martin E. Tew, 2nd, Lieut.	Newspaperman	Minneapolis

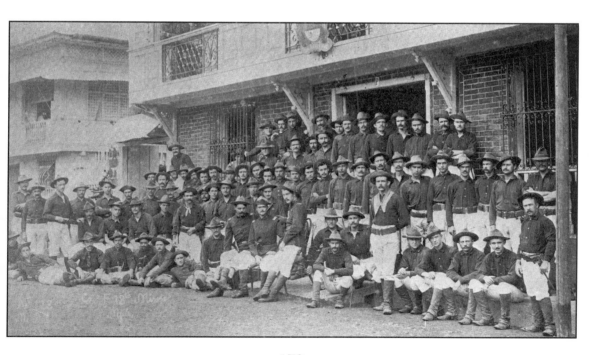

NAME	OCCUPATION	ADDRESS
Jas. B. Stafford, 1st Sergt.	Printer	Minneapolis
Julius I. Newhouse, Q. M. Sergt.	Painter	Minneapolis
Jas. F. Sorenson, Sergt.	Bagcutter	Minneapolis
Nelson Rardin, Sergt.	Engineer	Waterville
Myron W. Hingley, Sergt.	Railroadman	Minneapolis
Frank L. Vorce, Sergt.	Teamster	Minneapolis
Gustave A. Princell, Corp.	Bookkeeper	Minneapolis
Frederic A.J. Tudhope, Corp.	Newspaperman	Minneapolis
Bert P. Libby, Corp.	Bookkeeper	Minneapolis
Albert J. Chesley, Corp.	Nurse	Minneapolis
Gustave A. Brome, Corp.	Finisher	Minneapolis
Henry Deering, Corp.	Farmer	Minneapolis
Jas. Walsh, Corp.	Engineer	Minneapolis
Daniel W. Doyle, Corp.	Beltmaker	Minneapolis
Jesse J. Haw, Corp.	Bookkeeper	Minneapolis
Ivar Anderson, Corp.	Clerk	Minneapolis
Frank S. Bishop, Corp.	Teamster	Pilot Mound, Iowa
Geo. H. White, Corp.	Teamster	Minneapolis
Edw. J. Blakey, Corp.	Farmer	Minneapolis
Hector A. Christensen, Musician	Salesman	Minneapolis
Harry M. King, Artificer	Boiler-maker	Minneapolis
Daniel W. Kerr, Wagoner	Engineer	Minneapolis

PRIVATES

NAME	OCCUPATION	ADDRESS
Geo. A. Bryson	Barber	Minneapolis
Wesley L. Beedle	Engineer	Albert Lea
Wm. H. Bohanan	Printer	Albert Lea
Carl W. Colby	Student	Albert Lea
Roy M. Covey	Solicitor	Albert Lea
Benj. F. Chilson	Teamster	Albert Lea
Arthur G. Crosby	Farmer	Albert Lea
August Conrad	Teamster	Albert Lea
Adolph Dietz	Shingle-packer	Albert Lea
Malcolm De la Fere	Physician	Albert Lea
Charles E. De Laine	Engineer	Albert Lea
Ernest G. Everitt	Clerk	Albert Lea
Oliver D. Edwards	Lawyer	Albert Lea
Murvile E. Gates	Candy-maker	Albert Lea
Edgar A. Gibbs	Clerk	Albert Lea
Julius Goehner	Artist	Albert Lea
Wm. E. Gore	Cook	Albert Lea
Frank A. Green	Painter	Albert Lea
Fred L. Gregory	Reporter	Albert Lea

NAME	OCCUPATION	ADDRESS
William Goff	Teamster	Albert Lea
William Hagen	Printer	Albert Lea
Albert S. Hanson	Clerk	Albert Lea
Edw. J. House	Student	Albert Lea
Herman C. Helms	Candy-maker	Albert Lea
Frank H. Jessup	Salesman	Albert Lea
Victor Klingenberg	Harness-maker	Minneapolis
Gustave Lienau	Engineer	Minneapolis
Arthur W. March	Miner	Minneapolis
Wm. J. Marshall	Tailor	Minneapolis
Harry J. Monroe	Teamster	Minneapolis
Geo. D. Montfort	Lawyer	Minneapolis
Chas. E. Merriman	Clerk	Minneapolis
Frank F. Monahan	Bookkeeper	Rice Lake, Wisconsin
Wm. J. Nicolas	Carpet-layer	Minneapolis
Wm. A. Reynolds	Carpenter	Minneapolis
Lars Stai	Barber	Minneapolis
Carl L. Setchell	Student	Minneapolis
Wm. C. Slenker	Machinist	Minneapolis
Miles G. Slavin	Clerk	Green Isle, Wisconsin
Thos. Splan	Laborer	Minneapolis
Wm. B. Smith	Painter	Minneapolis
Leo T. Tobin	Clerk	Minneapolis
Geo. A. Werner	Painter	Minneapolis
Abraham Walker	Scaler	Minneapolis
Reuben J. Washburn	Farmer	Minneapolis
Michael Wolf	Butcher	St. Peter, Minn.

DISCHARGED

Chas. N. Clark, 1st Lieut.	Printer	Manila, P.I. (re-enlisted)
Carl L. Stone, 2nd Lieut.	Engineer	Manila, P.I. (re-enlisted)
Wm. H. Hatcher Q.M. Sergt.	Printer	Minneapolis
John E. Kaaro, Sergt.	Cabinet-maker	Minneapolis
Herbert A. Moulton, Sergt.	Teamster	Manila, P.I. (re-enlisted)
Earl G. Chamberlain, Sergt.	Student	Manila, P.I. (re-enlisted)
Samuel A. Rask, Corp.	Insurance Agent	Caledonia, Minn.
David A. Small, Corp.	Machinist	Minneapolis
Samuel J. Rardin, Corp.	Clerk	Manila, P.I. (re-enlisted)
Moses J. Le May, Musician	Laborer	Minneapolis
David (or Daniel) Allen	Clerk	Minneapolis
Roy T. Brown	Machinist	Manila, P.I.
Frank L. Bunker	Grocer	Minneapolis
Claude L. Freer	Miller	Manila, P.I. (re-enlisted)

Name	Occupation	Address
Edw. T. Fortier	Clerk	Minneapolis
Irvin D. Foster	Farmer	Manila, P.I. (re-enlisted)
Anton E. Johnson	Bookkeeper	San Francisco, California
Richard M. Knight	Machine Agent	Minneapolis
Geo. H. La Due	Fireman	Manila, Philippines
Chas. Little	Miller	Minneapolis
Harry A. Luxton	Reporter	Minneapolis
John F. Lynch	Printer	Manila, P.I. (re-enlisted)
Thos. D. Merrick	Clerk	Manila, P.I. (re-enlisted)
Leonard J. Nicolas	Draper	Minneapolis
Lorenzo A. Phillips	Waiter	Manila, Philippines
Carl J. Rusted	Student	Minneapolis
Wm. T. P. Sample	Salesman	Minneapolis
Samuel L. Sprouse	Farmer	Manila, P.I. (re-enlisted)
Chas. S. Stetson	Painter	Minneapolis
Chas. J. Swanson	Laborer	Manila, P.I. (re-enlisted)
Ira S. Towle	Laundryman	Minneapolis
Jos. Vosika	Cooper	Manila, P.I. (re-enlisted)
Chas. Warren	Salesman	Manila, P.I. (re-enlisted)
Edwin J. Walbourn	Carver	Manila, P.I. (re-enlisted)

TRANSFERRED

Lawrence J. Koerble	Telegraph Operator	To Bat. Sergt. Maj.

WOUNDED

Chas. N. Clark, 1st Lieut. . . . . Wounded in head at Guiguinto, April 11, 1899
Martin E. Tew, 2nd Lieut. . . . . . Flesh wound in right thigh at San Isidro, May 17, 1899
Albert S. Hanson . . . . Wounded in left shoulder at Manila, Aug. 13, 1898
Chas. Little . . . . Wounded in left leg at Manila, Aug. 13, 1898
Ira S. Towle . . . . . Wounded in both hands and left arm at Quinque, April, 21, 1899

DEAD

Jesse J. Cole	Killed at Sta. Isabel, P.I., April 10. 1899
Sidney T. Garrett	Died at Manila, Nov. 3, 1898
Frank C. Lewis	Killed in action near San Rafael, May 1, 1899
Vernon E. Taggart	Died of fever at Manila, May 23, 1899

Company G - Second Battalion

Name	Occupation	Address
Oscar Seebach, Capt.	Bookkeeper	Red Wing
Edw. S. Mellinger, 1st Lieut.	Telegraph Operator	Red Wing
Carl A. Anderson, 2nd Lieut.	Furniture Finisher	Red Wing
Arthur D. Danielson, 1st Sergt.	Clerk	Red Wing
Frank H. Erickson, Q.M. Sergt.	Clerk	Red Wing
Edw. L. Skoglund, Sergt.	Clerk	Red Wing
Edmund P. Neill, Sergt.	Carver	Red Wing
Frank A. Anderson, Sergt.	Laborer	Red Wing
Elmer M. Bassett, Sergt.	Bookkeeper	Red Wing
John T. Ek, Corp.	Clerk	Red Wing
Sidney S. Lundquist, Corp.	Bookkeeper	Red Wing
Geo. W. A. Buel, Corp.	Foreman	Red Wing
Ralph S. Melendy, Corp.	Photographer	Red Wing
Henry N. Jones, Corp.	Printer	Red Wing
Edw. E. Olson, Corp.	Photographer	Red Wing
Chas. J. Ahlers, Corp.	Potter	Red Wing
Carl J. Heglund, Corp.	Packer	Red Wing
Geo. J. Haustein, Corp.	Clerk	Red Wing
Olaf Benson, Corp.	Tinner	Red Wing

Name	Occupation	Address
John A. Fisher, Corp.	Poultry Raiser	Red Wing
Ralph L. Munger, Corp.	Student	Frontenac
Christ C. Bracher, Cook	Butcher	Red Wing
Chas. A. Wendler, Musician	Painter	Red Wing
Owen Leeson, Artificer	Railroadman	Red Wing
Jas. B. Webb, Wagoner	Cigar-maker	Red Wing

PRIVATES

Name	Occupation	Address
Gottlieb Amenda	Farmer	Clay Bank
Fred C. Allen	Cook	St. Paul
Olaf A. Anderson	Machinist	Red Wing
Henry Bammert	Carpenter	Red Wing
Ludwig R. Berg	Carpenter	Red Wing
Henry H. Bearbaun	Conductor	Red Wing
Frank A. Brecht	Laborer	Minnesota Lake
Carl J. Blawd	Teamster	Red Wing
Carl O. Bakke	Clerk	Red Wing
Harry Bolus	Farmer	Red Wing
Frank M. Crowel	Farmer	Red Wing
Albert F. Chinnock	Clerk	Decorah, Iowa
Albert Carlstrom	Potter	Red Wing
Arthur R. Clement	Student	Waseca
Homer C. Carey	Clerk	Minneapolis
John C. Clarke	Potter	Red Wing
Ernest H. Dahlberg	Machinist	Red Wing
Hjalmer Danielson	Teamster	Red Wing
John W. Ellstrom	Packer	Red Wing
Henry Freedlund	Potter	Red Wing
Chas. W. Fisher	Potter	Red Wing
Iver Fosse	Driver	Kenyon
John C. Foughty	Teamster	Hampton, Iowa
John G. Gerdes	Clerk	Red Wing
Robt. L. C. Geib	Undertaker	Red Wing
Everett J. Harding	Farmer	Bay City, Wisconsin
John C. G. Johnson	Clerk	Red Wing
Eugene S. Judd	Laborer	Diamond Bluff, Wisconsin
Wm. Am Jones	Printer	Red Wing
Theo Johnson	Laundryman	Red Wing
Victor C. Johnson	Cook	Red Wing
Andrew Jackson	Farmer	Red Wing
Victor Johnson	Brakeman	Red Wing

NAME	OCCUPATION	ADDRESS
Emil E. Jorgenson	Printer	Hutchinson
Edw. R. Kappel	Student	Red Wing
Hugh Kennedy	Student	Monticello
Alvie Mannix	Fireman	Red Wing
James F. Morrison	Laborer	Hager City, Wisconsin
Rudolph Nelson	Laborer	Red Wing
Cecil M. Nichols	Student	Minneapolis
Otto B. Olson	Potter	Red Wing
Francis J. O'Neill	Carver	Red Wing
Lawrence Penfold	Laborer	Red Wing
Gustaf Peterson	Carpenter	Ellsworth, Wisconsin
John T. Pewters	Carpenter	St. Paul
Frank D. Putnam	Student	Red Wing
Christ Quall	Teamster	Red Wing
Conrad F. Risch	Printer	Red Wing
Wm. G. Reid	Teamster	Red Wing
Wm. Roberts	Blacksmith	Red Wing
Albert M. Schouweiler	Clerk	Red Wing
Chas. W. Sterwart	Student	Red Wing
August Swanson	Laborer	Red Wing
Gottfried Swanberg	Farmer	Vasa
Chas. E. Stockwell	Laborer	Red Wing
Henry Seebach	Clerk	Red Wing
Bert E. Stockwell	Potter	Red Wing
Chas. Sundberg	Laborer	Red Wing
Geo. Tebbe	Packer	Red Wing

DISCHARGED

NAME	OCCUPATION	ADDRESS
Carl K. Reckner, Sergt.	Laborer	Red Wing
Fred'k W. Reichert, Corp.	Cooper	Red Wing
Geo. T. Rice, Musician	Printer	Red Wing
Geo. W. Baker	Student	Red Wing
Alfred H. Baldwin	Brakeman	Red Wing
Wm. H. Bell	Printer	Red Wing
Emerson Flansberg	Hostler	Red Wing
Oscar Fjellman	Mason	Hutchinson
Thos. Head	Student	Red Wing
Micheal Hempftling	Potter	Red Wing
John E. Johnson	Cook	Red Wing
Robt. C. Keefe	Potter	Red Wing
Gustaf P. Lundgren	Stone-cutter	Red Wing

NAME	OCCUPATION	ADDRESS
Aaron B. Newburgh	Bricklayer	Pine Island
John W. Newton	Musician	Pine Island
Fred Newcomb	Barber	Hutchinson
Fred Pa Delford	Barber	Red Wing
Leonard L. Phelps	Horseman	Hutchinson
Fred H. Scobie	Teamster	Red Wing
Benj. F. Tubesing	Machinist	Red Wing

TRANSFERRED

NAME	OCCUPATION	ADDRESS
Christian E. Gilbertson	Clerk	To Hosp. Corps
Chas. J. Hartman	Druggist	To Hosp. Corps.
John W. Lovgren	Clerk	To Hosp. Corps.

WOUNDED

Oscar Seebach, Capt. . . . . . . Wounded in lung in action at Manila, Aug. 13, 1898

Chas. J. Ahlers, Corp. . . . . . Wounded in left leg in action at Manila, Aug. 13, 1898

Geo. W. Baker . . . . Wounded in neck in action at Tondo, Feb. 23, 1898

Frank M. Crowel . . . . Wounded in right hip in action at Manila, Aug. 13, 1898

Robt. L.C. Geib . . . . Wounded in leg in action at Polo, March 26, 1899

Wm. A. Jones . . . . Wounded in left elbow in action at Manila, Aug. 13, 1898

DEAD

Frank A. Morley, 1st Lieut.	Died of rheumatism of the heart at Manila, Aug. 30, 1898
Chas. Burnsen, Sergt.	Died of wounds at Manila, Aug. 16, 1898
John H. Sell	Disappeared from transport at Manila, Aug. 1, 1898

COMPANY H - THIRD BATTALION

NAME	OCCUPATION	ADDRESS
Alfred W. Bjornstad, Capt.	Cashier	St. Paul
Frank C. Sauter, 1st Lieut.	Salesman	St. Paul
David H. Whitney, 2d Lieut.	Student	St. Paul
Martin A. Earley, 1st Sergt.	Collector	St. Paul
Alex Gray, Q.M. Sergt.	Glazier	St. Paul
Carl W. Albrecht, Sergt.	Clerk	St. Paul
Lloyd T. Smith, Sergt.	Plate Printer	St. Paul
Jos. P. McLeer, Sergt.	Clerk	St. Paul

NAME	OCCUPATION	ADDRESS
Theo. Simon, Sergt.	Inspector	St. Paul
Chas. E. Collet, Corp.	Student	Hamline
Louis F. Dow, Corp.	Salesman	St. Paul
Wm. A. Simmons, Corp.	Milkman	St. Paul
Bruno B. Klammer, Corp.	Teacher	Chaska
Wm. T. Larson, Corp.	Lineman	St. Paul
George Belden, Jr., Corp.	Student	St. Paul
Watkin W. Rosser, Corp.	Student	Hamline
Hacon B. Daniels, Corp.	Clerk	St. Paul
Wm. A. Hayes, Corp.	Machinist	St. Paul
Oscar F. Froberg, Corp.	Salesman	St. Paul
James H. Tucker, Corp.	Student	Hastings
John T. Kovec, Corp.	Boiler-maker	St. Paul
James O'Boyle, Cook	Butcher	South St. Paul
Oakes L. Ames, Musician	Photographer	Dassel
Thos. W. Chilton, Artificer	Carpenter	St. Paul
Darwin H. Mead, Wagoner	Teamster	St. Paul

PRIVATES

Chas. N. Albertson	Student	Hamline
Fred Boyd	Bricklayer	St. Paul
Warren D. Bowen	Printer	St. Paul

NAME	OCCUPATION	ADDRESS
Jno. Brabeck	Clerk	St. Paul
Edw. G. Bugton	Well-driller	Delevan
James Barrett	Clerk	South St. Paul
Geo. W. Bostrom	Classcutter	St. Paul
Wm. C. Boesel	Drug Clerk	St. Paul
Wm. Conway	Student	St. Paul
Almon L. Downing	Driver	St. Paul
John J. Duke	Engineer	Hastings
Percy K. Egbert	Barber	St. Paul
Henry J. Flecken	Clerk	Shakopee
Wm. K. Follmer	Clerk	St. Paul
Glen J. Gillmore	Farmer	Hagar City, Wisconsin
William J. Godske	Railroad Clerk	St. Paul
John Gunderson	Clerk	St. Paul
Jacob Hames	Brakeman	St. Paul
Harley F. Hammer	Student	St. Paul Park
Theo. Hansen	Painter	St. Paul
Oscar A. Johnson	Butcher	St. Paul Park
Robert C. Johnson	Student	Hamline
Edward J. Kelly	Teamster	South St. Paul
Theo. L. Kremmer	Driver	San Francisco, California
Maurice E. Keefe	Engineer	St. Paul
Joseph Kisch	Baker	St. Paul
Chas L. Kerr	Refiner	South St. Paul
Charles Lawrence	Mechanic	St. Paul
James G. Lynch	Machinist	St. Paul
Horace O. Lunsford	Farmer	Dassel
Joseph Lannen	Clerk	South St. Paul
Jno. L. Mangan	Conductor	St. Paul
Robt. A. Morrill	Student	Hamline
Peter L. Miller	Driver	St. Paul
Frank G. Nelson	Printer	St. Paul
Frank E. Packard	Student	Hamline
Louis J. Pope	Cigar-maker	St. Paul
James H. Rafferty	Fireman	Lanesboro
Roy G. Reynolds	Telephone Man	Minneapolis
Wm. Y. Richardson	Casemaker	St. Paul
Stanley S. Ruth	Laundryman	St. Paul
Frank C. Regan	Brakeman	St. Paul
Frederick Rathstock	Butcher	Mapleton
Mathias J. Ring	Clerk	Shakopee

NAME	OCCUPATION	ADDRESS
Howard M. Smith	Clerk	Hamline
Robt. H. Simmons	Horseshoer	St. Paul
Frederick Sorenson	Farmer	St. Paul
Frank E. Thomas	Laborer	Mapleton
Arthur R. Walker	Helper	St. Paul
Andrew J. Weidle	Stockman	St. Paul
Fred Widman	Clerk	St. Paul
Daniel P. Winther	Clerk	St. Paul
Julius L. Weyand	Musician	Colusa, California
Otto Yanke	Moulder	St. Paul

DISCHARGED

John C. Hardy, Capt.	Merchant	St. Paul
Leon J. Lambert, 1st Sergt.	Clerk	St. Paul
Linus F. Dee, Sergt.	Clerk	Manila, Philippines
Edw. O. Cowden, Corp.	Soldier	St. Paul
Victor J. Bergstrom, Corp.	Soldier	Manila, P.I. (re-enlisted)
Jonathan Boothby, Corp.	Student	Hammond, Wisconsin
Arthur A. Dorn, Mus.	Conductor	St. Paul
Jno. T. Blomberg, Wagoner	Soldier	Manila, P.I. (re-enlisted)
Fred Berndt	Soldier	Manila, P.I. (re-enlisted)
Francis H. Cariveau	Painter	St. Paul
John H. Dow	Painter	Manila, Philippines
Albert d'Arcy	Clerk	Manila, Philippines
Albert E. Erickson	Teamster	Rush City
Jas. H. Gilmore	Farmer	Hartland, Wisconsin
Ernest C. Hopkins	Soldier	Manila, P.I. (re-enlisted)
Jno. A. Johnson	Laborer	Washington, D.C.
Leonard Olson	Clerk	St. Paul
Charles Peake	Soldier	Manila, P.I. (re-enlisted)
Harry Postel	Barber	Minneapolis
Chas. W. Ryder	Mechanic	Hamline
Frank C. Smith	Cook	St. Paul
Gunnar Thorsell	Soldier	Manila P.I. (re-enlisted)
Lewis H. Wallace	Student	Drayton, North Dakota
Chas. H. Wallace	Student	Drayton, North Dakota
George R. Yorke	Machinist	St. Paul

TRANSFERRED

E. Mason Brown	Telegrapher	To signal corps.
Joseph Craigue	Drug Clerk	To Hosp. Corps.

Name	Occupation	Address
Edw. G. Ireland	Student	To Hosp. Corps.
Conrad F. Risch	Printer	To Co. G
Quincy R. Shoemaker	None given	To Co. B

Missing

Wm. J. Worthington	Driver St. Paul	Missing, June 7, 1899

Wounded

Alfred W. Bjornstad, Capt. . . . Wounded through body and muscles of back, Manila, Aug. 13, 1898

James Barrett . . . . Wounded in right shoulder at Maasim, May 4, 1899

Albert E. Erickson . . Wounded through left arm and body at San Miguel, May 13, 1899

Gunnar Thorsell . . . . Wounded in head at Manila, Aug. 13, 1898

Lewis H. Wallace . . . . Wounded in right shoulder at Manila, Aug. 13, 1898

Andrew J. Weidle . . . . Wounded in right forearm at Caloocan, Feb. 28, 1899

Dead

Albert E. Dennis	Typhoid fever at Cavite, Sept. 11, 1898
Chas. W. Schwartz	Typhoid malaria at Manila, Aug. 31, 1898

Company I - First Battalion

Name	Occupation	Address
Frank T. Corriston, Capt.	Lawyer	Minneapolis
Wm. J. Byrnes, 1st Lieut.	Clerk	Minneapolis
John F. Chambers, 2nd Lieut.	Clerk	Minneapolis
Ernest W. Langdon, 1st Sergt.	Architect	Minneapolis
Elwin G. Jones, Q.M. Sergt.	Engraver	Minneapolis
Harry S. Taylor, Sergt.	Salesman	Minneapolis
Chas. W. McQuery, Sergt.	Printer	Minneapolis
John D. Currie, Sergt.	Grain Inspector	Minneapolis
Wm. A. Pealock, Sergt.	Stage Mechanic	Minneapolis
Jas. S. Loudon, Corp.	Salesman	Minneapolis
Archie R. Priest, Corp.	Bookkeeper	Minneapolis
Earle A. Barker, Corp.	Jeweler	Minneapolis
Edw. B. McInnes, Corp.	Bookkeeper	Minneapolis
Arthur D. Holbrook, Corp.	Salesman	Minneapolis

NAME	OCCUPATION	ADDRESS
Wm. J. Kingsley, Corp.	Salesman	Minneapolis
Albert E. Bates, Corp.	Nailer	Minneapolis
Harry R. McKay, Corp.	Student	Minneapolis
Ernest A. Dunn, Corp.	Electrician	Minneapolis
Fred'k Ekman, Corp.	Railroadman	Detroit City
Anthony X. Schall, Jr., Corp.	Student	Minneapolis
Thos. J. Davis, Corp.	Clerk	Minneapolis
Geo. W. Dyer, Cook	Butcher	Delano
Geo. D. Montgomery, Mus.	Student	Hamline
Chas. L. Flannigan, Mus.	Printer	Waverly
Bert E. Smith, Artificer	Clerk	Minneapolis
Robt. M. Byers, Wagoner	Miller	Minneapolis

PRIVATES

John W. Ames	Student	Minneapolis
Vernon E. Bean	Decorator	Minneapolis
Walter M. Beck	Physician	Minneapolis
Alvin L. Buffington	Architect	Minneapolis
Allan Burrill	Steam Fitter	Hawley
Warren S. Clark	Salesman	Minneapolis
Wm. Z. Desmond	Barber	Minneapolis
Glenn A. Durston	Art Student	Minneapolis
Jessie F. Dyer	Clerk	Minneapolis

Name	Occupation	Address
Elmer E. Erickson	Carpenter	Delano
Chas. W. Fairchild	Clerk	Minneapolis
Merritte E. Fox	Shoe Finisher	Minneapolis
Allen Gilmer	Farmer	Howard Lake
Gerald G. Groves	Teacher	Howard Lake
August Guttenburg	Real Estate Agent	Minneapolis
Wm. H. Hall	Clerk	Minneapolis
Edwin E. Hawkins	Civil Engineer	Minneapolis
Peter P. Hegdahl	Printer	Minneapolis
John T. Hohoff	Clerk	Minneapolis
Albert J. Jefferies	Clerk	Minneapolis
Wm. B. Johnson	Clerk	Minneapolis
Wm. F. Kissinger	Butcher	Minneapolis
Geo. W. Kurtz	Printer	Delano
Wm. M. Laurel	Engineer	Minneapolis
Burt H. Libbey	Clerk	Minneapolis
Percy C. Libby	Student	Minneapolis
Scott J. Lintner	Stenographer	Minneapolis
Frank B. McAllister	Clerk	Minneapolis
Arthur J. McGregor	Carriage-maker	Minneapolis
Geo. M. McGregor	Student	Minneapolis
Chas. B. Marsh	Clerk	Farmington
Garrett L. May	Clerk	Howard Lake
Ralph L. Morgan	Clerk	Howard Lake
Alfred C. Murphy	Salesman	Minneapolis
Ambro S. Park	Lawyer	Minneapolis
Harvey S. Rogers	Clerk	Minneapolis
Glenn E. Smith	Teacher	Howard Lake
Wm. Steffes	Clerk	Delano
Wm. F. Steffes	Clerk	Minneapolis
Jesse L. Stegner	Lithographer	Minneapolis
Burt Thomas	Carpenter	San Francisco, California
Edwin N. Van Slyke	Clerk	Minneapolis
Jos. W. Weaver	Candy-maker	Minneapolis
Harold O. Wheeler	Salesman	Minneapolis
Oscar Wirtensohn	Shoe-maker	Minneapolis
Wm. W. Woehler	Student	Rochester
Wm. J. Works	Student	Hawley

Discharged

Name	Occupation	Address
Wm. P. Christian, Sergt.	Clerk	Minneapolis
Edw. A. Finnegan, Sergt.	Clerk	Minneapolis
Reuben R. McDermid, Sergt.	Clerk	Minneapolis
Harry F. Bedbury, Corp.	Clerk	Minneapolis
Otto S. Langum, Corp.	Clerk	Minneapolis
Walfred A. Ryberg, Corp.	Clerk	Minneapolis
John M. Roberts, Mus.	Student	Minneapolis
Allan R. Bartlett	Clerk	Minneapolis
David K. Christian	Clerk	Minneapolis
Jas. A. Creighton	Lumberman	Minneapolis
Albert M. Easthagen	Clerk	Minneapolis
Geo. R. Egbert	Clerk	Minneapolis
Geo. A. Gallagher	Student	Minneapolis
Nicholas W. Garratt	Clerk	Minneapolis
Allen A. Grimes	Student	Minneapolis
Isaac R.D. Hallowell	Insurance Agent	Minneapolis
Jas. R. Hull	Journalist	Minneapolis
John G. Hvoslef	Lawyer	Minneapolis
John J. Kelley	Cloth-cutter	Minneapolis
John A. Kenworthy	Clerk	Minneapolis
Newton E. Keyes	Dairyman	Minneapolis
Alex. H. McDonald	Tailor	Minneapolis
Jos. M. Moore	Clerk	Minneapolis
Wm. R. Overmire	Clerk	Minneapolis
Lennard A. Porter	Printer	Minneapolis
Geo. F. Rock	Cook	Minneapolis
Martin A. Saxton	Cloth-cutter	Minneapolis
Robt. N. Sherman	Clerk	Minneapolis
Otho W. Smith	Salesman	Minneapolis
Ernest E. Wheelock	Salesman	Minneapolis

Transferred

Jenner P. Chance	Medical Student	Hospital Corps
Harry E. Sutton	Student	Hosptial Corps

Wounded

Fred'k Ekman, Corp. . . . . Wounded in both legs near Banlac, March, 1899
Edw. B. McInnes, Corp. . . . . Wounded in right hand near Banlac, March 25, 1899
Walfred A. Ryberg, Corp. . . . . Wounded in left arm at Guiguinto, April 11, 1899
Allen A. Grimes, Private . . . . Wounded in head near Banlac, March 25, 1899
Lennard A. Porter . . . . Wounded in right hip near Banlac, March 25, 1899

DEAD

Wm. W. Ray, Corp.	Dead of pneumonia at San Francisco, May 30, 1898
Archie R. Patterson, Mus.	Killed in action at Manila, Aug. 13, 1898
Verne A. Barker, Private	Died of smallpox at Manila, Feb. 23, 1899
Amasa J. Hawkins, Private	Died of smallpox at Manila, Dec. 3, 1898
Edw. J. Sutton, Private	Died of smallpox at Manila, March 9, 1899
Robt. L. Van Eman, Private	Died of smallpox at Manila, Feb. 20, 1899

COMPANY K - SECOND BATTALION

NAME	OCCUPATION	ADDRESS
Edwin M. Conrad, Capt.	Merchant	Stillwater
John J. Walsh, 1st Lieut.	Bookbinder	Stillwater
Geo. H. Grant, 2nd Lieut.	Printer	Stillwater
Harry M. Howard, 1st Sergt.	Clerk	Stillwater
Horace L. Keefe, Q.M. Sergt.	Printer	Stillwater
Walter W. Koons, Sergt.	Electrician	Stillwater
Wm. H. Arthur, Sergt.	Tinner	Stillwater

NAME	OCCUPATION	ADDRESS
Michael T. Nolan, Sergt.	Laborer	Stillwater
Carl J. Johnson, Sergt.	Tanner	Stillwater
Peter C. Peterson, Corp.	Molder	Stillwater
Mathew C. McMillan, Corp.	Student	Stillwater
Jas. C. Pratt, Corp.	Butcher	Stillwater
Max W. Hoppe, Corp.	Clerk	Stillwater
Nelson O. Marsh, Corp.	Student	Stillwater
Robt. M. Coles, Jr., Corp.	Musician	Stillwater
Harry J. Staples, Corp.	Log-scaler	Stillwater
John M. Nolan, Corp.	Laborer	Stillwater
John Connelly, Jr., Corp.	Laborer	Beaver Falls, New York
Angus J. McDonald, Corp.	Woodsman	Stillwater
Terrence Cook, Corp.	Laborer	Stillwater
Ernest C. Korn, Corp.	Barber	Stillwater
Chas. A. Peterson, Cook	Cook	Stillwater
Daniel L. Carroll, Musician	Clerk	Stillwater
Martin L. Carey, Musician	Clerk	St. Paul
Wm. H. Rutherford, Artificer	Farmer	Stillwater
Napolean F. Parrent, Wagoner	Farmer	Stillwater

PRIVATES

Wm. T. Alexander	Printer	Stillwater
Godfrey J. Anderson	Shoemaker	Rockford, Illinois
Clemens T. Arndt	Clerk	Stillwater
Sep. A. Balzart	Laborer	St. Paul
Stewart P. Barton	Laborer	Marine Mills
Paul F. R. Behnke	Molder	Minneapolis
Otto A. Beiging	Carpenter	Stillwater
Harry E. Borroman	Laborer	Stillwater
Daniel Brophy	Laborer	Minneapolis
Wm. G. Brotherton	Riverman	Stillwater
Lewis P. Burlingham	Clerk	Stillwater
Arthur L. Chambers	Clerk	Stillwater
Jas. A. Clapperton, Jr.	Laborer	Stillwater
Chas. E. Connors	Blacksmith	Stillwater
Chas. S. Clewell	Student	Stillwater
Frank H. Curtis	Teamster	Stillwater
Merle F. Chapel	Student	Minneapolis
Harvey C. Downs	Laborer	Menomonie, Wisconsin
Raymond R. Downs	Druggist	Stillwater
Chas. E. Elmquist	Laborer	Marine Mills
Wm. H. Foster	Dairyman	Stillwater
Wm. B. Fuller	Lumber-man	Freeborn

NAME	OCCUPATION	ADDRESS
Wm. A. Garen	Teamster	Stillwater
Oscar J. Grant	Sashmaker	Stillwater
Geo. W. Gordon	Clerk	Stillwater
Harry J. Haggerty	Laborer	Stillwater
Jas. J. Haggerty	Student	Stillwater
Louis E. Hartong	Butcher	Columbia City, Wash.
Thos. J. Henry	Laborer	Stillwater
Frank E. Hinds	Student	Stillwater
Bernard M. Hinz	Laborer	Stillwater
Newton Hobbs	Laborer	Marine Mills
Warren J. Hoehne	Sawyer	Stillwater
Jas. A. Hughes	Boiler-maker	Stillwater
Wm. H. Husting	Butcher	St. Paul
Harry S. Jenks	Farmer	Stillwater
Chas. C. Johnson	Machinist	Minneapolis
Geo. A. Kearney	Horseshoer	Stillwater
Jas. H. Keefe	Painter	Stillwater
Gilbert S. Kelly	Laborer	Eau Claire, Wisconsin
Elmer C. Kinyon	Farmer	Withrow
Fred'k N. Knapp	Farmer	Stillwater
Stephen La Furgey	Laborer	Stillwater
Nathan N. Lanners	Cook	Stillwater
John E. Lawson	Plasterer	Stillwater
Chas. J. Luhmann	Painter	Stillwater
Donald D. Mac Rae	Printer	Morgan
Hector McNeil	Woodsman	St. Paul
Daniel P. McDonald	Stenographer	Stillwater
Jas. C. McGee	Woodsman	Stillwater
Edw. F. McGillin	Laborer	Stillwater
Patrick McLeod	Lumber-man	Stillwater
Chas. T. Newman	Farmer	Winthrow
Axel Olsen	Farmer	Maple Island
Emil E. Pankonin	Drayman	Stillwater
Louis W. Reiter	Farmer	Scandia
Wm. F. Russell	Boiler-maker	Stillwater
Thos. J. Ratican	Lumber-man	Stillwater
Clinton W. Rutherford	Farmer	Stillwater
Walter C. Scheela	Shoemaker	Stillwater
Albert G. Secker, Jr.	Wheelwright	Stillwater
Wm. H. Sinnott	Printer	Stillwater
Ernest G. Smith	Lumber-man	Stillwater
John F. Scott	Laborer	Stillwater

NAME	OCCUPATION	ADDRESS
Wm. E. Spindle	Laborer	Stillwater
Andrew G. Shoquist	Clerk	Stillwater
Ernest P. Thompson	Laborer	Stillwater
Gustaf A. Thornquist	Saw Setter	Stillwater
Benj. F. Thelen	Student	Stillwater
Frank T. Tobisch	Florist	Stillwater
Otto A. Wachsmuth	Shingle-worker	Stillwater
Michael M. Walsh	Laborer	Stillwater
Jas. E. Walsh	Laborer	Stillwater
Jas. F. Walls	Farmer	Stillwater
Otto H. Wurdeman	Student	Stillwater
Roy E. Webster	Engineer	Stillwater

DISCHARGED

NAME	OCCUPATION	ADDRESS
Wm. B. Burlingham, Sergt.	Clerk	Stillwater
Geo. A. Brewsaugh	Engineer	Stillwater
Chas. A. Glaser	Laborer	Stillwater
Clarence L. Kinyon	Farmer	Stillwater
Albert G. Schuberg	Laborer	Stillwater
Wm. F. Seigler	Cooper	Stillwater
Henry E. Wallace	Musician	Manila, Philippines
John T. Whelan	Clerk	Stillwater

PROMOTED

Jos. P. Masterman, Capt.   To Major, May 27, 1899

WOUNDED

Wm. B. Burlingham, Sergt. . . . . Wounded in left knee at Norzagaray, April 24, 1899
John J. Connelly, Corp. . . . Wounded in right hip at Mariquina Road, March 25, 1899
Jas. C. McGee . . . . Wounded in left hand at Mariquina Road, March 25, 1899
John T. Whelan . . . . . . Wounded in right side at Mariquina Road, March 25, 1899

DEAD

Paul J. Rode   Died of fever at Manila, June 28, 1899

COMPANY L - SECOND BATTALION

NAME	OCCUPATION	ADDRESS
Alfred S. Morgan, Capt.	General Agent	Minneapolis
Harry D. Lackore, 1st Lieut.	Electrician	Minneapolis
Hugh R. Scott, 2nd Lieut.	Clerk	Minneapolis
Louis B. Bassett, 1st Sergt.	Farmer	Minneapolis
Frank A. Neyhart, Q.M. Sergt.	Clerk	Minneapolis
Harry B. Shears, Sergt.	Student	Pepin, Wisconsin
Chas. A. Steele, Sergt.	Shoe-maker	Minneapolis
Arthur R. Neyhart, Sergt.	Electrician	Minneapolis
Otto Sougstad, Sergt.	Bookkeeper	Milwaukee, Wisconsin
Paul E. Donaldson, Corp.	Clerk	Minneapolis
Eric Okerlund, Corp.	Electrician	Duluth
Robt. Long, Corp.	Railroadman	Minneapolis
Jas. F. Myers, Corp.	Horseshoer	Minneapolis
Gust. Peterson, Corp.	Bookkeeper	Minneapolis
Arthur D. Purcell, Corp.	Farmer	Watson, Missouri
August Anderson, Corp.	Farmer	Minneapolis
Fred'k J. Podas, Corp.	Candy-maker	Minneapolis
Bert Devinney, Corp.	Laborer	Minneapolis

NAME	OCCUPATION	ADDRESS
Fred S. Buck, Corp.	Nailer	Minneapolis
Adam Hotchkiss, Corp.	Lineman	Minneapolis
Ellsworth Christensen, Corp.	Miller	Minneapolis
Henry Endewardt, Cook	Laborer /	Minneapolis
Ernest Lee, Musician	Miller	Minneapolis
Carl Fieldstad, Musician	Dairyman	Lisbon, North Dakota
Jas. Sullivan, Artificer	Horse-trainer	Minneapolis
Wm. McDermott, Wagoner	Engineer	Minneapolis

PRIVATES

Roy Arnerson	Candy-maker	Minneapolis
Elmer H. Bassett	Farmer	Rushmore
Hartley A. Berry	Laborer	Minneapolis
Stephen J. Brennan	Painter	Lancester, Wisconsin
Frank Brereton	Clerk	Minneapolis
Edw. Bougie	Roofer	Minneapolis
Peter Callan	Teamster	Minneapolis
Norman H. Cavan	Teamster	Minneapolis
Chas. F. Conrad	Telegraph Operator	Minneapolis
Henry A. Davies	Farmer	Minneapolis
Jos. Dushek	Clerk	Morris
Sibert Eggen	Wood-worker	Minneapolis
Willard Emerson	Teamster	Minneapolis
Peter J. Fallon	Cap. Vol. of America	San Francisco, California
Arthur H. Gerrish	Grain Sampler	Minneapolis
David D. Gonser	Student	Minneapolis
Edw. M. Griffin	Stone-cutter	Minneapolis
Conrad Guenther	Painter	St. Paul
Sigurd Halvorson	Carpenter	Minneapolis
Oscar Hawley	Teamster	Minneapolis
Chas. Henriksen	Blacksmith	Minneapolis
Wm. Hoadley	Grain Sampler	Minneapolis
Christ J. Holland	Painter	Willmar
Chas. H. Jacquinet	Electrician	Minneapolis
Robert Jacquinet	Cigar Maker	Minneapolis
Anton Johnson	Laborer	Minneapolis
John D. Jones	Machinist	Minneapolis
Geo. Kahl	Laborer	Minneapolis
Theo. R. Kunitz	Druggist	Minneapolis
Hjalmar Lundin	Farmer	Lindstrom
Jas. Madden	Painter	Minneapolis

NAME	OCCUPATION	ADDRESS
John Metke	Printer	Deer River
Frank Merrill	Bookkeeper	St. Paul
Michael J. Murphy	Printer	Minneapolis
Henry S. Opsahl	Grain Sampler	Minneapolis
Jarvis L. Parks	Veterinary Surgeon	Fort Fairfield, Maine
John Paulsrud	Farmer	Nielsville
Chas. Peters	Cook	Minneapolis
John A. Peterson	Laborer	Minneapolis
Daniel Petrie	Machinist	Minneapolis
Ernest E. Rider	Engineer	Vineland
Revenell S. Stephens	Painter	St. Paul
John C. Shillock	Landscape Gardener	Minneapolis
Fred E. Sine	Salesman	Minneapolis
Arthur L. Smith	Butcher	Minneapolis
Peter Sorenson	Farmer	Minneapolis
Hilfred L. Thomasson	Harness-maker	Morris
Louis Ulmer	Butcher	Minneapolis

DISCHARGED

NAME	OCCUPATION	ADDRESS
Chas. R. Head, 1st Sergt.	Clerk	Minneapolis
Roland A. Gray, Corp.	Photographer	Minneapolis
Gustaf H. Ahlberg	Laborer	Minneapolis
Alfred E. Anderson	Painter	Minneapolis
Wm. H. Aylesworth	Engineer	Minneapolis
Fred R. Buri	Stenographer	Manila, Philippines
Wm. Cooper	Miner	Minneapolis
Walter J. Cork	Salesman	Minneapolis
Thos. P. Davis	Mechanic	Minneapolis
Thos. R. Davis	Iron Worker	Minneapolis
Chas. Felton	Teamster	Minneapolis
Harry M. Glazier	Clerk	Minneapolis
John F. Hauck	Student	Manila, Philippines
Richard H. Kelly	Photographer	Minneapolis
Michael J. Lyons	Miller	Manila, Philippines
John W. McCormick	Teacher	Minneapolis
Wm. F. McGilnton	Painter	Minneapolis
Charles J. McWilliams	Cook	Minneapolis
Wm. Moore	Salesman	St. Paul
Jeremiah Mullen	Switchman	Minneapolis
Chas. W. Nelson	Clerk	Minneapolis
Benj. Ohman	Farmer	Minneapolis

NAME	OCCUPATION	ADDRESS
Louis Olimb	Clerk	Manila, Philippines
Christopher Opdahl	Waiter	Manila, Philippines
Patrick Ryan	Teamster	Manila, Philippines
Wm. Saylor	Shoemaker	Minneapolis
Thomas W. Short	Salesman	Minneapolis
Fred'k Still	Stone Cutter	Minneapolis
Geo. F. Tenney	Undertaker	Minneapolis
Jas. Vetenburg	Butcher	Minneapolis
Warren Whiteman	Miller	Manila, Philippines

MISSING

Joe Walsh   Missed at Manila. June 9, 1899

WOUNDED

Adam Hotchkiss, Corp. . . . . Wounded in left knee at Bigaa, April 11, 1899
Harry M. Glazier . . . . Wounded in left thigh at Mariquina Road, Mar. 25, 1899
Richard H. Kelly . . . . Wounded in left shoulder at Bocaue, April 11, 1899
Geo. Kahl . . . . Wounded in head at Cingalon Church, Aug. 13, 1898
Wm. Moore . . . . Wounded in head at Cingalon Church, Aug. 13, 1898
Benj. Ohman . . . . Wounded in left leg at Caloocan, Feb. 10, 1899
Ernest E. Rider . . . . Wounded in left hand at Cingalon Church, Aug. 13, 1898
Geo. F. Tenney . . . . Wounded in head at Cingalon Church, Aug. 13, 1898
Louis Ulmer . . . . Wounded in neck at Cingalon Church, Aug. 13, 1898

DEAD

Fred W. Buckendorf	Died of wounds at Baliuag, May 6, 1899
Henry Dickson	Died of fever at Cavite, Aug. 16, 1898
Edward Pratt	Died of smallpox at Manila, March 25, 1899
Wm. Sullivan	Died of fever at Honolulu, July 17, 1898
Frank F. Weirauch	Died of smallpox at Manila, Oct. 1, 1898

COMPANY M - SECOND BATTALION

NAME	OCCUPATION	ADDRESS
Jas. E. McKelvy, Capt.	Sheriff	St. Cloud
Leigh D. Bruckart, 1st Lieut.	Reporter	Minneapolis
Henry J. Limperich, 2nd Lieut.	Teacher	St. Cloud
Iver M. Engerbretson, 1st Sergt.	Clerk	Lowry
John B. Pattison, Q.M. Sergt.	Law Student	St. Cloud
Wm. H. Lawrence, Sergt.	Miller	Wabasha
Herbert W. Getchell, Sergt.	Teacher	Annandale
Jos. J. Kramer, Sergt.	Deputy Sheriff	Melrose
Herbert M. Fischer, Sergt.	Expressman	St. Cloud
Grant E. Getchell, Corp.	Driver	Aberdeen, South Dakota
Fred'k E. Schacht, Jr., Corp.	Student	Fergus Falls
Harry M. Mickley, Corp.	Conductor	St. Cloud
Frank W. Richardson, Corp.	Stone Cutter	Merrillan, Wisconsin
Julius L. Hendrickson, Corp.	Quarryman	St. Cloud
Asa C. Maxson, Corp.	Draughtsman	St. Cloud
Arthur Johnson, Corp.	Farmer	Melrose
Edw. O. Lentz, Corp.	Barber	St. Cloud
Wm. Osgood, Corp.	Broommaker	St. Cloud
Geo. A. Arness, Corp.	Teacher	Terrace
Frank A. Paulius, Corp.	Bartender	St. Cloud
Daniel Thursdale, Corp.	Clerk	St. Cloud
Jos. H. Capser, Corp.	Bartender	St. Joseph

NAME	OCCUPATION	ADDRESS
Eugene Robbins, Mus.	Laborer	Melrose
Walter D. Matheney, Mus.	Photographer	St. Cloud
Henry G. Lempe, Artificer	Laborer	Monticello
Wm. D. Whiting, Wagoner	Farmer	St. Cloud

PRIVATES

Frank R. Balder	Laborer	St. Cloud
Wm. J. Balder	Laborer	St. Cloud
Edw. J. Brick	Clerk	St. Cloud
Alex. T. Burns	Packer	St. Cloud
Wm. N. Bonnelle	Carpenter	St. Cloud
Frank Briol	Wagon-maker	Albany
Robt. A. Bursch	Laborer	Hanover
Peter Brandenburger	Carpenter	St. Cloud
Orrin Benson	Teamster	Dassel
Jas. F. Brown	Stone-cutter	St. Cloud
Wm. J. Donken	Iceman	St. Cloud
Andrew Denzer	Painter	Le Sueur
John Danzl	Car Repairer	Melrose
Wm. J. Fox	Steam-fitter	St. Cloud
Carl T. Franklin	Painter	St. Paul
Egidius J. Fehr	Student	St. Cloud
Chas. L. Fisher	Teamster	Melrose
Robt. Flick	Baker	Minneapolis
Geo. E. French	Machinist	St. Cloud
Oscar Frykman	Teamster	Minneapolis
Rich'd F. Gehm	Teacher	St. Cloud
Albert H. Gillis	Painter	Minneapolis
Bertrand G. Hines	Motorman	St. Cloud
Geo. W. Harding	Photographer	Darwin
Edw. J. Heyser	Railroadman	St. Cloud
Carl I. Hendrickson	Quarryman	Acton
Paul Huberty	Laborer	Albany
Fred'k Hohnes	Deputy US Marshall	St. Cloud
Merton E. Hall	Moulder	Owatonna
John Johnson	Car Repairer	Eagle Bend
August J. Kruse	Student	Belgrade
Ole Kvinge	Carpenter	Minneapolis
Eugene Lorance	Bartender	Harrington, Nebraska
Math Lemm	Farmer	Luxemburg
Wm. Latzka	Teamster	Alexandria

NAME	OCCUPATION	ADDRESS
Chas. O. Lindquist	Shoemaker	Sauk Rapids
Fred W. Lewis	Carpenter	St. Cloud
John L. Lempe	Farmer	Monticello
Wm. C. Lindley	Printer	Sauk Rapids
Herbert A. Morrison	Clerk	St. Cloud
Chas. C. Madison	Clerk	St. Cloud
Edw. T. Millane	Laborer	Benson
Stephen Nuerenberg	Liveryman	St. Cloud
Axil Newdall	Student	Springfield
John P. O'Brien	Blacksmith	St. Cloud
Jas. O'Hara	Laborer	Melrose
Wm. F. Pohl	Student	St. Cloud
Geo. F. Peterson	Cook	St. Cloud
Geo. Pracna	Musician	Minneapolis
Miche E. Redmann	Butcher	Melrose
Martin Reider	Farmer	St. Joseph
Geo. H. Robinson	Student	St. Cloud
Frank J. Ruff	Farmer	Arban
Peter F. Roller	Teacher	St. Cloud
Wm. J. Rooney	Drayman	St. Cloud
Geo. M. Ramey	Farmer	Dassel
Judson O. Smith	Engineer	Fairhaven
Frank W. Sipe	Lineman	St. Cloud
Jos. H. Steffes	Butcher	St. Cloud
Peter H. Schumacker	Clerk	St. Cloud
Jos. A. Theilen	Barber	St. Cloud
John Torker	Blacksmith	Brockway
Geo. H. Tyler	Fireman	Melrose
Henry Tenvoorde	Carpenter	St. Cloud
Otto B. Varner	Stage Carpenter	St. Cloud
Jas. P. Walsh	Student	St. Cloud
John F. Wheeler	Painter	St. Cloud
Wm H.Z. Wheeler	Miller	St. Cloud
Lambert Weis	Lumberman	Stillwater
Fred W. Zertler	Driver	St. Paul

DISCHARGED

Andrew W. Anderson, Sergt.	Student	Manila, Philippines
Walton C. Graham, Corp.	Machinist	Kalamazoo, Michigan
Roy M. Blood, Corp.	Broommaker	St. Cloud
Arthur G. Briederly	Teamster	Manila, Philippines

NAME	OCCUPATION	ADDRESS
Martin A. Bertramsen	Barber	Albert Lea
Paulinus G. Huhn	Joiner	St. Cloud
Chas. E. Michaels	Telegraph Operator	Melrose
Wm. G. Reichmuth	Painter	Manila, Philippines
Fred T. Thompson	Cook	Manila, Philippines

TRANSFERRED

Herman H. Gehm	Mechanic	To Hosp. Corps.
Arthur W. Riches	Musician	To Non-Com. Staff

DESERTED

Robert Burns — Deserted at Honolulu, Aug. 10, 1898

WOUNDED

Egidius J. Fehr . . Wounded in breast, left arm and right hip at Tondo, Feb. 23, 1899
Oscar Frykman . . . . Wounded in groin at Tondo, Feb. 23, 1899
Paulinus G. Huhn . . . . Wounded in left breast at Mariquina, March 25, 1899

DEAD

Geo. H. Cootey — Died of smallpox at Manila, Oct. 4, 1898
Wm. H. Pilgrim — Died of Dysentery at Manila, June 23, 1899

Bibliography

Books

Blegen, Theodore C., *Minnesota: A History of the State,* St. Paul: North Central Publishing Company, 1975.

Blount, James, *The American Occupation of the Philippines, 1898-1912*, New York: Putnam, 1913.

Bowe, John, *With the 13th Minnesota: In the Philippines*, Minneapolis: A. B. Franham Printing and Stationary Company, 1905.

Brands, H.W., *The Reckless Decade: America in the 1890s,* New York: St. Martin's Press, 1995.

Breslin, Jimmy, *Damon Runyon*, New York: Ticknor and Fields, 1991.

Brown, Charles Henry, *The Correspondents' War: Journalists in the Spanish-American War,* New York: Scribner, 1967.

Burnquist, Joseph A. A., *Minnesota and its People, Vol. III*, Chicago: The S. J. Clarke Publishing Company, 1924.

Cooper, Jerry M., *Citizens as Soldiers: A History of the North Dakota National Guard,* Fargo: The North Dakota Institute for Regional Studies, 1986.

Cosmas, Graham A., *An Army for Empire: The United States Army in the Spanish-American War,* Columbia: University of Missouri Press, 1971.

Davies, Kenneth M., *To the Last Man: The Chronicle of the 135th Infantry Regiment of Minnesota,* St. Paul, Minnesota: The Ramsey County Historical Society, 1982.

Emery, Michael and Edwin Emery, *The Press and America: An Interpretive History of the Mass Media,* Englewood Cliffs, New Jersey: Prentice Hall, 1988.

Everett, Marshall, *Exciting Experiences in Our Wars with Spain and the Filipinos,* Chicago: Quadrangle Books, 1964.

Faust, Karl, *Campaigning in the Philippines,* New York: Arno Press, 1970 [c1898].

Finzer, W. E., *The Official Records of the Oregon Volunteers in the Spanish American and Philippine Insurrection,* Salem, Oregon: J. R. Whitney, State Printer, 1903.

Fitch, William C. and General McC. Reeve, *13th Minnesota Vols.: Historical Record in the War with Spain,* Minneapolis: Price Bros. Printing Company, 1900.

Foner, Philip S., *The Spanish-Cuban-American War and the Birthright of American Imperialism, 1895-1902,* New York: Monthly Review Press, 1972.

Folwell, William Watts, *A History of Minnesota, Vol. III,* St. Paul: The Minnesota Historical Society, 1969.

Gates, John Morgan, *Schoolbooks and Krags: The United States Army in the Philippines, 1898-1902,* Westport, Connecticut: Greenwood Press Inc., 1973.

Gould, Lewis L., *The Spanish-American War and President McKinley,* Lawrence Kansas: University Press of Kansas, c1982.

Graff, Henry F., *American Imperialism and the Philippine Insurrection: Testimony Taken from Hearings on Affairs in the Philippine Islands before the Senate Committee on the Philippines, 1902,* Boston: Little, Brown, 1969.

Halstead, Murat, *The Story of the Philippines,* Chicago: Our Possessions Publishing Co., 1898.

Healy, David F., *US Expansionism: The Imperialists Urge in the 1890s,* Madison: University of Wisconsin Press, 1970.

Holbrook, Franklin F., *Minnesota in the Spanish-American War and the Philippine Insurrection, Vol. 1,* Publications of the Minnesota War Records Commission, St. Paul: The Riverside Press, 1923.

Ingalls, John J., *America's War For Humanity: A Complete History of Cuba's Struggle For Liberty,* New York: N.D. Thompson Publishing Co., 1898.

Karnow, Stanley, *In Our Image: America's Empire in the Philippines,* New York: Random House, Inc., 1990.

Keller, Allen, *The Spanish-American War: A Compact History,* New York: Hawthorn Books, 1969.

Kelly, Thomas, III, *The U.S. Army and the Spanish American War Era, 1895-1910,* Carlisle Barracks, Pennsylvania. US Army Military History Research Collection, 1974.

Kunz, Virginia Brainard, *Muskets to Missiles: A Military History of Minnesota,* St. Paul: Minnesota Statehood Centennial Commission, 1958.

LeRoy, James Alfred, *Americans in the Philippines,* 2 Vols. New York: AMS Press, 1970.

Linderman, Gerald F., *The Mirror of War: American Society and the Spanish-American War,* Ann Arbor: University of Michigan Press, 1974.

Linn, Brian McAllister, *The United States Army and Counterinsurgency in the Philippine War, 1899-1901,* Chapel Hill: University of North Carolina Press, 1989.

Mahon, John, *History of the Militia and the National Guard,* New York: MacMillan, c1983.

March, Alden, *The History and Conquest of the Philippines and Our Other Island Possessions,* Philadelphia: John C. Winston, 1899.

Miller, Richard H., *American Imperialism in 1898: The Quest for National Fulfillment,* New York: Wiley, 1970.

Miller, Stuart Creighton, *Benevolent Assimilation: The American Conquest of the Philippines, 1899-1903,* New Haven: Yale University Press, 1982.

Millis, Walter, *The Martial Spirit: A Study of Our War with Spain,* New York: Houghton Mifflin Co., 1931.

O'Toole, G.J.A., *The Spanish-American War, An American Epic-1898,* New York: Norton, 1984.

Offner, John L., *An Unwanted War: The Diplomacy of the United States and Spain Over Cuba, 1895-1898,* Chapel Hill, North Carolina: The University of North Carolina Press, 1992.

Pier, Arthur Stanwood, *American Apostles to the Philippines,* Freeport, New York: Books for Libraries, 1971.

Pomeroy, William J., *American Neo-Colonialism: Its Emergence in the Philippines and Asia,* New York: International Publishers, 1970.

Pratt, Julius W., *Expansionists of 1898: The Acquisition of Hawaii and the Spanish Islands,* Chicago: Quadrangle Books, 1964.

Quirino, Carlos, *Filipinos At War: The Fight for Freedom from Mactan to Bessang Pass,* Philippines: Vera-Reyes, Inc., 1981.

Roth, Russell, *Muddy Glory: America's "Indian Wars" in the Philippines 1899-1935,* West Hanover, Massachusetts: Christopher Publishing House, c1981.

Schirmer, Daniel B., *Republic or Empire; American Resistance to the Philippine War,* Cambridge, Massachusetts: Schenkman Publishing Company, 1972.

Seib, Philip, *Headline Diplomacy: How News Coverage Affects Foreign Policy,* Westport, Connecticut: Praeger Publications, 1997.

Severo, Richard and Lewis Milford, *The Wages of War: When America's Soldiers Came Home—From Valley Forge to Vietnam,* New York: Simon and Schuster, c1989.

Sexton, William Thaddeus, *Soldiers in the Sun: An Adventure in Imperialism,* Harrisburg, Pennsylvania: The Military Service Publishing Co., c1939.

Smith, Joseph, *The Spanish-American War: Conflict in the Caribbean and the Pacific, 1895-1902,* New York: Longman, 1994.

Stanley, Peter W. A., *Nation in the Making: The Philippines and the U.S., 1899-1921,* Cambridge: Harvard University Press, 1974.

_____, *Reappraising an Empire: New Perspectives on Philippine-American History,* Cambridge: Harvard University Press, 1984.

Stephenson, George, *John Lind of Minnesota,* Minneapolis, Minnesota: The University of Minnesota Press, 1935.

Stickney, Joseph, *The Conquest of the Philippines by the United States, 1898-1925,* London: Putnam and Sons, 1926.

Strait, N. A., *Alphabetical Lists of Battles, 1754-1900: War of the Rebellion, Spanish-American War, Philippine Insurrection, and All Old Wars with Dates,* Detroit: Gale Research Co., 1968.

Tew, Martin E., Lt., *Official History of the Operation of the 13th Minnesota Infantry, U.S.V. in the Campaign in the Philippine Islands.* S.I.: S.N., 1899.

Trask, David F., *The War with Spain in 1898,* New York: MacMillan, c1981.

Venzon, Anne Cipriano, *The Spanish-American War: An Annotated Bibliography,* New York: Garland, 1990.

Walsh, John, *The Philippine Insurrection, 1899-1902: America's Only Try for an Overseas Empire,* New York: Watts, 1973.

Welch, Richard E., *Response To Imperialism: The United States and the Philippine-American War, 1899-1902,* Chapel Hill: University of North Carolina Press, 1979.

White, Trumbell, *Pictorial History of Our War with Spain for Cuba's Freedom,* Freedom

Publishing Co., 1898.

_____, *Our New Possessions*, Minneapolis: Creore and Nickerson Publishing Co., 1898.

Wildman, Edwin, *Aguinaldo: A Narrative of Filipino Ambitions*, Boston, Lothrop Publishing Company, 1901.

Wilkerson, Marcus Manley, *Public Opinion and the Spanish-American War: A Study in War Propaganda,* Baton Rouge: Louisiana State University Press, 1932.

Wolff, Leon, *Little Brown Brother: How the United States Purchased and Pacified the Philippine Islands at the Century's Turn*, Garden City, New York: Doubleday, 1961.

Young, James Rankin, *History of Our War with Spain: Including Battles on Sea and Land,* Washington D.C.: Office of the Librarian of Congress, 1898.

_____, *Reminiscences and Thrilling Stories of the War by Returning Heroes,* Chicago, Illinois: World Bible House, 1899.

Newspapers

The Duluth News Tribune, January 1 - April 25, 1898.

Mankato Daily Free Press, January 1 - April 25, 1898.

The Minneapolis Tribune, April 1898 - October 1899.

Moorhead Daily News, January 1 - April 25, 1898.

Red Wing Daily Republican, April 1898 - October 1899.

St. Cloud Times, April 1898 - October 1899.

St. Paul Pioneer Press, January 1898 - October 1899.

Stillwater Gazette, April 1898 - October 1899.

Unpublished Material

Anderson, August, 1859-1918, Correspondences, Minnesota Historical Society, St. Paul, Minnesota.

Baker, Mouraine, ed., Dear Folks at Home: Wright County's View of the Spanish-American War, p. 1-26, Minnesota Historical Society, St. Paul, Minnesota.

Bell, James Hughes, 1825-1892, Papers, Minnesota Historical Society, St. Paul, Minnesota.

Burlingham, Lewis Preston, 1879-1951, Papers, (Member of Co. K, 13th Regiment, Minnesota Vol. Inf.), Minnesota Historical Society, St. Paul, Minnesota.

Cressy, Charles A., 1861-1916, Papers, (Minister with the 13th Regiment), Minnesota

Historical Society, St. Paul, Minnesota.

Frankel, Hiram David, ed., Company "C," First Infantry Minnesota National Guard: Its History and Development. Brown, Treacy, and Co. Minnesota Historical Society, St. Paul, Minnesota.

Gardner, Henry Rufus, 1842-1913, Papers, (Scrapbook of clippings relating to the Spanish-American War), Minnesota Historical Society, St. Paul, Minnesota.

Hallowell, Isaac R. D., 1899? Scrapbook, Minnesota Historical Society, St. Paul, Minnesota.

Heilbron, Julius, 1860-1940, Papers, Minnesota Historical Society, St. Paul, Minnesota.

Jacobsen, Joseph, The Heroes of the 13th Minnesota U.S.V.: grand march and two step. Minneapolis, F.O. Williams, 1899.

Kahlert, Alexander J. 1898, Diary (Served with the 13th Minnesota Inf.), Minnesota Historical Society, St. Paul, Minnesota.

Keatley, C. E., 1898-1934, Scrapbook on the Thirteenth Minnesota Regiment in the war with Spain, Minnesota Historical Society, St. Paul, Minnesota.

Kridler, Bert, Pride of Minnesota: march-two-step, Graceville, Minnesota: Bert Kridler Music Co., c1899.

Lawson, John E., 1898-1899, Papers (member of the 13th Minnesota Inf.), Minnesota Historical Society, St. Paul, Minnesota.

Lind, John & Norman., 1870-1933. Papers. Minnesota Historical Society, St. Paul, Minnesota.
McKelvy, James E., 1863-1908, Papers, Central Minnesota Historical Society, St. Cloud, Minnesota.

_____, 1898, Letters, Stearns County Historical Society, St. Cloud, Minnesota.

Neill, Edmund P., 1898-1899, Letters (Member Co. G, 13th Minnesota Inf.), Minnesota Historical Society, St. Paul, Minnesota.

Stone, Carl L., 1890-1920, Letters (Member 13th Minnesota Infantry), Minnesota Historical Society, St. Paul, Minnesota.

Thirteenth Minnesota Regimental Association, Pamphlet Collection 1923-1932, Central Minnesota Historical Center, St. Cloud, Minnesota.

United States, Army, Minnesota, 1900? Souvenir, Co. I, 13th Minnesota Volunteer Infantry, Minnesota Historical Society, St. Paul, Minnesota.

Government Documents

Minnesota. Governor, "Records, 1895-1898," Minnesota Historical Society, St. Paul, Minnesota.

Minnesota. Office of the Adjutant General, "National Guard expedition files, 1898-1900," Minnesota Historical Society, St. Paul, Minnesota.

_____, "State Report, 1900, Volume II," Minnesota Historical Society, St. Paul, Minnesota.

_____, "Spanish-American War military service records, 1898-1900," Minnesota Historical Society, St. Paul, Minnesota.

_____, "Spanish-American War miscellaneous records, 1898-1900," Minnesota Historical Society, St, Paul, Minnesota.

_____, "Spanish-American War muster rolls, 1898-1899," Minnesota Historical Society, St. Paul, Minnesota.

Minnesota War Records Commission, "Spanish-American War history files, 1898-1923," Minnesota Historical Society, St. Paul, Minnesota.

Journals and Periodicals

Agnew, James, "Private Longden and the Medical Corps Of 1898," *Military Review,* 59, no. 7 (1979): pp. 11-21.

Arcilla, Jose S., "The Fall of Manila: Excerpts from a Jesuit Diary," *Philippine Studies,* 37, no. 2 (1989): pp. 192-214.

Burdett, Thomas, "The Memorable March of the 3rd Infantry from San Miguel to Balinag," *Military Collector & Historian* (Fall 1974): pp. 145-148.

_____, "A New Evaluation of General Otis' Leadership in the Philippines," *Military Review* (January 1975): pp. 79-87.

Carmony, Donald and Karen Tunnenbaum, "Three Years in the Orient: The Diary of William R. Johnson, 1898-1902," *Indiana Magazine of History,* 63, no. 4 (1967): pp. 263-298.

Chapman, Gregory, "Taking Up the White Man's Burden: Tennesseans in the Philippine

Insurrection, 1899," *Tennessee Historical Quarterly,* 47, no. 1 (1988): pp. 27-40.

Chaput, Donald, "Private William W. Grayson's War in the Philippines, 1899," *Nebraska History,* 61, no. 3 (1980): pp. 355-366.

Clymer, Kenton, "Not So Benevolent Assimilation: The Philippine-American War," *Reviews in American History* (December 1983): pp. 547-552.

Cosmos, Graham, "Military Reform After the Spanish-American War: The Army Reorganization Fight of 1898-1899," *Military Affairs* (February, 1971): pp. 12-18.

Coterini, Dino, "Repeating Ourselves: The Philippine Insurrection and the Vietnam War," *Foreign Service Journal* (December 1977): pp. 11-32.

Friedel, Frank, "Dissent in the Spanish-American War and the Philippine Insurrection," *Massachusetts Historical Society,* 81 (1969): pp. 167-184.

Gates, John, "War-Related Deaths in the Philippines, 1898-1902," *Pacific Historical Review,* 53, no. 3 (1984): pp. 367-378.

Gillett, Mary, "Medical Care and Evacuation during the Philippine Insurrection, 1899-1901," *Journal of the History of Medicine* (April, 1987): pp. 169-185.

_____, "U.S. Army Medical Officers and Public Health in the Philippines," *Bulletin of the History of Medicine* (1974): pp. 182-187.
Ginsburgh, Robert, "Damn the Insurrectos," *Military Review* (January 1964): pp. 58-70.

Grant, Roger, "The Fighting First: The First South Dakota and Nebraska Volunteers," *South Dakota History,* 4, no. 3 (1974): pp. 320-332.

Hall, John, "The Philippine War: The Diary of Robert Bruce Payne, 1899," *Nebraska History* (Winter 1988): pp. 193-198.

Harper, Frank, "Fighting Far From Home: The First Colorado Regiment in the Spanish-American War," *Colorado History* (1988): pp. 2-11.

May, Glenn, "Why the United States Won the Philippine-American War, 1899-1902, *Pacific Historical Review,* 52, no. 4(1983): pp. 353-377.

Mickelson, Peter, "Nationalism in Minnesota During the Spanish-American War," *Minnesota History* (Spring 1968): pp. 1-12.

Mischal, Adam, "'Young and Adventurous': The Journal of a North Dakota Volunteer in the Spanish-American War, 1898-1899," *North Dakota History,* 60, no. 1 (1993): pp. 2-20.

Pomeroy, William, "'Pacification' in the Philippines, 1898-1913," *France-Asie Asia* (1967): pp. 427-446.
Poplin, Richard, "The Letters of W. Thomas Osborne," *Tennessee Historical Society*

(June 1963): pp. 152-169.

Reilly, Margaret Inglehart, "Andrew Wadsworth, a Nebraska Soldier in the Philippines, 1898-1899," *Nebraska History* (Winter 1987): pp. 183-199.

Rystad, Garan, "The Philippine Struggle for Independence and Its Effects on American Expansionism at the turn of the Century," *Revue Internationale D'Histoire Militaire,* 70 (1988): pp. 107-129.

Saum, Lewis, "The Western Volunteer and 'The New Empire,'" *Pacific Northwest Quarterly* (January 1966): pp. 18-27.

Smith, Ephrain, "'A Question from Which We Could Not Escape': William McKinley and the Decision to Acquire the Philippine Islands," *Diplomatic History,* 9, no. 4 (1985): pp. 363-375.

Smith, Joseph, "The Splendid Little War of 1898: A Reappraisal," *History,* 80, no. 258 (1995): pp. 22-37.

Strobridge, William, "Rendezvous in San Francisco," *Tennessee Historical Quarterly* (Summer 1974): pp. 204-209.

Thiesson, Thomas, "The Fighting First Nebraska: Nebraska's Imperial Adventure in the Philippines, 1898-1899," *Nebraska History* (Fall 1989): pp. 210-272.

Trussell, John, "A Pennsylvanian in the Philippines," *Pennsylvania History,* 44, no. 2 (1977): pp. 117-144.

_____, "Pennsylvanian Volunteers in the Spanish-American War," *Military Collector and Historian,* 38, no. 3 (1986): pp. 98-109.

Index